JOYOUS ANARCHY

The Search For Great American Wines

Also by William E. Massee

THE ART OF COMFORT
WINES OF FRANCE
(in collaboration with Alexis Lichine)
WINES AND SPIRITS
WINE-FOOD INDEX
PASTA PRONTO
MASSEE'S GUIDE TO AMERICAN WINES
MASSEE'S WINE HANDBOOK
EATING AND DRINKING IN EUROPE

JOYOUS ANARCHY

The Search For Great American Wines

By

William E. Massee

G.P. Putnam's Sons

New York

The quotation from "A Natural Miracle" by
Berton Roueché is reprinted by kind permission
of *The New Yorker* from their issue of September 20, 1976.

LIBRARY OF CONGRESS CATALOGING IN PUBLICATION DATA

Massee, William Edman.
  Joyous Anarchy.

   1.   Wine and Wine Making—United States. I. Title.
TP557.M37   1978   641.2'2'0973   77-26007

SBN: 399-12069-6

PRINTED IN THE UNITED STATES OF AMERICA

*To Andre Tchelistcheff
and Charles Fournier,
who made sense of chaos*

CONTENTS

Part I:
Wines and Vines

An American Wine Sampler

"The trouble is that you never list the wines you really like," said a friend and constant critic. There are always one or two selections for every winery, it was pointed out, with mentions of others in the text.

"But the list should be in front of the book, one after another, so you don't have to paw through the whole thing," said the critic. Then you wouldn't need to read the book, he was told. "You would if you wanted to know more, and the where of it and the how, and why," said my friend.

Here they are, then, right up front, selections of wines I like, region by region, winery by winery—a buying guide. What's more, they are wines you can get in every major market. There are many other grand wines from small wineries—wines that win prizes—but they are produced in small quantities; distribution is limited; prices are high. The ones listed here are a good sampling of American wines, good buys because most of them cost less than five dollars.

Any two or three of those listed would be good for a dinner party. The lists can be used to start a wine cellar. For scarcer wines, limited bottlings to be sought after, the book will help you in making up your own lists, which will be the best of all. Taste tells.

13

99 WINES TO LOOK FOR
(A SELECTION OF AMERICAN WINES GENERALLY AVAILABLE IN MAJOR MARKETS)

	WHITES	REDS
MENDOCINO		
Parducci	Chenin Blanc	Petite Sirah
	French Colombard	Carignane
Cresta Blanca	Sauvignon Blanc	Zinfandel
Weibel	Green Hungarian	Zinfandel
SONOMA		
Sebastiani	Sylvaner-Riesling	Barbera
	Pinot Chardonnay	Cabernet Sauvignon
Sonoma Vineyards	Chardonnay	Pinot Noir
	French Colombard	Cabernet Sauvignon
Souverain	Colombard	Cabernet Sauvignon
	Chardonnay	Petite Sirah
Geyser Peak	Pinot Chardonnay	Zinfandel
Korbel	Chardonnay	Cabernet Sauvignon
Simi	Chenin Blanc	Pinot Noir
Pedroncelli	Gewürztraminer	Zinfandel
NAPA		
The Christian Brothers	Pinot Chardonnay	Cabernet Sauvignon
	Napa Fumé	Pinot St. George
Robert Mondavi	Fumé Blanc	Cabernet Sauvignon
	Pinot Chardonnay	Table wine
Beaulieu Vineyards	Beaufort	Beau Velours
	(Pinot Chardonnay)	(Pinot Noir)
	Beauclair (J. Riesling)	Beau Tour (Cabernet)
Louis Martini	Mountain Pinot Ch.	Cabernet Sauvignon
	Mountain Folle Blanche	Mountain Barbera
	Mountain White	Mountain Red
Beringer Brothers	Fumé Blanc	Pinot Noir
	Traubengold	Barenblut
Charles Krug	Chenin Blanc	Claret
Sterling	Chenin Blanc	Pinot Noir

14

SANTA CLARA & MONTEREY	WHITES	REDS
Paul Masson	Emerald Dry	Rubion
	Pinot Blanc	Baroque
San Martin	Johannisberg Riesling	Pinot Noir
Almadén	Pinot Chardonnay	Grenache Rosé
Mirassou	Monterey Riesling (Sylvaner)	Zinfandel
	Gewürztraminer	Gamay Beaujolais
Monterey Vineyards	Del Mar Ranch	Gamay Beaujolais

LIVERMORE		
Wente Bros.	Le Blanc de Blancs	Pinot Noir
	Pinot Blanc	
	Sauvignon Blanc	Gamay Beaujolais
Concannon	Dinner Wine	Petite Sirah
	Sauvignon Blanc	Cabernet Sauvignon

THE NORTHEAST		
Gold Seal	Chardonnay	Catawba Red
Widmer	Cayuga White	Pinot Noir
	Moore's Diamond	Cabernet Sauvignon
Great Western	White Niagara	Chelois

THE NORTHWEST		
Ste. Michelle	Johannisberg Riesling	Pinot Noir

* * *

SPARKLING WINES	
Gold Seal	Blanc de Blancs
Schramsberg	Brut
Hanns Kornell	Sehr Trocken
Korbel	Brut
Domaine Chandeon	Cuvée de Pinot Noir

FORTIFIED WINE
Ficklin Port

LOW-PRICED WINES (under $3)
Sonoma Vineyards French Colombard
Sebastiani Green Hungarian
Paul Masson Pinot Blanc
Paul Masson Rubion
Louis Martini Mountain Red
Widmer's Naples Valley Foch

The Best Bottles: High, Sloping and Slender

"Nobody knows anything about American wines and nobody wants to admit it," said the retailer with a little wine shop in the village. "A few read about a wine, usually a six-dollar bottle and when they say that's too much and I suggest another, they think it's a con. The kids don't trust me because I'm gray; women don't trust me because I'm male; and men don't trust me because they don't trust anybody."

There, there, I said.

"Not knowing is great. You can always find out. Finding out is exciting. People think they should know about wines, that they are hicks if they don't. But they think knowing about wines is high-class, like knowing how to play polo or sail a yacht or eat caviar—all snob. You know what I do?"

What? I answered.

"I pull out a Zinfandel or a Côtes-du-Rhône. Three dollars, how can they go wrong? 'Everybody says enjoy,' I say, 'so enjoy.' I pull out a Chenin Blanc and a Muscadet. 'Enjoy,' I say. You know what they do?"

No, I responded.

"They buy the French and run and I never see them again. They're afraid to know, ashamed to find out. Who cares if you don't know? But what they're missing!"

17

William E. Massee

It's too bad, I replied.

"It's a crime. You know what I'd like to do? Grab a customer and pull out a bottle of Bordeaux. 'See the high shoulders on the bottle?' I'd say. 'Wines in bottles like that are dry.' Then I'd pull out a Burgundy bottle. 'See those sloping shoulders?' I'd say. 'The wines are fruity.' I'd pull out a Rhine wine. 'See how tall and skinny it is?' I'd say. 'Wines like that are flowery.'"

You mean start at the beginning, said I.

"Exactly. 'Buy a mixed case,' I'd say, 'six reds and six whites, all from California, costing under forty dollars for the lot, the price of a night out. Stay in once in a while, drink them up. Then buy another case. Drink that. By the time you have finished, you'll begin getting the idea. Trust me.'"

Do they? I asked.

"Are you kidding?" demanded the retailer. "They think it's a con. They think I'm being paid by the Californians when actually I make more profits on imports. I'd really start them off on the wines of Napa or Sonoma—not the whole region. And the prices would be averaged—I'd put in a couple of five-dollar bottles and several two-dollar bottles."

You could start with one grower or shipper, I suggested.

"Then they'd really think it's a con. You've given me an idea. I'm going to make up a list of wineries by districts—the biggest ones—and let people pick their own bottles. If they go over thirty-five bucks a case I'll suggest substitutes."

Later he sent me a list, thanking me for the idea, and instructing me to add tasting terms, particularly words like *body*, and to say what *sweet* meant, and *dry*. Here is his list. The matters of taste are in that section, Part IV, page 249.

CALIFORNIA GROWERS AND SHIPPERS WITH WIDE DISTRIBUTION
(A SELECTIVE LIST OF PREMIUM PRODUCERS)

NAPA
The Christian Brothers
Robert Mondavi
Louis Martini
Beaulieu Vineyard

SONOMA & MENDOCINO
Sebastiani
Sonoma Vineyards
Korbel
Souverain

18

Joyous Anarchy

Beringer Brothers
Sterling Vineyard
Charles Krug
Inglenook

Pedroncelli
Geyser Peak
Parducci
Cresta Blanca

LIVERMORE, SANTA CLARA & MONTEREY

Wente Bros.
Concannon Vineyard
Mirassou
Paul Masson
San Martin
Almadén
Monterey

America's Ten Best Wines

"California's like Burgundy in the old days when Frank Schoonmaker used to bustle around among the peasants, trying to pick up fifty cases from one, a hundred from another," said the wine buyer, gazing into the depths of his snifter, where a spoonful of Cognac from Ragnaud waited. "Burgundy was easy. All you had to know was French, and how to select the right *pièce*, and how to talk the peasant out of his wine. He could sell all his wines twice over, but Schoonmaker was such a good taster that the peasant was proud to be selected. Schoonmaker always had to pay top price, agree to take wines in off years, even pay in advance."

Never interrupt rememberings. With the grandest of Cognacs before us, it was easy to keep quiet and wait.

"California's worse. At least in Burgundy, you just tasted Chablis for a day, or Volnay, going from cellar to cellar. Just one wine, from different vineyards, different makers. When you found a barrel you liked you marked it with a chalk. And it was all Chardonnay for whites or Pinot Noir for reds. Not in California. You run around like a nut."

The buyer swirled his little pool, sniffed it, and whistled in a tiny sip. He swallowed and waited, smiling fondly at the half-teaspoonful left. I nodded at the waiter, who headed for the bar to get the bottle.

21

"You don't realize what it's like until you start driving around. Just take Napa. There are lots of little wineries up in the hills and you might get the idea that you could find some good Chardonnays by going around and tasting. Forget it.

"Somebody decided in the Sixties that you needed forty acres to make a vineyard practical, so that you could produce maybe six thousand cases a year. Wineries started up with that minimum in mind. Vines take four years to mature, so a new winery has to buy grapes. And every winery wants to have Cabernet and Riesling and Pinot Noir, as well as Chardonnay. Then maybe they want some Sauvignon, too, some Zinfandel or Petite Sirah—they're fashionable now—and maybe some Chenin Blanc. So he's making four wines, at least, maybe eight, and then an ordinary red or white to take care of his too-young grapes or any extra gallonage from his main varieties. He has to run all over to various growers for his grapes, all of which mature at different times and require different handling. A Burgundian makes Chardonnay or Pinot Noir and that's it. He gets to know the grape, how it grows in different vineyards, how to handle it in different vintages. He makes it barrel by barrel and keeps each separate. But not in Napa."

The waiter poured an inch in his snifter, a dollop in mine. We swirled and sniffed. I sniffed too hard and my nose tingled.

"They blend all their Chardonnay together and maybe they get a couple of hundred cases. The same with Cabernet, and so on—not enough to supply people who buy direct from the winery, let alone California, let alone restaurants, let alone the whole United States."

The wine buyer sipped. I joined him. Intense, ethereal, lingering.

"They've got German winemakers up there in the hills, and randy young Davis graduates, and guys who get it all from books, and sons of old-timers who pumped wines as soon as they could walk. All sorts of ideas about how to make the wines. You know what? They're all little shippers."

I looked startled.

"Sure they are. They buy grapes, don't they? And lots of them buy wines. And they tend the wines, like a Burgundian *éleveur*. Then they market them under their own label, these blends, like a *négociant*. But not just Burgundy, not just Pinot Noir and Chardonnay. They make Bordeaux, too, Cabernet and Sauvignon, and Loire with Chenin Blanc, and

22

Rhine wines with Riesling. Maybe they've got some Traminer or Sylvaner, so they make wines like the Alsatians. They're all little shippers."

But they make lots of good wines, it was necessary to interject. This was a mistake. The wine buyer thumped his snifter.

"So what? It's anarchy up there. People making all kinds of wines, all different ways. I can't buy just Chardonnay. They want me to buy Cabernet, too, and Zinfandel, maybe the whole line. And they keep changing the way they make the wines—one year full, the next year light, one year lots of wood, the next year none. They drive you crazy."

He swirled and took a big sip for emphasis and choked. I took a small sip to hide my grin.

The wine buyer let out a big breath, panted some, then took a sip of cold coffee and cleared his throat.

"It's all this American go, go, go that's wrong. You've got to be the best in everything. You've got to outdo the Burgundians and the Bordelais, and the Rhinelanders. They want to be better than Lafite or Montrachet or Bernkasteler. And the soils are different, the climate, everything. They ought to settle down and be happy to make good wines. Then maybe all my running around would pay off and I could get a few thousand cases of good Chardonnay instead of a few hundred."

The wide range is great for wine drinkers, I said, all the experimenting, all the effort to be best.

"Who cares? Who even knows about it? People still ask me if there really are some good wines from California. And when I say try Chardonnay from Heitz or Montelena, maybe Chappellet's Chenin Blanc or Dry Creek Fumé Blanc, they ask how much. 'Five dollars a bottle,' they say, 'ten dollars—are you crazy?' They won't take a chance for that much money. Restaurants balk at listing the wines because too few of their customers know them. And if they do get a wine going, the restaurant owners can't get a second shipment, so they get disgusted and go back to Sancerre, or whatever. They settle for a good Burgundy shipper's blend, like Louis Latour's Cuvée Blanc, which retails for five dollars, but it's good and the restaurant can be sure of getting it."

Maybe some of the California wines are better, I suggested, more exciting, real discoveries.

"Maybe, but mighty few people are going to get the chance to find out. The lots of wines are too small, there are too many names, there's no con-

23

tinuity. It's anarchy out there. It's like Burgundy in the Fifties, only more confusing, and the wines are harder to come by. The wines are there but I can't market them. You can't market anarchy.''

Joyous anarchy, I said. Wine lovers will find the wines, somehow. They'll get marketed, somehow.

"Not when you hide your light under a bushel,'' said the wine buyer. "Not when the wines don't even get out of California.'' He looked at his watch.

It was after three. We struggled up and walked out into the sunlight, blinking. The wine buyer was flying to Paris that night. I went home.

There was a call from a publisher. "How would you like to do a book on American wines?'' One of mine is on the market right now, I told him. "You wrote it five years ago,'' said the publisher. "There must be lots of new wines.'' There are, said I. "Well?'' said he. It's anarchy out there, said I. "Swell,'' he said, "tell me all about it.''

On the first Sunday in July I took off for San Francisco. Again.

THE GRAPES: NOBLE AND EXCEPTIONAL

America's ten best wines are known by the grapes from which they come, so a list should make them easier to find:

WHITE WINES	RED WINES
Folle Blanche (or Chenin Blanc)	Gamay Beaujolais (or Napa Gamay)
Sauvignon Blanc	Barbera
Pinot Blanc	Pinot Noir
Riesling	Merlot
Chardonnay	Cabernet Sauvignon

The trios heading each list are the noble vines of the world's greatest wine regions: Burgundy, Bordeaux and the Rhine. Pairs ending the lists produce better grapes in California than they do in their home regions and wines from them are discoveries not to be missed.

Already there is confusion. Some of America's most unusual wines are left out, particularly those reds from California's own grape, Zinfandel, and its companion, Petite Sirah. Many rank their wines right after Cabernet. They warrant separate consideration. For comparison's sake, the list focuses on the noblest vines of Europe's greatest regions and on those that do better here than abroad.

Folle Blanche: Rare and Delicious. White wines are appealing because they can be drunk by themselves and are served cold; they are less complex than reds and are drunk young. Starting with the discoveries, Folle Blanche produces a fresh, tart wine.

A grape of the lower Loire, it is hard to grow, forming tight bunches subject to mildew and rot. Now it is being replaced in Cognac, Armagnac and the Midi, so about the only source is California, where Louis Martini has about the only commercial planting. Folle Blanche is worth singling out because it is so good—better than Muscadet, which dominates the home region—but also because it shows up the difficulty of getting many of our best wines. This can be frustrating.

Chenin Blanc: From Dry to Sweet. One might better seek out wines easy to come by that are as good as those from Europe and popular with our growers, like Chenin Blanc.

This grape of the Middle Loire—where it is also called Pineau de la Loire—produces Vouvray, Saumur and Savennières, among others. Our dry versions are tart—some say they are crisp—and are fruitier than their French cousins. Like them, many of ours are lightly sweet to bring out their floweriness, although this quality is not now fashionable. The sweet savor is pleasing when Chenin Blanc is served with scallops or chicken or spicy dishes. And here is another complication—where a particular grape produces a wide range of wines. Those scorning sweetness and those who think sweetness isn't stylish will miss many fine wines by avoiding Chenin Blanc. For zealots of the dry, the driest of the Chenin Blancs is from Dry Creek, while those from Chappellet and Sterling Forest are almost as dry.

Sauvignon Blanc and Aliases. To be logical, if not orderly, consider the grape of the Upper Loire, Blanc Fumé. The local name hides the fact that this grape is the great Sauvignon Blanc of Bordeaux, which produces superb wines in California, lighter and more elegant than many of those from France. For no reason at all Sauvignon Blanc from California has never been popular in the market place. Robert Mondavi got the idea of calling it Fumé Blanc; this had instant appeal. The round, lingering wines are now more popular than the French wines from the same grape, the Graves and Blanc de Blancs of Bordeaux, the Pouilly-Fumé and Sancerre of the Loire. You cannot judge by name alone.

To ease confusion, the grape and the wines will be called Sauvignon here. Full and dry, they are marvelous with fish and fowl, with flavorful veal and pork dishes. Seek for those of Wente, Concannon, Sonoma Vineyards. Dry and lighter Sauvignons are superb with Italian and other Mediterranean dishes and with many of the mélanges from Oriental cuisines. Look for Mondavi's Fumé Blanc and Almadén's Blanc Fumé. Marvelous with any dish made with fruit or those sweet sauces often served with duck or pork are soft and flowery versions like Spring Mountain or Château Beaulieu of BV.

Pinot Blanc: An Intermediate to Look For. Back to the discoveries on the list: look for Pinot Blanc. It produces an outstanding California wine superior to those from Burgundy, where the grape is overshadowed by the Chardonnay. There are many wines overshadowed by more famous neighbors. They are called intermediate wines by the trade, hard to sell, like a vintage rated only good. Pinot Blanc is one of the best intermediates to look for, invariably outstanding. The full, fruity wine of Wente should be bought whenever found, although Mirassou or Almadén may be more readily available. (Chenin Blanc used to be marketed as White Pinot until its true name became known and it now appears only if a shipper has built a market under the misnomer or is trying to fool the public.)

Riesling and Company. Perhaps the most confusing white wine on the list is Riesling, from grapes that produce all the greatest wines of the Rhine. In California, the wines are called Johannisberg Riesling or White Riesling and these are the names to look for on labels. The confusion comes because California wines labeled Riesling are made from the less-distinguished grape called Sylvaner. The practice should stop and the only way to stop it is to pass up all California wines labeled simply Riesling. Here, the great grape of the Rhine and the Moselle will be called, properly, Riesling, the intention being to simplify matters.

There is further confusion because a California cross is called Emerald Riesling, and there is another called Grey Riesling, fashionable in San Francisco, made from a mediocre French grape called Chauché Gris.

There are so many good Rieslings from the Rhine, say importers, why bother in California? Because growers can't stand being outdone; true Rieslings are popular; they can be drunk by themselves and are good with smoked or spicy meats; they can be made dry and flowery. When the grapes are left long on the vine Late Harvest Rieslings can be made sweet and fruity. Look for BV, Louis Martini, Sonoma Vineyards—or a dozen others.

Chardonnay. Chardonnay, the grape in all of Burgundy's finest white wine vineyards, is California's present glory. The wines are often marketed as Pinot Chardonnay, once the official name of the grape. The best of them come from small producers and are expensive, often $10 a bottle. They are enormous, fragrant, fruity wines of remarkable distinction. The less prestigious wines from the large producers are excellent, perhaps better with fish and fowl—and by themselves—than the more expensive and more overpowering bottlings. When priced around $4, those of The Christian Brothers, Paul Masson and Almadén are some of California's best buys.

* * *

A list plunges you right into the middle of things, but when there are a dozen Chardonnays on the shelf, a score of Rieslings, where do you begin? Be sure that when you have tried one you have not tried them all. Variety in excellence is the joy of wine.

"Ten-best" lists leave out a lot. (Maybe for this reason alone, wines are rated on a basis of 20.) But even with the short list of whites, we can set up some guidelines for buying wines:

- Many good wines are rare; remember there are alternatives.
- Many wines from the same grape have different names; the names are easy to get to know, so learn them.
- Wines from the same grape vary over a wide range; try several.
- Names of great grapes are stolen or borrowed for lesser wines; beware.
- Many good wines are intermediates, overshadowed by more famous ones; look for them.
- Many good wines are simply out of fashion; don't be put off by light sweetness.

•Wines from a single grape vary widely in price; remember that some of the less-expensive may taste best with meals.

And that's just considering the white wines. Other matters of judgment are obvious. It is interesting to compare wines from different places but from the same grape, just to note the differences, not necessarily to find out which is better. Wines are best compared price for price: when a high-priced wine excels, that's to be expected; but when a low-priced wine stands out, that's cause for triumph. Many good wines at low prices are good for drinking regularly. Many good high-priced wines, their complex tastes demanding attention, are most pleasing when you have them once in a while; they are in the class of caviar, smoked salmon, rib roasts of beef.

Two different wines are more attractive at a meal than two bottles of the same. The more variety, the better. Wines for the table taste best with food. A pleasant way to find out about them is to try two or three with something simple. A plate of cold cuts, a chicken or a stew brings out the tastes of the wines. So will cheese. Wines' tastes vary with the different foods. One can be more critical when the wines are tasted against each other, without food, in the traditional way of wine tastings. The first aim, though, should be pleasure.

* * *

White wines are easier to taste because they are less complex, but reds eventually interest people more. The widest range is among the Cabernets, a grape of Bordeaux whose wines take years to mature, becoming the most complex of all wines. Comparing them is difficult because of wide variations. Like wines from other grapes, inexpensive versions should be drunk, if the wines are unfamiliar, strictly for pleasure. Less-complex red wines are considered first.

Gamay and Company. Gamay Beaujolais tastes fruity and fresh and delicious, something like a light Burgundy from Santenay or Savigny, but with perhaps less distinctiveness. French chefs love to serve the Beaujolais from Southern Burgundy because its sprightly taste when young is properly quenching and does not attract attention to itself—and away from the food, particularly the light dishes of modern French cuisine.

28

Californians believed they had the peer of this in their Gamay Beaujolais, but the grape so called in California may be a relative of the noble Pinot Noir, the grape that produces all the great Burgundies. No wonder, then, that it tastes so good, particularly when young.

Napa Gamay, now being called Gamay Noir by some producers, is considered to be the actual grape of Beaujolais or close to it. The Gamay, like most grapes, turns out to be a family, but the one in Beaujolais is the Gamay Noir à Jus Blanc, where it excels and produces Chiroubles and Juliénas, Fleurie and Saint Amour, Brouilly and Chénas, Moulin-à-Vent and Morgon. These are considered to be the best young wines in the world, meant to be drunk before the following vintage, preferably right from the cask; only the last two in the list improve with a year or two in bottle. The California version is softer than the Beaujolais of France (because it seems to have less fruit acids) and may thus be more appealing to some.

There is no need for bewilderment just because the two wines have similar names and are close in taste. Both are attractive wines, especially when they come from the North Coast counties. Winemakers from Mendocino to Monterey produce fine bottlings, some trying to achieve softness in the wine, others trying to attain fruitiness. The variations are appealing, and dinner parties are more interesting when a pair of them are served one after another, rather than two bottles of the same wine.

With a preference for young fresh wines, especially with roasts, stews and light sauces, (Napa) Gamay Noir is attractive. There is a tendency to choose the youngest and fruitiest available from Napa or Monterey, those from Sonoma and Mendocino seeming soft. Try Robert Mondavi's Napa Gamay.

The Gamay Beaujolais is even softer. Try Wente's Gamay Beaujolais.

Neither wine seems to get high praise from California tasters, perhaps because most of them are attracted by fuller and fruitier wines. Eastern tasters prefer lighter, drier wines than these two, and one can hope that they would be so made, if only for contrast with others. Both wines lend themselves to experiment—by makers and by tasters. Potential is there.

The wines sell for a little more than $3 a bottle and are good ones for tasting against European wines in the same price range.

California Gamays are most like the regional wines of Burgundy, those marketed under the names of districts or townships. While those from California are softer and lighter than their French peers, they are often more carefully made; they are usually better than wines sold here as Beaujolais or Beaujolais Supérieur. Here's a list of California-Burgundy comparisons:

GAMAY BEAUJOLAIS
Côte de Beaune-Villages
Santenay
Auxey-Duresses
Savigny
Givry
Mercurey

NAPA GAMAY/GAMAY NOIR
Beaujolais-Villages
Macon Rouge

NOTE: Pinot Noir is being planted more and more in Eastern Europe, and bottles from Hungary, Yugoslavia and Rumania are beginning to appear on the market. Those costing less than $3 a bottle are often comparable to Gamay Beaujolais.

Barbera. Barbera makes a full, dark red in Italy's best wine region, the Piedmont, the alpine foothills bordering France. In California the wines are perhaps more rounded and fruitier, not being kept so long in cask. A good wine with just the amount of sharpness for hearty pot roasts and pungent spaghetti sauces, it is quenching and not so overpowering that it attracts attention to itself and away from the food.

A lot of Barbera is planted in the hot Great Central Valley around Fresno, where it was used for blending into California's idea of Chianti. Big shippers in the valley began putting the name on labels when Barberas from Napa and Sonoma began attracting attention. The valley wines are rarely more than ordinary, but those under $3 are reminiscent of Italian jug wines. Gallo's Barbera of California may be the driest of those around $2. Those with some sweetness rank higher in tastings, for instance, G & D Fior di California Barberone. They taste best chilled, or perhaps with ice and a squeeze of lemon.

Barberas from cool North Coast counties can be superb. They are among the best buys on the market. Look for those of Louis Martini and Sebastiani, particularly. Our Barberas seem to have a little less fruit than the Freisa of the Piedmont, for instance, perhaps resembling more the Rhônes like Gigondas and Cairanne, which have more body and are generally drier.

Tasters are quick to note that California wines generally seem to be more flowery or fruity than similar European wines. Once noted, though, exceptions crop up time after time. Much of this is a matter of winemaking style or even local custom. Winemaking varies from year to year, not only because of vintage differences, but because of more sophisticated control of fermentation. In California, particularly, there is constant experimentation, if only because there are so few control laws. The giant producers find a market for a particular wine, then cater to it. Small producers try to get more and more out of a grape, leaving it up to individuals to find the distinctive wines. Barberas, particularly, are a widely varying family of wines and are a comparatively inexpensive group worth exploring, selling for $3 or so. They are generally much lower in price than the popular Cabernets and Pinot Noirs.

Pinot Noir. The Pinot Noir produces all of Burgundy's great reds—dry and fruity wines. California versions tend toward the flowery and experts say it is because the soil is not calcareous, lacking in chalk or lime. Some say the northern part of the Napa Valley is too warm for the grape; but try those from Louis Martini and BV, from Monterey Vineyards or Wente. Superb with steaks.

Merlot and Cabernet Sauvignon. Cabernet Sauvignon and Merlot are the great Bordeaux grapes and they are equally distinguished in California. There are more than 25,000 acres of Cabernet, only 4,000 acres of Merlot. Because of variations in winemaking, age of vines and vineyard soil and climate, the range of wines is enormous. Prices start at $3 and rise to $10 and more. The wines should be dry, somewhat fruity but not flowery, and subtle. Try Paul Masson, Sebastiani or The Christian Brothers for wines under $4. Compare them with Rumania's Premiat, Yugoslavia's Adriatica, one of those from Argentina or Chile, and Bordeaux blends like De Luze's Club Claret, Sichel's My Cousin's Claret or any of those from a leading shipper. For those under $6 try BV or Louis Martini, Korbel or Parducci, Weibel or Sonoma Vineyards.

Merlot produces a softer and fruitier wine more quickly ready than Cabernet and is the predominant grape in the Pomerol district of Bordeaux. It is grown in Bordeaux vineyards along with Cabernet. Most plantings are still young, but try the wine of Sterling Vineyards, and look out for blends of the two.

31

Cabernets, particularly, are wines to try with abandon, assuming that one can be abandoned about bottles costing $4 and up. As a group, they are the world's most graceful red wines and those of California are among the best.

* * *

Our list of ten grapes stretches to a dozen when Chenin Blanc and Gamay Noir are added, but there should be many more. Some of the world's best grapes have not been given a good try in the United States. There are a few experimental plots and wines from them should be tried whenever they are available.

The Syrah of the Rhône produces magnificent, full wines like Hermitage and Côte Rôtie. They should do splendidly in California because the climates are similar, producing wines for roasts, grilled meats and hearty stews. The only extensive planting is in the Napa Valley at Phelps Vineyards.

Another excellent and similar red is the Nebbiolo of Italy—where it produces the big Barolos, full Gattinaras and lighter Barbarescos in the Piedmont and the Valtellinas of Lombardy: Sassella, Grumello and Inferno. The grape and its wines are also called Spanna in Italy; many sell for under $4, and moderately priced wines could be produced in California. There are no substantial plantings.

There are other red grapes—the Bikaver of Hungary, the Cabernet Franc of Bordeaux, the San Gioveto of Chianti—but white wine grapes offer as alluring a promise.

The most exciting is the Viognier of the Rhône, which provides us with Condrieu and that rare but marvelous dry white, Château Grillet. There is the Roussanne of Hermitage and Crozes-Hermitage, producing full, golden wines. There is the Trebbiano of Italy, which produces a sound wine and is used for Soave along with Garganega, which is even better. In France, Trebbiano is called Ugni Blanc, where it is planted in Cognac and also makes the Riviera white of Cassis. Wente has a little of it, but nobody has yet considered the others.

Then there is Pinot Gris, called Tokay in Alsace, Auxerrois in various parts of France, Rülander in Germany and Pinot Grigio in the mountains north of Venice, where it makes distinctive light wines. With so many names it should be a hit in California, but it is not planted because it is light in acid.

Certainly, a list of best wines could be expanded with Syrah and Nebbiolo, Viognier and Roussanne. They will be planted, along with the others, during the Eighties, to be awaited with great expectations.

Top American Jug Wines

"They cut off the peaks and fill the valleys," said the old professor, passing his hand over the four glasses of Haut Brion like a benediction, up over the '45, down to the '42, high above the '37, higher still over the '34. "The glory of wines is change from vintage to vintage, as the wine-maker brings out the essence of each season's grapes. When a shipper pours all the little châteaux into his vat, sturdy wines with soft ones and so on, you achieve only a plateau of sameness."

How that appealed to my sense of rightness—there should be no limits on righteousness, particularly among shippers—but virtue is costly.

"Blending's the nature of wines," declared the shipper, "and has been since the beginning. A wine too sharp to drink can be blended with one that's too soft and you end up with something pretty good. When you bottle a hundred small châteaux separately you get wines with minor distinctions most people don't notice. Each wine costs more, at least a dollar or more per bottle, and think of all the names, all the labels, all the paperwork. By blending I can market one wine at a better price. Even if I take out the ten best of a hundred I have trouble marketing them." He was indignant. "Here's a glass of my claret—it costs you fifty cents—and here's a little château that costs seventy-five. Tell me it's better by half."

35

It wasn't.

"Most wines need blending. They blend in the vineyards in Bordeaux, planting Cabernet Franc and Petit Verdot and Merlot and Malbec in the vineyard with Cabernet Sauvignon. Champagne wouldn't be Champagne unless you blended the juice of Pinot Noir with Chardonnay or the product of one vineyard with another. Four grapes are used to make Chianti, over a dozen for Châteauneuf-du-Pape. Sémillon and Sauvignon are used to make Sauternes. You blend to make good wines—free run with press wine, young wines with old—it's a matter of balancing stocks."

It's also a matter of stretching wines, of hiding flaws, of getting rid of undrinkable wines.

"A blend is better than its parts, as one wine brings out the best in others. A heavy, tannic wine you wouldn't drink can taste wonderful when blended with a light, flowery wine that would be insipid if tasted by itself. A master blender can take ten uneven wines and make one desirable wine out of them. That's what it's all about."

The shipper's claret was good, no doubt about that, if not remarkable. The little château wasn't remarkable, either. How about great wines?

"Are there a hundred Bordeaux vineyards worth separate bottling? A hundred Burgundies, a hundred Mosels? Would you pay ten dollars and up a bottle, wait years for them to develop? You drink such wines once a month, if you're lucky. What about every day?"

We drink jug wines, four dollars for half a gallon.

"If you spent five dollars or even six you'd drink twice as well," said the shipper accusingly. "Spend maybe thirty cents a glass and you could forget all about little châteaux and boutique wineries and premium varietals." He took himself off in a light huff, somewhat nettled, perhaps the proper state for a shipper selling a million cases a year.

The professor's rightness seemed sensible for his generation, although it scarcely suited ours and the shipper's desire to fill the valleys but leave a hundred peaks in the world's great wine districts. Four dollars seemed plenty to pay for a jug, particularly when you can't be sure another dollar or so would mean much better wines.

"You can't be sure, that's the catch," said the housewife. "We drink one jug until it changes or we grow tired of it, then I shop around for another. If the new one's too bland, we put ice in it, a twist or squeeze of lemon, maybe some soda water. If it's too sharp, as occasionally one of the Blanc de Blancs will be, we mix it with the bland. I scarcely ever buy a six-dollar jug."

Blending your own is one way. Trying the six-dollar blends is another. Doing both is easy. Pour glasses of your regular, and before that's gone pour a second glass of a better wine. It's nice to taste both, more interesting because the wines bring out different tastes in the food.

"That's fine, but it still doesn't solve the problem. Why can't we get nice young fresh wines, the way they do in Europe? Rosé on the Riviera is wonderful; you buy it by the demijohn and it's gone in a couple of days. But it doesn't taste the same when you buy it here. Beaujolais tastes better in France; so do all the country wines. We get nothing like those little Rhine wines. It's a shame."

The wines are fresh because they come straight from the cask. When they're bottled, that's just for convenience in getting them to market; they are drunk within days of the bottling. They aren't in bottle long enough to lose freshness

"That's true," said her housemate. "We liked a Muscadet we had in Paris and we brought back a bottle, but it wasn't as good as we remembered when we opened it. We thought it was us."

It was the wine. Certain wines improve in bottle, especially those from the famous grapes and famous districts. But most wines are best when drunk within a year of the vintage, right from the cask. They aren't lesser wines, only different.

"Why can't California give us wines like those we drink abroad?" demanded the housewife. "That's what I want. That's what everybody wants. I'd pay six dollars for them."

"No you wouldn't," said her mate, "not when you know the same thing would cost you half as much in France. You'd be mad."

"Maybe not. You drink wine all the time in Europe. That's unusual here. If the wine were better we'd drink more."

Our jug wines are better, but different. They cost more because we drink one bottle a month and the French drink a dozen. It's the fault of our fathers, who settled for beer and whiskey. A generation ago importers insisted that a wine should be able to hold together on the shelves for a year and more. That meant high alcohol, over twelve percent, and lots of tannin, lots of fruit acid. Those were big wines, and the best, and that's what we got used to drinking. When California began making good wines in the Sixties they copied the wines from Europe. The closer they got, the better they sold. They'd disappear from the shelves in a week. So now they don't need to be so strong or so sturdy.

"Then why don't they make them?" demanded wife.

Because you won't even try them; you stick to your four-dollar jugs, said I smartly.

"Aha," said her mate.

"If you don't tell me about them, how am I to know?" asked the housewife calmly, pouring a little more of the jug into my glass.

She had me there.

You can't blame the wines on the market, but only on the maker. The two may get together in the jugs.

The first difficulty was size. The producers wanted to sell jugs to get rid of surplus wines and to tap the beer and soft drink markets, so they began offering cheap blends by the gallon. Those jugs wouldn't fit into a refrigerator; customers held out for half-gallon jugs; and this size, more or less, became popular. Half a gallon equaled two bottles and a half, from 60 to 64 ounces, depending on how it was filled. About the same was the European bottle of two liters, a little more than two quarts, or about 68 ounces. Customers paid scant notice to differences in size, but the half-pint variation made it possible for producers to vary quality and price—by 10% or so. Customers ignored this.

The magnum, or double bottle of about 50 ounces, was popular; it looked properly generous on the table, not gross like a jug. People willingly spent four dollars for a magnum, even when they balked at five dollars for a jug. Market experts earned tidy sums explaining why wine priced the same could sell more in one size or the other; depending on their stocks of bottles, some producers stuck to jugs, others switched to magnums.

As for the wine, 12% alcohol was good and any more was better—customers noticed that. If you called it "Chablis," that meant a white wine, sort of dry. If you called it "Burgundy," that meant a red wine, sort of dry. If you called it "Claret," that meant a sort of drier red; "Chianti" meant a sort of less-dry red. Oh yes, and "Rhine" meant a sort of less-dry white. Actually, you could put any wine in the jugs, just so you watched the colors; if you mixed them, you had "rosé." And you called them all "dry."

This arrangement suited producers, who put into the jugs whatever was left over. Customers didn't seem to mind, so long as the price was right and the alcohol high. Snobbish eastern markets preferred the "drier" "Chablis" or "Claret"; the rest of the country went for the other jugs. Market experts made tidy sums analyzing markets.

This California success also stirred up European producers, so their importers began bringing in jugs from Spain, Italy, France, high in alcohol and somewhat drier. Whites were "Blanc de Blancs" or "Macon Blanc" or "Bianco" or whatever, reds were "Claret" or "Bourgogne Rouge" or whatever, and the word IMPORTED was in large type. These sold well. Competition is the spice of trade.

The secret was residual sugar. The California wines had 1% or so of sugar in the wines, which made them taste pleasingly soft. You wanted dry, you bought the imports, which tasted sharper. Many customers, though, said the wines were too dry. More residual sugar was the answer, 3% or so, and the wines were called "mellow." They were given Italianate names, because you didn't notice the sweetness with tomato sauce or ketchup. Mellow wines sold everywhere.

This drove European shippers wild again. You want sweet, said the importers, we'll give you sweet. As the Seventies waned, eight out of ten bottles coming from Europe were sweet Portuguese rosé, sweetish Spanish Sangria, sweet and puckery Italian Lambrusco, slightly sweet German Liebfraumilch. IMPORTED was big on the label.

These were wines to serve with anything. You could even serve them by themselves, without food, drink them any time at all, morning, noon and night. Over a million cases are drunk each week. Unknown carloads of California "dry" and "mellow" wines wash down millions of hamburgers and fried chickens each day. All together they account for nine bottles out of ten drunk in North America. Market experts make bundles by showing how the sale is making America into a wine-drinking continent.

And why not?

If you can't get fresh, young wines without sweetness, you drink what you can get, just so long as it quenches thirst. You want sour, drink beer.

There are light wines coming because there is so much good wine in the world, particularly in California. At least 25,000 acres of good wine grapes have come into bearing in the past couple of years, over 50,000 during the Seventies. Over in Sonoma at mid-decade, August Sebastiani found himself with something like a million gallons of premium wines, vats full of Cabernet and Chardonnay and Pinot. He put them in half-gallon jugs. You can't do that, said the trade, you're upsetting prices. Customers loved it. Now most major wineries are putting the famous grape names on jugs.

At the same time, businessman Norton Simon ventured into the wine business by buying San Martin, the big winery down in Santa Clara. (His acquisitors urged him to buy Sonoma Vineyards, and when he decided against it they resigned and bought it themselves.) At San Martin, somebody began inquiring about light wines, and soon on the market could be found 11% Johannisberg Riesling and some others. They began moving through trade channels so fast, the winery had trouble keeping up. Why not put them in jugs, somebody suggested. Market experts began a study, while up in Sonoma the new owners watched closely . . . The trouble, of course, is the size of the jug. A half-gallon takes up a lot of room in the refrigerator; the magnum is too tall. Change the refrigerator, say the winemakers, so the refrigerator people are making a market study. Let's shorten the big bottle, say winemakers. That's being studied, too, while customers wait . . .

Customers are wising up some, particularly now that women are doing most of the buying. You don't have to buy many jugs to realize that the only difference between California Burgundy and California Claret is the name and that the wine varies from batch to batch and maker to maker. Those from the best winemakers taste a little better than those from ones with lesser reputations, at least sometimes. The more market-wise producers, those that seem to consult market experts least, are beginning to think that they need their own names to identify their wines. Brands, you might call them, like Grand Marque and Mouton Cadet of Bordeaux, Soleil Blanc and Chantefleur of Burgundy. Surely, market experts can discover that brand names have a future in America, just as wines do.

Until the names get sorted out, here's a list of jug wines on the market that are worth trying and comparing.

CALIFORNIA JUGS AND EUROPEAN PEERS (MAGNUMS OF 56.2 OUNCES UNLESS NOTED)

CALIFORNIA WHITES
Around $4
Pedroncelli Sonoma White, ½ gal.
Gallo Sauvignon Blanc
Inglenook Navalle Chenin Blanc
Los Hermanos Chardonnay
Louis Martini Mountain White

IMPORTED WHITES
Around $4
Villa Banfi Roman White
Barberini Colli Albani White, 68 oz.
Folonari Soave, 67 oz.
Victori Pinot Chardonnay
Cartier Blanc de Blancs

40

Around $6
Robert Mondavi White Table Wine
Sterling White
Fetzer Premium White
Sebastiani Mountain Pinot Chardonnay

Around $6
Marino Frascati, 60 oz.
Bonfils Ugni Blanc de Blancs
Cantina Sociale de Soave Bianco
   di Verona (Schoonmaker) 67 oz.

CALIFORNIA REDS

Around $4
Gallo Barbera
Inglenook Navalle Zinfandel
Christian Brothers Claret, 50 oz.
Los Hermanos Gamay Beaujolais
Villa Armando Vino Rustico, 50 oz.
Pedroncelli Sonoma Red, ½ gal.

IMPORTED REDS

Around $4
Villa Banfi Roman Red
Folonari Valpolicella, 67 oz.
Ecu Royale Claret Reserve
Cartier Rouge
Soderi Chianti, ½ gal.
Rubino Mellow Red

Around $6
Robert Mondavi Red Table Wine
Sebastiani Mountain Cabernet
   Sauvignon, ½ gal.
Sterling Red
Fetzer Premium Red
Louis Martini Mountain Red, ½ gal.
Sonoma Vineyards Zinfandel, 50 oz.

Around $6
Bonfils Coteaux du Languedoc, 64 oz.
La Belle Epoque Bordeaux Red
Dourthe Freres Grand Marque
Bertani Valpolicella
Segesta Mellow Red, ½ gal.
Juan Hernandez Burgella, ½ gal.

HANDLING THE JUGS

Lay in a half-dozen screwtop bottles and some stickers. And a funnel. When you buy a jug, pour the wines into the screwtop bottles. Use the funnel, and write the name of the wine on the stickers and stick them on the bottles. The air that gets to the wine while you are pouring is good for the wine. Wine lovers used to decant all wines (into carafes) before serving. Be sure you fill the screwtop bottles as full as possible because air in contact with wine for a long time will spoil the wine. Those who open a jug and pour from it for a few days until the wine is gone will discover that the wine tastes poorer with each passing day. In full-up screwtops the wine will keep for years and maybe even get better.

This may sound like a dumb thing to do, even a nuisance, but it's easy to tire of a jug wine. By putting it in smaller bottles, serving a couple of different ones at a meal, perhaps, the wine will be interesting longer. Besides you get rid of the jug, which is awkward. Some jugs are handsome enough to make into lamps. At our house, nearly all the lamps are jugs. When you have enough lamps, start throwing away the jugs. Empty jugs take up a lot of room.

A JUG WINE BUFFET

This can be a hamburger outdoors, or some salami, cheese and good bread. Jug wines don't call for anything special; they go with what you've got. When you are thirsty, it is pleasant to have two or three different jug wines around so they won't become monotonous and because one may go better with what you are eating than another.

Allow three glasses per person, and pour about three ounces per glass. For a crowd larger than eight, allow two glasses per person, but have an extra jug or two on hand to allow for great thirst.

Have ice and lemons on hand for those who want to make Spritzers; let guests make their own blends of wine and soda. If you have a lot of white wine, put out a bottle of bitter Vermouth like Campari: white wine and Campari and soda, with ice, is a marvelous quenching drink. So is Kyr, made by adding a dollop of the currant liqueur, Cassis, to a glass of white wine, perhaps with ice and soda. Some people like white wine and quinine, or tonic water.

For the first grand day of spring, you might set out a plate of raw asparagus and whatever other raw vegetables you can get, along with the cheese and salami. You could thin some mayonnaise with water for a dip, or make one with a teaspoonful of dry mustard, some of the white wine, some cream and chopped chives. A bowl of fruit, particularly strawberries, is delicious with a glass of white wine. Pears and apples are good with white wine and cheese.

Olives drained and dribbled with olive oil, then stirred with slices of orange, taste splendid with red wine.

In autumn, nothing is better with red wine than roasted chestnuts.

In winter, bring wine to a simmer with a couple of cloves and a sprinkle of nutmeg, add a sprinkle of sugar to taste, pour into mugs and stir with a cinnamon stick. If the mug cools too much, heat the wine again by sticking a hot poker into it. Use either red or white wines for these punches. Add hot water if the drink is too strong, a little brandy or liqueur if the drink is too weak. With bread and cheese and fruit, there's no need to cook.

Good Wines, Good Buys

VIEWPOINT: AN IMPORTER LOOKS AT MID-VARIETALS

"They planted all the wrong grapes," said the importer when I complained about high prices for Californian. "Just when the country's venturing beyond jugs, they plant costly vines for cold climates in warm-weather vineyards, pricing themselves right out of the market. The few wine buffs willing to pay ten dollars a bottle, or even five, are going to play safe and buy European. It's crazy, all those Cabernets and Pinots and Rieslings. They'll have to rip them out."

We were tasting some '21 Rhines gathered by a couple of buffs, grand-father wines amber as old Sherries. There was that dark brown taste, without any syrupy tang, good with walnuts and Gruyère and Jarlsberg and tough bread. There were changing hints of fruit and flower in the ripe sweetnesses of these survivors of a vintage unequaled for fifty years. Hearty ghosts, to be judged finally only when the '71s are half a century old—by our grandchildren.

"They're trying to make things like this in California right now," said the importer, "to cop gold medals in some wine Olympics of the future. And there isn't even a race on. It's dumb, when what people want is a nice three-dollar bottle for dinner."

Good grapes are better than bad, said I, absently, between sips of a

43

Riesling and a Traminer, both pretty much alike. Maybe the Traminer was fruitier.

"That's not the point," said the importer. "They get yields of maybe three tons an acre from the shy bearers and when they push for more or stretch by blending they make bland wines. And then they go in for those nutty crosses with high yields for the hot vineyards, like Ruby Cabernet, when there are dozens of good-bearing Mediterranean and Balkan grapes they haven't even tried."

With so much Cabernet and such they could drop prices, said I. Maybe the Riesling taste lingered longer.

"They can't," said the importer. "The wines cost too much to make. Grape growers don't change. They make the same mistakes over and over again. Look at Burgundy. Look at Bordeaux.'

They cost too much, too, I said, The Traminer tasted less tired, maybe, and it was a lesser grape, too.

"The French get a nice trade going and then the speculators move in, skimming off the best wines and jumping prices, which people finally refuse to pay, so the boom busts and the cycle starts over."

That keeps a lot of new wines coming on the market, I said. The walnuts and the cheese tasted good with the wines, just as they do with Port. Ought to drink Port more.

"And what the new wines do is confuse," said the importer. "A store owner can't keep track of Spanish, Italian, Hungarian, Chilean, Yugoslavian—you name it —and so he concentrates on a few blends and popular names and bargains. So people buy Liebfraumilch and Lambrusco, Sangria and Portuguese rosé, and never know what they're mis sing."

"Are there any really good California wines we're missing?" asked one of the buffs. We were back where we started. More or less.

They certainly planted the wrong grapes to begin with, poor ones that made bad wine. It's helpful to know why they planted all the wrong grapes in California—in order to avoid them.

Spanish padres brought Spanish vines up from Mexico, planting them at every mission along El Camino Real, the royal road that ran up to the Sonoma Valley, north of San Francisco Bay. There are still some 6,000 acres of Mission grapes abounding, bringing down the level of every blend they go into.

Equally vile is Alicante-Bouschet, a cross named after its developers, who wanted a heavy bearer for the French Midi. A *teinturier*, or dyer, its red juice darkens pale wines and its high alcohol strengthens weak ones. Planted all over California to provide home makers with dark juice during Prohibition, there remain 6,400 acres of them, 10 square miles, still being used for stretching and coloring.

A horde of mass-production grapes were planted out in the great valley of the San Joaquin, partly for stretch wines, but also for distilling into brandy. At least a dozen varieties remain, more than 50 square miles of them, so that raisin and table grapes can be made into wine. Half of California vineyards are in raisin grapes (nearly 250,000 acres) and table grapes (nearly 70,000 acres).

Most widely planted is Thompson Seedless, called the 3-way grape because it can be used not only for raisins but for table grapes and for wine, growers and shippers insist, despite all criticism. Old 3-way went into the Sneaky Pete of the Depression, the sweet Muscatel and Sherry and Port that was the cheapest form of alcohol—from 14% to 21%. It went into the lighter wines for the pop generation of the Sixties, all those with the funny names, and into untold bottlings before and since. All that color and stretch wine from mass-production grapes—they came to be called standard grapes, although most of them were below any creditable standard—was used for making into marketable wines and even into brandy and industrial alcohol.

Old 3-way is certainly a wrong grape, as are any table or raisin grapes that make their way into wines. Marketed as California Chablis or Burgundy or Rhine, or given an Italianate name or a brand name, they become soda pop substitutes with alcohol. But some of the standard wine grapes did well in the San Joaquin. Importers would like to see them planted in the cooler vineyards under their own names, replacing the noble vines that compete with imports. Many of them can make superior wines to compete with European regionals.

The importer was not complaining about past sins, but about competition. Bordeaux can supply him with all the Cabernet he needs, the Rhine with Rieslings, Burgundy with Pinot and Chardonnay. The cool-climate vineyards around San Francisco Bay and down the coast may be cool enough only in places to be ideal for those noble vines, but skill and science have extended the range. California wines compete with European.

45

The coast vineyards are rarely as cool as those in Europe, nor do the vines get as much light. The wines are softer, less distinctive, age more quickly. The wines are different.

A truism is that the noble vines do best at the extremity of the growing range, where the vines are stressed. The vines are not under stress so much in California—but the growers are. Past success urges them on. What has come into being is a new family of wines, like the great wines of Europe, but different. The wines themselves cannot easily be compared, but levels of excellence can be.

A favorite question is, Which do you prefer, Burgundy or Bordeaux? Experts answer that it is good to have both. Today a new region enters the reckoning. Isn't it nice we have all three?

Even Prohibition served California well. Many of the mass-production grapes were pulled out. And there was time for much consideration as to what to plant when Repeal came along in 1932. Vines were needed for the San Joaquin, and the new wine department of the University of California at Davis began making crosses. A number of hybrids were developed, several producing palatable wines; Ruby Cabernet and Emerald Riesling are the most widely planted (18,000 acres and 3,000 acres), but there are Centurion (1,400 acres), Carnelian (2,400 acres), Flora (500 acres) and at least a promising score still in experimental plots. Grapes developed for hot climates may revolutionize the wine world before the turn of the centruy, thanks to all those lousy grapes that once grew in the San Joaquin.

There was still another boon. Most California wine a generation ago was so bad that native pride anguished. The postwar generation of winemakers just had to come up with something good. There had been the odd spectacular bottle here and there for the past hundred years. Certainly intelligence and effort could pay off. In the Sixties they began doing so.

The new region of California began doing well with the noble grapes, which they began calling varietals or premium wines to distinguish them from wines named after European regions, which they called generics. Then California began doing well with other grapes.

There was Gewürstraminer, for instance, and Sylvaner, secondary grapes of the Rhine. Labeled with grape names, they were certainly premium varietals. And what about Zinfandel and Petite Sirah, unknown or unheralded in Europe. And even lesser grapes that produced vast quanti-

46

ties of good wine, what about them? They came to be called mid-varietals because they were cheaper.

The rule seemed to be that if the wine cost over $4, it was premium. If the wine cost under $4 it was a mid-varietal. If the label had a grape name on it, the wine was premium. If the wine bore the name of a European region, it was not premium, but a generic. Such confusion.

At least they were getting away from old 3-way and friends.

How do you judge the wines? Price is a good criterion. Reputation of the bottler is another. Grapes that do well in California, like Barbera, are discussed in the following pages.

Some of these good wines are considered separately, as good buys. A second group can be made up of good wines that can be drunk casually—salad wines or picnic wines—whenever you come upon them. They are more consistent than the generic wines, better than generics if only because they are more precisely labeled.

Below are grapes considered mid-varietals, whose plantings have been extended over the past decade. The chart shows acreage (40 acres or larger) of mid-varietals in 10 leading counties noted for superior wines.* Smaller plots can be considered experimental.**

	Barbera	Carignane	Colombard	Grenache	Petite Sirah	Zinfandel
Alameda			95		50	135
Lake					40	320
Mendocino		2,200	1,000	90	500	1,100
Monterey	200	120	470	610	2,200	3,200
Napa		450	600	50	1,000	1,500
San Benito		235		200		200
San Luis Obispo	70					1,100
Santa Barbara						60
Santa Clara		200	120	100	20	200
Sonoma	50	1,500	200	60	1,000	3,800
TOTALS	300+	4,700+	3,500	1,100+	5,000	12,000

*Figures from various sources, rounded off. Totals also rounded off.

**Compared to total acreage for these grapes, these figures are modest, although confidence is being shown in all but Barbera, the most promising of the lot.

The following grapes have been widely planted in this decade:

VARIETY	SIXTIES ACREAGE	SEVENTIES ACREAGE
Barbera	1,600	20,000
Carignane	24,000	30,000
Colombard	6,000	26,000
Grenache	12,000	20,000
Petite Sirah	3,000	13,000
Zinfandel	17,000	30,000

These grapes are producing remarkable wines in cool vineyards. Zinfandel and Petite Sirah are often considered to be fine wines when planted in cool vineyards.

Unique Wines: Zinfandel and Petite Sirah, Sylvaner and Gewürztraminer, Grenache

America has some of the world's most exotic wines, astonishing and delightful, a new world to those used to the ordinary bottlings of Europe, those regional blends of Bordeaux, Burgundy, Italy and the Rhineland. The history of disappointment has been such that even most Americans are unaware of what can be found. Lief Ericson was so awed by the grapes abounding that Vinland seemed the only suitable name, but then, his crew made wine in the hollow of a rock. It was awful, and continued to be for a thousand years. This present generation is seeing promise fulfilled. There is, for example, Zinfandel.

Zinfandel. Nobody knows where it came from, maybe the Rhône or Italy or even Russia, but almost certainly it came to America with Agoston Haraszthy during the Civil War. He was Hungarian, and after several trials, he set up Buena Vista on a Sonoma hillside with a good view. The grapes he had there made horrors, so he talked the newly independent state into backing a European trip in search of vines. He brought back thousands of cuttings but the war was raging and nobody cared. The state refused to pay him for his twigs; he couldn't sell the cuttings; finally he gave them away to neighbors. Among them was Zinfandel, or so they say. Nobody knows for sure because the tags were lost. Disgusted, Agoston left sons Arpad and Attila with the winery and took himself off to Nicaragua to try

48

his hand with coconuts and rum. He fell into a river and was devoured by crocodiles, a lesson to those who try to make a fortune from wines. Maybe you don't even get coconuts.

Zinfandel persisted, showing that Haraszthy had had the right idea in the first place. It began replacing Mission in vineyards. The vine flourished without much care, bearing heavy bunches that easily made into wine that wasn't bad at all, no matter how careless you were. It was dark red in color, had a fruity smell and taste that reminded you of berries, and tasted like a Beaujolais or Chianti when young, like a Rhône or Piedmont after a few years in cask, like a claret after a long stay in bottle. Used as a stretch wine and for blending, it fell into disrepute, considered to be not much above the Mission, but a few winemakers kept the faith.

A newspaperman named Frank Bartholomew bought Buena Vista in the Forties and decided to see what could be done with Haraszthy's best-known grape, perhaps something more than the country wines made by the Italian settlers all around him. Up in Mendocino, Parducci had the same idea, as did Louis Martini, over in Napa. By the Sixties just about everybody was making Zinfandel and claiming to be the birthplace of the vine. Grapes from irrigated vines out in the Great Valley were made into wines for jugs of California Burgundy and California Claret. Over in Napa, light wines like Beaujolais came forth as Mountain Red. In Sonoma they made Chianti types; up in Mendocino, Piedmont types, long in cask, were produced. Small wineries made Late Harvest wines from raisinized grapes, sometimes 17% in alcohol; others made wines from grapes attacked by botrytis, the noble mold, almost reminding you of Port.

"I don't like Zinfandel," states the one who has tasted a couple, which is like saying you don't like sex because your first girl got lipstick on your chin and made you feel funny.

Some Zinfandels still display the old California style—wines that are flowery and fruity, smelling and tasting of wood most usually identified as cedar, with a heaviness from alcohol and an underlying sweetness. This was the taste of Central Valley grapes fermented and aged in redwood. That old redwood taste, Easterners call it, looking down their noses, even holding them.

Not much redwood remains in California wineries, and even overbearing grapes from the central valley are cool-fermented in stainless steel. These cheapest of Zinfandels, even with 2% or 3% of the grape sugar left in the wine, taste rounded and full, great spaghetti wines. Bottles that have been kept for several years, which cost originally less than two dollars, develop a sturdy taste and lose sweetness. They are meant to be drunk young, to appeal to the American sweet tooth, to have the common touch, but when five years old, the taste is intriguing and reminiscent of fine old wines from anywhere—not great, but not bad, either.

There are many Zinfandels to choose from, at least one hundred new ones every year. Even five-year-old wines may cost less than four dollars. Ordinary Zinfandels, in jug or bottle, are good buys. They taste best chilled—perhaps half an hour in the refrigerator—and they can be lightened with a couple of ice cubes and a squirt of soda. A lemon peel cuts any sweetness, a squeeze of lemon sharpens the taste. Fixed to your taste, these Zinfandels are really wines that go with anything. Not fish, of course, or seafood.

Nearly 30,000 acres of Zinfandel flourish in California, but not much more than a third are in the cool counties. Only there, are the wines truly delightful; and only then, when the vines are pruned well so that yields are kept down, the winemaking is expert, and storage is not in redwood. (Of course, now that the old California taste has begun to disappear, many are nostalgic for it. Not me.) Given those basics, Zinfandel is the best wine of California. It is also the best buy in all the world of wines.

"Cabernets are better," say the winemakers, "and just wait, we're going to do wonders with Pinot Noir. We've scarcely begun with the Gamays, not to mention Merlot." "Those are different, not better," you answer. "Why compare apples and oranges?" The query is ignored. "Zinfandel's OK," is the response. "Some are good; a few are even great wines that can live a long time and develop subtleties."

It's just Zin, is the unspoken final comment, familiar, even fine, but not Cabernet. Anybody can make a good Zin; not many can make a great Cabernet. It's like saying Louis Armstrong was a great jazz trumpeter but he couldn't play classical. He could, too. With joy.

An eastern argument goes that we have all the Cabernets anybody could want from Bordeaux. It's a pleasure to see what the grape does elsewhere, particularly when it is cheaper, but you don't need seven million cases of Cabernets at prices starting at four dollars, which is what California is producing now, with more to come.

You do need the almost twelve million cases of Zinfandel, priced from two dollars up. (The most expensive Zinfandel currently availiable is

Ridge Lytton Springs, under seven dollars. This is twice the cost of most of the premium Zinfandels.)

Getting to know Californian is easy with Zinfandel. You cover the range of vineyards and winemaking in half a dozen bottles. Starting a tasting course, the lead taster (more like the trailbreaker on a dog team than a teacher) is wise to go to the best shop around and have the owner pick out six Zinfandels. What the other tasters like shows preferences and prejudices which suggest what the rest of the tasting sessions should be. One wine not to miss is Pedroncelli's Sonoma Zinfandel at about three dollars. If that's not available, try for the Zinfandel from the San Francisco retailer and importer, Bercut-Vandevoort, who found Pedroncelli's wine and buys much of it for his own label. Failing that, try for Nichelini's or Louis Martini's, over in Napa. In any event, get one from each of the cool counties and maybe Roma, Guild, Franzia or Gallo from the Great Valley.

Zinfandel is too much wine for people used to bland Italian jugs or cheap Rhine wines. There is too much taste. It's one wine that should be served with bread and cheese and even salami at a tasting. The cheese should be a hard one, a slicing cheese like Swiss or Cheddar. Some food makes the wine seem more familiar, less startling.

If Zinfandel could be traced to a home in Europe, it might win more respect. Perhaps it is a seedling or a mutation, for vines have to come from a cutting to breed true. Vineyardists call such a wayward offspring a sport, a name to fit. Latest word is that Zinfandel came from southern Italy, which is no boon, because that is a region of cheap wines.

Petite Sirah. Petite Sirah is another grape that is California's own, certainly a sport. Once it was traced to a Rhône grape, the Duriff, now outlawed there, so it came to be called the Petite Sirah, after the noble vine it resembles. Not despised at all in California, it makes a strong and balanced red, sometimes startling in its depth of flavor and robustness. Deep in color, it was used as a blending wine, until James Concannon noticed that the wine had some distinction and began bottling it separately. The Concannon Petite Sirahs of the Sixties were marvels and they are better today. Parducci began making very full Petite Sirahs up in Mendocino ("They'll last fifty years," says John), and neighboring wineries began experimenting. Today there are a score on the market, from some 13,000 acres, producing over five million cases.

The wine needs age in cask and bottle, at least three years, even twice that, most of those marketed being full-bodied and lasting. The wine is usually well cleared before bottling, but tastes better when it has been decanted two hours or more before it is drunk.

If a grape possibly from the Rhône does so well, the Syrah demands attention. After all, there are scarcely 20,000 cases of Côte Rôtie, scarcely 30,000 of Hermitage, the two great reds of the Rhône. (Châteauneuf-du-Pape produces some 800,000 cases, some good, all overpriced.) The trouble with the Syrah is that grapes drop from the bunch before they ripen, an ill called *coulure*, which reduces yield. Bravely, Phelps Vineyard has a bearing plot that produces a full and subtle wine, sure to encourage others to plant more. In the Eighties, Syrah will be one of the best wines of California. Meanwhile, Petite Sirah is abundantly available.

Sylvaner. Californians used to big flower and fruit may think their native ferments are like those of the Mediterranean. Easterners find them much stranger, as exotic as gypsy vintages from Hungary, stout Balkan pressings, Rumanian treadings, Crimean mysteries. The wines are wild, conjuring Bohemian delights of painters' studios, sculptors' lofts—Left Bank, Latin Quarter and Soho in every glass. They call for goulash and sausages, venison haunches, bread torn from the loaf and fruit eaten out of hand, as men wander and maidens dance. Bacchus would have loved them.

Bacchus loved the hills, as Livy said, and vines came from the east to European slopes, out of Persia, across the Carpathians, by way of the Danube or the Tyrol. Sylvaner was surely one of these, making a fresh and agreeable wine in Austria, getting more austere as it moves west through Bavaria and into Alsace. There it becomes the wine for smoked meats, dumplings and sauerkraut, when beer is not enough.

The trouble with Sylvaner is that is is not very assertive, just fruity and pleasant. It is the most widely planted vine in Germany, dominating in the Rheinpfalz and in Franconia, where it is called Franken Riesling and makes Frankenwein. (In Switzerland it is called the Johannisberg.) In California, where it is thought to be not much more than fair, it is called Riesling, to give it tone; the name is legal, though confusing, and should be abandoned. The vine has been crossed successfully with the true Riesling and the crosses are called Main Riesling or Müller-Thurgau; the two grapes warrant exploration.

It is well to bear in mind that there is also the Grey Riesling, a wine popular in San Francisco, but actually the Chauché Gris of France, where it is little considered. A cross developed at Davis, called Emerald Riesling has become popular as Paul Masson's Emerald Dry. California should really do something about its names for wines.

Sylvaner is best of the lot and deserves having its own name on labels. There are almost 1,500 acres, but most of it goes into blends, which is too bad. A good wine ought not to be used to make poor wines into something mediocre. Sylvaner could be as popular here as it is in Europe, a simple *vin de carafe*.

Gewürztraminer. When something with more taste than Sylvaner is called for, a wine with more presence, one that is more beguiling, open a bottle of Gewürztraminer. The spicy grape is a special strain of a vine that comes from the mountains north of Venice, named for a town once known as Tramin, now Termeno. The grape excels in Alsace, where its wines are soft and almost too spicy for some—until they try it with choucroûte garnie or sauerbraten, roast duck or something from the pig.

In California, Gewürztraminer is not quite so highly perfumed, which can be a blessing, because its aroma can fill a room. There are some 220 acres in California, a five-fold increase during the decade, a sign of its growing popularity. The name is sharp but the wine is soft and the spicy character is quickly evident, while the acidity is not. Some think the wine is more herbal than spicy, reminiscent of basil or oregano in intensity. The wine does not taste best with dishes containing those herbs, but with those that include sage or thyme, spices or fruits. Sour dishes with some sweetness contrast well with it. Gewürztraminer is a special wine.

Grenache Rosé and Company: Pinks No Longer Pallid. Rosés are made from black grapes, the juice being left with the skins just long enough to pick up some color. White wines are made from red wine grapes by separating the juice from the skins right after pressing; Champagnes use the white juice of Pinot Noir for their blends, there being no problem at all in making a fine wine in this fashion. This rarely seems to happen when it comes to rosés.

Rosés are generally considered to be bland little wines scarcely worth serious attention. For a generation wine drinkers have turned up their noses at them. They are supposed to go with anything; they are certainly served with everything. The best taste like a light red wine, even look like one, and these deserve more recognition than they get. Slowly, attitudes are changing.

The best from France comes from Tavel, where the grape is Grenache. The best from Italy is made from the Grignolino. Both are grown in California, 20,000 acres of the first, a doubling during the decade, and some 150 acres of the second, which is better.

Grenache Rosé from Almadén was the wine that started America on its wine-drinking way a generation ago. It swept the country, imitators followed, and when Almadén began making a big thing of grape names on the label, others did, as well.

Rosé can be beautiful.

Nothing looks more marvelous on a table than a glass of rosé. Fresh from the cask, rosé is delicious, as anyone who has summered on the Riviera is only too glad to tell you. Some of the Tavels are quite marvelous, as are some of the orange wines from the Loire that are called rosés.

Almadén's Grenache Rosé was almost dry. The other big wineries called in market experts to find out why it was so popular. It's not quite dry, said some marketers, so their wineries made a drier rosé. It's a little sweet, said other marketers, and their wineries made a sweeter rosé. More is better. All sold, but nobody caught up with Almadén, which was selling thousands of cases.

Gallo consulted nobody. They made a rosé like Almadén's, one drier and one sweeter. They sold thousands of carloads. It's the American way.

Gallo thought all of this was great. More rosé would be greater. They made Gypsy Rose. They made Pink Chablis. They made Boone's Farm Strawberry Hill, using apples. They made Red Rosé. They made Pink Champagne. More carloads.

Eager Europeans and avid importers flung themselves on the market, copying everybody. Today there must be a hundred rosés available, at least one from every wine district on earth. Some are not so dry. Some are not so sweet.

The popularity of pink wines has influenced some of our best winemakers to try their hands. There is a challenge, because rosés do not have to be bland, or sweet with residual sugar. They can be made so that they are full of fruit acids, light in alcohol, tempting and quenching. They can be marketed so that they are sold within six months of the vintage, as appealing as any wine straight from the cask.

Any shop has a wide range. New bottlings are the ones to look for, and those from producers whose other wines you like. A great advantage is that they are cheap, many selling for under $3 a bottle. If you get an insipid one by mistake, some lemon, ice and soda water—or the addition of a sharp red or white—can make it palatable.

Of special interest are pink wines made from Zinfandel, and there are others from Cabernets, Pinot Noirs and various other red grapes.

The point is that the pink wines should not be scorned merely because of color. There are good bottles to be found, attractive wines for picnics and casual meals.

Salad Wines

VIEWPOINT: DIETING WITH WINES

"All I eat these days is salads," said the lady of a certain fullness, with a sigh. "At first, I was miserable—all that lettuce and cottage cheese and carrots. Then I had to go to California for a few days. It changed my life. They serve salads first."

I like salads, I interposed.

"They serve wine with the salads. Good wines. They use raw zucchini in some, with anchovies. Raw mushrooms and spinach and bacon. Fennel with cucumber. Sliced endive. They vary salads much more than we do. With the wines, they're marvelous. So now I always have salad first, with wine, and if I want something more—which I rarely do—then I have something grilled or maybe some cheese. And more wine. I'm down ten pounds. You ought to say something about salad wines."

SALAD WINES FOR SALAD DAYS, AND EUROPEAN PEERS

The simple French meal with wine—something to start with, a fish or meat course or both, salad, cheese and fruit, maybe dessert—is only a couple of generations old. It is a Parisian meal, adapted by city people from older customs of court and country—imitations of the great ban-

57

quets of the rich, sophistications of the hearty dishes from the farms. It is a marvelous meal, easily expanded with extra courses or special dishes to glorify the season or the guest, easily reduced to bread, cheese and wine—and maybe something from the *charcuterie*. The pork butcher provides all sorts of delicacies for a first course, as the *pâtisserie* supplies dessert. The French family buys pâté or pastry, only making them for special occasions. The market varies the meals, with a new mushroom or vegetable or cheese every week—seasonal joys. And always a simple wine.

The wines we drink so casually, the classed growths of Bordeaux, the great and first growths of Burgundy, rarely appear on French tables. It's usually a Beaujolais or Rhône or Midi for red, a Macon or Muscadet or Sylvaner for white—brand wines from the grocery store. All other wines are special.

The pattern evolved out of the restaurants, where you ordered course by course. Salad—invariably greens with oil and vinegar—stopped the wine drinking, which could start again with the cheese. The meal ended with the salad; the evening began with the cheese.

It's an odd pattern—and it was broken in California, where the salad came to be served first. This may have started in restaurants, to give diners something to eat while the orders were being prepared. It scarcely took hold in the East, where you drank cocktails and highballs until the orders were served.

Some of us still like the French way, with courses and small portions, a glass of white wine or a light red with the first, a glass of fuller or older wine with the main course, a rest during the salad, another glass with the cheese. A meal lasts for hours.

Most of us grew up eating the American way, with everything on the plate, and second helpings. This is still meat-and-potato country, with vegetables on the side, and much of the time there's no room for salad—and scarcely time for wine. Some of us are happy with a glass or two sipped along the way, and when we do have room for salad we go on drinking the wine, even finishing it with dessert. Wines don't taste their best this way; salads get set aside. Sometimes salads are the best part of the meal. Vinegar makes the wine taste bad, we are told, so we cut down on the vinegar. And still we hesitate to have a bite of salad with the main course, because salad is bad with wine. It was a great leap to freedom when Californians decided wine was fine with salad—good, ordinary wine.

Serving salads first, when you're hungry, is a fine way to stir your appetite for what's coming, like the rustle of a curtain going up. It is a leisurely start to a meal, the bustle of tossing and passing plates serving as an overture. After a few forkfuls a sip of wine tastes good.

Italians have eaten so all along; so have country people everywhere. A meal begins with a bang, as the bottle of wine is set on the table. There are clinks as the glasses are poured, lifted, sipped—and then everybody looks to the cook to see what's coming.

There's antipasto while you wait.

The way we eat is as much habit as custom, so people who come to like wines after growing up on fruit juice and soda pop find themselves changing old patterns. This can be upsetting, though pleasurable.

Think of Chaplin, snowbound in the Yukon, carefully turning his shoelace on a fork as if it were a strand of spaghetti. And no wine. Watch the tourist in a Paris bistro as he considers the small slice of steak on his plate and the smaller serving of potatoes, and no vegetable on the side. See the Midwesterner in the south examining the grits piled beside his bacon and eggs. Note the look on the New Englander's face as the Texas waitress pours the coffee before she takes the order.

Such ways have much to do with drinking wine.

We take wine much too seriously—and miss the fun. Wines don't go with salads? Of course they do.

Set out a plate of sliced tomatoes, scallions, celery, pimiento and pepper strips, black and green olives, a couple of kinds of salami, some ham, slices of a couple of kinds of cheese, some anchovies and sardines. Open a bottle of French Colombard or Gray Riesling, or both, and a bottle of Ruby Cabernet or Carignane, or both. Break off a crust of bread . . .

What's for dinner? That's it.

In your favorite little French restaurant call for the hors d'oeuvre cart and it's little dishes of artichoke hearts, ratatouille, céleri remoulade, haricots vinaigrette, shrimp, herring . . . In the East you can get Maréchal Foch or Chelois for reds, Delaware or Aurora for whites, and then there's Sémillon and Emerald Riesling, Barbera or Grignolino.

What else? Skip dinner. How about a dessert?

Women order this way much of the time, claiming diet as an excuse. The real reason is that a couple of bites of various foods full of taste is satisfying and even exciting. Common sense or mother wit leads to such eating, delicious with a glass of wine or two.

All of it is salad fare, as is a Scandinavian smorgasbord or an American buffet. Every country has its version of this way to start a meal, made up of things that go into salads. Most of them taste best with simple wines.

Most wines are salad wines, young, fresh and quenching. Only a few are meant for formal meals, wines that call for aging in wood and bottle. These last get more attention, even though young wines are more versatile and less demanding. Young wines taste good with whatever is around. Any floweriness or fruitiness contrasts with or complements the food—the salty and sour, the bitter and sweet, the oiliness or chewy textures. Only when the food is too sweet, too sour—too strong in taste—does a sip of wine taste poorly. So we mute the taste of strong foods with a bite of bread—and the wine tastes good again.

Salad wines help to loosen us up about eating and drinking. We use our senses first of all as guards, like a child sipping his first soda pop. Then we use our senses to explore, like the child venturing on to root beer, ginger ale, lemonade.

The wine industry appreciates this very well, with their Cold Duck, their apple wines, their Sangrias. Because they are wine-based drinks, winemakers say they are a transition from soda pop to real wines. They are actually a substitution for soft drinks, drunk mostly apart from meals, and lead not at all to table wines in a natural and automatic progression.

But salad wines do lead the drinker to those aged wines that develop subtleties from time in wood and bottle. Most people are delighted with salad wines, content to have them with whatever goes on the table. Once you discount soda-pop substitutes, their number accounts for nine wines out of ten, including

- Jug wines without pronounced sweetness.
- Wines costing less than $3 a bottle.
- Wines intended to be drunk young.
- Wines with brand names.
- Wines from grapes not considered noble.

They taste fine with salads, simple or composed. The mere listing seems to be putting them in a lesser category. But to say they are for casual drinking, everyday drinking, is to mark them as the best of wines, like good bread or good cheese. Aged wines taste best now and then, at a meal served at a table with congenial company, that most civilized of ceremonies, ranking with weddings, baptisms, anniversaries, coronations and funerals.

Salad wines are for picnics and firesides, beaches and canoe trips, suppers and lunches, sandwiches and snacks, fishing and sailing. Here is a list of some, easily expanded by any you find on a shop shelf anywhere.

WHITES

AMERICAN VERSIONS	EUROPEAN VERSIONS
Mountain White	Blanc de Blancs, Aligote

Quenching, pleasant. Good with cold cuts, clams, vegetable and tuna and seafood salads.

Chasselas	Fendant, Gutedel, Zwicker, Schoppenwein

Bland, pleasant, good with quiche or fondue, salads with cheese.

Colombard	Vin blanc, Grinzing, Verdicchio, Vermentino

Slight bitterness, pleasing sharpness. Good with seafood salads, egg salads, cold cuts.

Emerald Riesling	Graves, Frascati

Pleasant, quenching. See Mountain White.

Grey Riesling	Italian or Spanish jug whites

Bland, pleasant. With antipasto or salads with antipasto ingredients, rice salads.

Sauvignon Vert	See Colombard

Often bitter, somewhat harsh. With sausages, smorgasbord, potato salads.

Sémillon	Graves, Vino Blanco, Vino Bianco, Furmint

Soft, lightly sweet. Excellent with ham or any spiced or smoked meats, in or out of salads.

Sylvaner   Silvaner, Franken Riesling,
                                           Verdiso, Pinot Grigio
    Soft, rounded. Good with smoked meats, salads with cheese.

Veltliner   Termeno, Vermentino,
                                           Grinzing
    Sharp, lightly spicy. Good with ham, salami, salads containing them.

Ugni Bland, Trebbiano   Soave, Frascati,
                                           Blanc de Blancs
    Balanced, fresh, attractive, good with salads containing fish or seafood, spiced or smoked meats.

REDS
AMERICAN VERSIONS   EUROPEAN VERSIONS
Mountain Red   Spanish or Italian jugs
    Pleasant, quenching, soft. Good with potato or noodle salads containing meat or cheese.

Barbera   Bardolino, Valpolicella
    Full, dark, pleasantly sharp. Good with antipasto, Italian mixed salads.

Carignan   Vin rouge, vino rosso
    Fruity, dry, pleasant. See Barbera, Mountain Red.

Gamay   Macon Rouge, Côtes-du-Rhône
    Bland, pleasant. Good with meat, cheese salads.

Grenache   Any dry rosé, or light red.
    Best as rosé, light, quenching. Drys are good with meat salads, half-drys with seafood salads, chicken.

Pinot St. George
    Like Gamay; sometimes sharp. See Gamay.

Ruby Cabernet   Bordeaux Supérieur, Chianti
  Soft, dry, bland. Good with potato or macaroni salads, dev-
  illed eggs, pizza.

Valdepeñas   Vin rouge, vino rosso
  Light, pleasant enough. See Gamay.

Zinfandel
  Belongs on any list of American wines. See all of above.

Part II:
The Grand Experiment

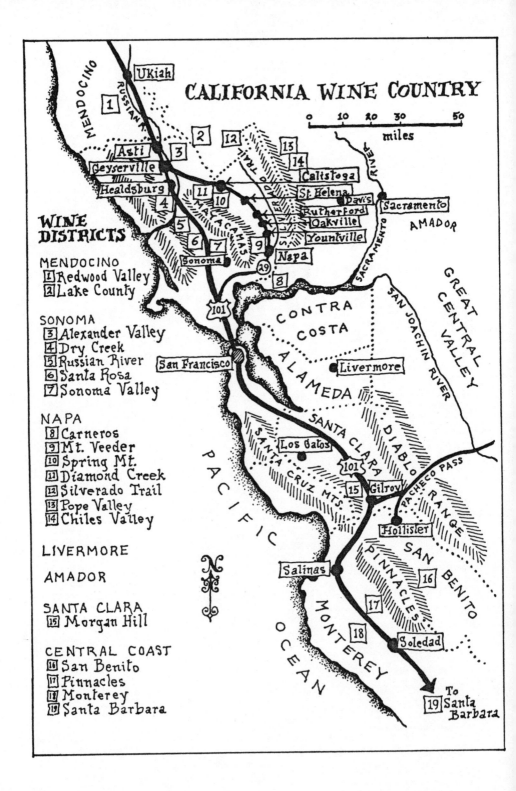

CALIFORNIA WINE COUNTRY

0 10 20 30   50
miles

WINE DISTRICTS

MENDOCINO
1 Redwood Valley
2 Lake County

SONOMA
3 Alexander Valley
4 Dry Creek
5 Russian River
6 Santa Rosa
7 Sonoma Valley

NAPA
8 Carneros
9 Mt. Veeder
10 Spring Mt.
11 Diamond Creek
12 Silverado Trail
13 Pope Valley
14 Chiles Valley

LIVERMORE

AMADOR

SANTA CLARA
15 Morgan Hill

CENTRAL COAST
16 San Benito
17 Pinnacles
18 Monterey
19 Santa Barbara

Ukiah
MENDOCINO
RUSSIAN R.
Asti
Geyserville
Healdsburg
Calistoga
St. Helena
Davis
Rutherford
Oakville
Yountville
Sonoma
Napa
Sacramento
SACRAMENTO RIVER
AMADOR
GREAT CENTRAL VALLEY
CONTRA COSTA
ALAMEDA
SAN JOAQUIN RIVER
101
San Francisco
Livermore
SANTA CLARA
Los Gatos
SANTA CRUZ MTS.
DIABLO RANGE
PACHECO PASS
Gilroy
Hollister
SAN BENITO
PINNACLES
Salinas
MONTEREY
Soledad
PACIFIC OCEAN
N
To Santa Barbara
MAYACAMAS
29

California: One More Time

"Are there any really good wines in California?" asked my seatmate, as we finished a sort of stew over Kansas. I took a sip of Almadén's Cabernet Sauvignon that the airline had graciously served me for a dollar, and nodded.

"I mean as good as what we get from Europe," she said, crossing her legs and taking another sip of Scotch in lieu of dessert, which was a square of something yellow on the bottom and something pink on the top, with flecks. I nodded again, and smiled.

"Which ones do you like?" she said, lighting a cigarette. You can't just sit there, reading the flight magazine; talking is better.

They come from the premium wineries around San Francisco. That's what they call the smaller wineries whose prices start around three dollars a bottle. The biggest of these, over nine million cases a year, is Almadén. Paul Masson sells around five million, Inglenook over three million, The Christian Brothers over two million. Sebastiani used to be less than a million, but they put some top premiums in jugs and doubled in size and may do so again. Lots of the premiums are going to double in size.

"Why?" she asked, sipping her Scotch.

We're drinking our own wines now. They're making wines that don't

67

need aging, especially whites. And rosés are getting good. New vineyards are coming in.

"Which are best?" Not that she cared, still doubting.

Napa used to have most of the best grapes but now they are spread around. There's Sonoma Vineyards and Korbel, Cresta Blanca in Mendocino, Mirassou in Monterey. They all make a quarter to half a million cases, as do Louis Martini and Beringer Brothers in Napa. All of them have special bottlings. Those making up to two hundred thousand cases are Robert Mondavi, BV and Krug in Napa, and Monterey Vineyards, which is growing.

"What's size got to do with it?" interjected my seatmate, eager to stop the flow.

The smaller, the more distinctive, supposedly. Sterling in Napa can produce about a hundred thousand cases, Sonoma has Souverain, Simi and Geyser Peak, Mendocino has Parducci; down south is San Martin.

"The smaller, the more expensive," my companion said.

Wente and Concannon in Livermore make fifty thousand cases, many under four dollars. Rutherford Hill in Napa, Firestone in Santa Barbara, will be the same size. Wineries that make twenty-five thousand cases have to charge more, like Heitz or Freemark Abbey, Chappellet or Phelps, in Napa. Château Montelena and Spring Mountain are a little smaller, but growing. Sonoma has Pedroncelli and Château St. Jean, there is Ridge down in Santa Cruz.

"That's too many, already," she said. "And they try to supply the whole country?"

Some get out to the big cities, and any store can order them. Even some of the fifteen-thousand-case wineries get around, like Burgess and Stag's Leap in Napa or Chalone in Monterey.

"And all of them make wines as good as those from France?" A bore is bad enough, her look said, but a liar is worse. I nodded.

Lots of Bordeaux châteaux make less than five thousand cases. Some Burgundy growers only make a couple of thousand cases and they sell here. You ought to try Mayacamas or Caymus, Clos du Val or . . .

"You're not drinking your wine," she said accusingly.

There are twenty Cabernets I like better, but it's as good as lots of those from Europe. Only it tastes different.

"Exactly," she said, triumphantly. "All flowery and funny and sweet."

Not all of them. French judges in a Paris tasting ranked Cabernet from Ridge a little above Léoville-las-Cases and Mayacamas a little below, in the '71 vintage. In '73 Chardonnays, Château Montelena was tops, outranking a Meursault Charmes, Spring Mountain outranked a Beaune Clos des Mouches. A '72 Veedercrest matched a '72 Puligny-Montrachet Les Pucelles. And the judges got all mixed up as to which were French and which were Californian.

"I read about that, and the '72 wasn't any good for Burgundy whites; the '71 wasn't so hot for red Bordeaux. It wasn't fair."

But the judges couldn't tell the best Californian from the French. Wines from Chalone and Freemark Abbey were right in there with the French whites; Stag's Leap and Clos du Val were right in there with the reds. Vintages were different because the wines round out faster in California, but the judges had trouble picking out where the wines came from.

"Comparing the wines is dumb. You'd have to compare wines that cost the same, for starters, then you'd have to compare wines that are equally ready to drink. Even then, you're only comparing quality and by the time you've worked that out the wines are off the market.'

Agreed. But lots of American wines are made in the European styles and they're often cheaper. Then there's the California urge to bring out the tastes of the grapes as they grow in California, new styles that are good, new wines that anybody would like.

"Why are you so hot on American wines?" she said suspiciously.

Because they are exciting; there are new wines coming on the market all the time; there's experiment everywhere, and change. Besides, I'm going to write about them.

"I see," she said, snuffing out her cigarette in my armrest. She leaned back and closed her eyes. Obviously, I had to get my axe well ground before we landed and she was leaving me to do it.

"Didn't you like your wine?" asked the stewardess as she took my tray. It was fine, fine, I answered. Seatmate smiled. But she didn't open her eyes.

HELENE WILL MEET YOU AT DOWNSTAIRS CURB IN A BEAT-UP BLUE CONVERTIBLE ABOUT NOON ITINERARY DRAFT ALSO AVAILABLE THEN (signed) HARVEY

—telegram from Wine Institute

"I don't see why Harvey had to call it beat-up; it works fine," said Helene, as she maneuvered out into the traffic headed for San Francisco. "Jim is secretary of the shows they put on in Stern Grove, all free and out-of-doors. You sit around and have picnics and he's got some of the wines from the new district around Santa Barbara and along the Mission Trail. They call it the Central Coast. The concert's the 'Evolution of the Blues.' They're taking it to New York."

I said that was nice. Three thousand miles to go to a concert. I ought to get up into Napa and start tasting.

"Have you toured the wineries before?"

* * *

The first time was 25 years ago. I thought about that as we drove to the grove. Almadén was riding high then with its Grenache Rosé and other wines with grape names on the label, so it was time to spread the word that California had something. The vineyards were being crowded by Santa Clara bedroom communities and Frank Schoonmaker was looking south between the devil and the hawk, the Diablo and Gavilan highlands in San Luis Obispo. Eight bottles out of ten are ordinary, I was told, just as in France, where less than 20% of the vineyards, scarcely 600,000 acres, come under control laws. The best vineyards were up in Napa, maybe 12,000 acres, and I had to talk to Tchelistcheff at Beaulieu, Louis Martini, Jack Daniel at Inglenook, the Mondavis at Krug. There wasn't much else. They gave me a car and a map . . .

Beaulieu was right on the road at Rutherford and Bacchus was smiling because Tchelistcheff was climbing out of a pickup as I parked. On the tailgate he drew a map of Napa with a twig.

"For five miles around us, almost down to the town of Napa, almost up to the town of St. Helena, over east to the Silverado Trail and west to the Mayacamas range, it's like Bordeaux. A solid region two. Over at the wine college at Davis, Doctors Amerine and Winkler have drawn up temperature charts comparing California to the great European regions. Around here is the place for Cabernet Sauvignon and Sauvignon Blanc.

"Region one is like Burgundy and Champagne and the Rhine. That's below Napa near the north end of San Francisco Bay, the Carneros region. There's the place for Burgundy's Pinot Noir and Chardonnay, the Riesling of the Rhine. Up in the hills above Silverado and in the Mayacamas range it's also region one. For every thousand feet of height you get a hundred miles of north, and some of the vineyards are two thousand feet above sea level.

"Region three is like the Rhône, or the Piedmont in Italy. Here the extent is from around St. Helena up beyond Calistoga, where the Napa Valley ends. The farther from the bay the warmer. Cool ocean air sweeps up the valleys all along the coast, tempering midday heat. Fogs roll in during the afternoon, swirling around knolls and outcroppings. So we have isolated pockets of coolness, microclimates, where Loire Valley grapes like Chenin Blanc do best, or California's own grape, Zinfandel. You can taste the differences in the wines. Come along."

The wines were more fruity, more flowery, softer, than what I was used to.

"Wines mature more quickly here because of the volcanic soil. There's more gravel west of the road, richer soils east, but you can recognize the Rutherford taste. We still seek the right root stocks so growth won't be too rampant. And we bring out the taste of the grape. Our wines are unique and good. Twenty years from now they will be even better."

I crossed the road to Inglenook, where John Daniel's German winemaker was fermenting and aging wines in redwood casks. All the wines tasted cedary—that redwood taste. I drove up to the shack outside of a big warehouse of a winery and there Louis Martini told me about bringing out the taste of the grape and about the mountain vineyards and plans for stainless steel fermenters. I drove up to Charles Krug, where Peter Mondavi told me about experimenting to make dry white wines and Bob Mondavi talked about using European oak and methods to get complexity into the wines, but it was hard to change old practices . . .

Back in New York, I wrote about the new wines coming. Almadén decided I was writing too much about the future, too much about other wineries. The book died.

* * *

We were swinging through the hills up to San Francisco, still looking like a mound of oyster shells with new skyscrapers sticking up to make it look more like every other city.

Early in the Sixties I wanted a big section on California for a handbook on wines in general and the Wine Institute had me out. Bob Mondavi, just back from Europe, picked me up and we went to Dobo's for dinner. We started with Olympia oysters and Stony Hill Chardonnay.

"I can always taste my own wines, but I want to taste Stony Hill because I've just come from Burgundy. Michael's over there now; you haven't met him, but he's my oldest and he loves wines. A summer in Burgundy's just what he needs. You know that nobody from here ever goes there. Martini doesn't; Andre hasn't been back for years; John Daniel says he has enough of wines when he's here. Nobody knows how the other half lives. I go every chance I get."

He sniffed the wine, swirled the glass, sniffed again.

"Now that's Chardonnay, beautiful, but it's not Meursault and it's not Montrachet. It's Napa hill wine." He swirled, sipped, whistled in. "Taste that fruit, and the flower in the nose. But so light. And needs more acid. Here, let's taste Andre's; he's making one with a lot of oak and another one with a little. And we ought to taste Louis Martini's from his Carneros vineyard, and maybe we ought to get one of Ramonet's from Chassagne-Montrachet. Not to compare, just to see differences. I like the Burgundy style, but a lot of the wine making is sloppy. . . ."

We needed more oysters and then we had some Rex sole. Racks of lamb came next, then cheese, to go with the Cabernets. First was one of Andre's, then an Inglenook, then an Almadén, then one of Louis Martini's. Mondavi tried to find a good Bordeaux, but they were all too old or too young. He settled for a bottle of Lee Stewart's Souverain.

"There are half a dozen vineyards up in the hills and they produce some marvelous bottles. Nobody ever gets a chance to taste them out of the state, but you ought to get up there and see what's coming."

We left the restaurant after midnight. We would have left earlier, but Bob wanted to taste a few Pinot Noirs with the cheese.

The next night I slept beside the vineyards at Mayacamas, 2,600 feet high. You could see the glow of San Francisco. The sleeping bag made the vineyard dog uneasy and after I settled down he came over and curled up beside me, guarding me against the deer and rabbits. The next day I went over to Stony Hill, across the valley to Stewart's Souverain on Howell Mountain, then down the Chiles Valley where Louis Martini was putting in vines, on to Nichelini, who made the best Zinfandel. I went over into Sonoma to Buena Vista and Sebastiani, up the Russian River to Korbel, sleeping under redwoods every night. Back in Napa I stopped to taste the sparkling wines of Hanns Kornell, and watched the sun go down in the Pacific that night at Point Reyes, just made into a National Sea-shore. I had a bottle of Kornell Brut to sip as the sun went down . . .

* * *

Back in New York, I put a list of wineries in the book, those you could get nationally like Martini and Wente and Korbel, and those that you could get in California, which was all the rest. To most of the country, California meant Almadén, Paul Masson and The Christian Brothers among the premium wineries, an occasional bottle of BV or Inglenook. Every few months through the Sixties word came of another new winery, of new vineyards in Sonoma and Mendocino and south in Monterey.

The Pont Neuf began having wine dinners and I talked about Champagne at one of them. An engineer for one of the networks came up and began talking about Joe Heitz and Donn Chappellet and Sterling, how Travers had taken over at Mayacamas and Jack Davies was rebuilding Schramsberg. All names to me, not wines.

A publisher called about doing a book on American wines. *You can't get them*, I said. "Let's have lunch," he said. *I want to bring along a guy who knows about California wines*, I said. *Name of Flaherty; he'll tell you.* "Bring him along," said the publisher. We met at the Forum of the Twelve Caesars. Through the poached salmon and veal medallions I explained carefully how impossible it was to get good wines. They hogged them all in San Francisco. Publisher asked engineer what he thought.

Flaherty sipped his Montrachet. "I go to California every other month or so, with a toothbrush and two suitcases. I leave Wednesday morning and by Friday afternoon the business is done, so I go up into Napa and stay with Joe Heitz. Sunday afternoon I fill the two suitcases with wine and fly back. I can tote maybe twenty bottles. I have a deal with the stewards and sometimes I can get an extra case aboard. There must be hundreds of guys like me."

The publisher drained his glass. "Could you leave next week?"

The Wine Institute had me out again, this time with a guide. It was November '69 and Napa vineyard land, bare, was $4,000 an acre. I toured Sonoma, Mendocino, Livermore, Santa Clara, San Luis Obispo, Monterey and the Great Central Valley. In Fresno I talked to Ernie Gallo, tasted Ficklin Port nearby, dined at the Imperial Dynasty in Hanford. I wrote through February, back in New York, then flew out to San Francisco.

Napa Valley vineyard land was $6,000 an acre; Cabernet was $600 a ton. I revised the book in '73. Cabernet was $1,000 a ton.

NEW WINES: SANTA BARBARA AND THE CENTRAL COAST

The concert was in an evergreen gulch, with a row of picnic tables in front of the stage and people sitting on the grass all around and far up the slope under the trees. All shades of blue, from jeans and workshirts and quilted jackets, with splashes of red from sweaters; faces looked tan in the light; children ran around; the band blared jazz as the dancers and singers belted forth. We had a table and Jim lifted up a jug with a plain white label, a name written vertically along one side.

"The best jug wine in California, James Arthur Field Chenin Blanc. Very popular. This is what California is drinking."

It chugged into clear plastic glasses. I sniffed and wrote "perfumed, good cellar quality. Thin. Light fruit . . . Half dry. Pleasant." Jim handed around box lunches: ham, salami, chicken salad, potato salad, a roll.

"We get these from a great deli. Good with this German potato salad. They make two kinds of potato salad, but I like this one best."

It tasted of potatoes and wasn't sweetened. The wine did taste good with it. Jim brought up a long, thin bottle like those used in Alsace, green.

"This is HMR Chenin Blanc '75. That's Hoffman Mountain Ranch and this is one of their first wines. Another new one is Firestone, but all these are going to be Hoffman so you can see what one winery is doing. Firestone won't be in national distribution for a while, but Hoffman's just beginning."

"And then the blues came up from New Orleans to Memphis," called out the announcer, "up to Beale Street." The band blared. As we sipped, the band got to Kansas City, Chicago, Harlem, the dancers and singers moving to Big Bill Broonzy, Handy, Satchmo . . .

I dreaded tasting the Chenin. It was going to be sweet, you could tell from the flowery aroma. I tasted. Not too sweet! I wrote "OK. Nice clean nose, fresh as if from cask. Fruity, full (no damn California flower), good tannin, but some sweet. Good with ham." What would you serve it with?

Jim sipped. "I like it with sole, pan fried, and with a squeeze of lemon. It's great with scallops."

74

Helene nodded. "But I like it best with cheese and fruit, not with a meal. The winemakers say they like Chenin Blanc with a little sweetness to bring out the taste of the grape. It's a fine wine with Chinese dishes."

A breeze blew the smell of eucalyptus to us, lemony and pungent. California has smells different from the rest of the country; they live different, drink different, eat different. What did you have for dinner last night?

Jim looked surprised, then laughed. "It was simple, nothing much, there was some leftover chicken. Helene put it in a cream sauce, with some mushrooms and artichoke bottoms. We had a Geyser Peak Cabernet with it. Good."

Helene said "Jim's really the cook. Friday night he did some shrimp in butter, then flamed it with rum. Buttered noodles and avocado salad. We had it with HMR Chardonnay. The Hoffmans serve their Chardonnay with bouillabaisse."

Jim pulled up a bottle and showed me the label, HMR Zinfandel '75. There was a price sticker, $4.50. "Zinfandel's California's own wine and Santa Barbara is its home; that's what they say. Good with beef and barbecues. You going to put recipes in your book?"

Mostly what goes well with what. The country's full of good cooks, but good American wines have been so scarce that few know what to serve with them. What you do west of the Rockies may give us ideas east of the Rockies.

"You can drink this young Zinfandel the way you do a Beaujolais or Côtes-du-Rhône. Old Zinfandels are different, more like claret."

The Zinfandel had a rich nose. Nice and dry. Good tartness. Not too heavy, nice balance. Tannin stays nicely. I like this.

"It's a well-made wine. Tchelistcheff is adviser to both Hoffman and Firestone, and he talks to all the winemakers, exchanging notes. There are twenty wineries along the Mission Trail in our group, and you'd get maybe twenty different Zinfandels. It's like jazz: everybody plays their own way."

The band was playing boogie-woogie. Jazz was America's greatest contribution to the world, out of Africa. Maybe wines would be another, out of Europe.

We sat there, listening to the jazz, sipping the wines, looking around at the people in blue with tan faces, thousands of them, having a good time in the afternoon.

We all went to dinner later, to a place once famous for its wine lists, even more famous for its food. Most of the wines on the list weren't in the cellar. Things started out fine, a plate of shrimp and spareribs and bits of ham with a Stony Hill Chardonnay I won't describe because it's impossible to get. I ordered a rack of lamb, which was ordinary, and there was a Cabernet from Buena Vista that had been mishandled in the making and the cask as well as in the restaurant. We had no dessert; the restaurant was having an off night. By ten o'clock I felt it was time to report that I was suffering from the three-hour time lag and went back to my hotel.

I was bright-eyed at six, of course, and started off for Mendocino, just as my itinerary said I should.

Mendocino: The Few Become Several

Off to see Parducci. The wonderful wizard of Ukiah. He isn't alone now. Nor is he the farthest north; a family winery has gone in a few miles north and plantings have begun over in Anderson Valley.

"We're getting out of prunes," said the orchard man ten years ago. "The hops are long gone—they had too much taste. There's still the sheep, but they'll go when the fever hits." Mendocino is still wild summer country for city people over on the coast, still mostly ranchers inland. And prunes. Enough vineyards for a while.

Parducci. The winery's just off the freeway, built into a slope so that grapes can go into crushers on the high side and juice can run into fermenters ranged below, then into big oak and redwood aging vats. Adolph Parducci moved up from Sonoma after Repeal and began growing tonnage from high-yielders, like his neighbors. Like them, he made some wines for roadside sale, the rest going in bulk to the giants. Two of his four sons wanted to make premiums and began in the Fifties.

Ukiah started out by serving the lumbermen chopping down the redwoods, its Main Street changing from wood to stone when shepherds brought their flocks to the bared hills, and the few side streets going in when plum orchards and hop farms took over the lowlands and valleys. There are still many sheep ranchers' wives, calling themselves the Bo-

Peeps. They produced *Mountain Lamb Cookery* in the Sixties, which Parducci sells in the tasting rooms along with leaflets from the local historical society about the Pomo Indians. The Indian legends create a subtle mythology of several worlds that mingle the spirits of the twisting valleys and their redwood flanks with those of sea and shore.

The Bo-Peeps put their ranch versions of recipes from Scotch, Basque and Mediterranean forebears in a ring binder, whose hardboard covers are courtesy of the local lumberyard. The lamb recipes include a section on smoking mutton and what to do with it, and include wine suggestions, such as Rhines with roasts and chops. Parducci recommends Petite Sirah, or maybe Zinfandel.

John Parducci is the winemaker and his first success was a full, dry French Colombard from the old vines, then Zinfandel, then Petite Sirah. Nobody else was bottling their own and his big wines were novelties. Brother George was pleased with sales. The two other brothers wanted to go separate ways but there was no money to buy them out, which John complained about one day when he was cashing a check in the local bank. "You can have what you need," said the bank. "But we don't have money," said John. "We have," said the bank, and financed purchase and expansion. John and George still don't know who it was that backed their notes at the bank. No matter. The good wines are paying off.

There are some 400 acres of vineyards now, much of it planted in Pinot Noir and Chardonnay. Further from the bay, Mendocino is warmer than Napa or Sonoma. Called mostly a region three, Rhône and Mediterranean grapes might be expected to do best. What's more, Burgundians believe in maturing wines in oak; Parducci doesn't. Bringing out the taste of the grape is an old California tradition; Parducci honors it. Some wines are fermented in oak or redwood vats, but many of these are aged in stainless steel. None of the classical ways had produced much interesting Pinot Noir. Parducci's would be interesting, anyway; too bad if lots of flower and a certain sweetness was what seemed to be California style.

I asked him what about that, and John Parducci opened a Colombard that had just been bottled. "Nice flower, green and clean. Soft, light, sweet in taste," read my notes.

"There's point eight sugar left in that," said John," less than one percent. I can dry 'em up in two minutes but the white wines wouldn't be half as appealing." The taste has to round out to be complete; that is the idea. He opened another bottle.

"This is our Mendocino Riesling. It's really Sylvaner, but nobody buys it when it's called that and we could sell twice as much Mendocino Riesling if we had it. Low residual sugar. It's a fine aperitif wine, but bring it to the table and taste it with cheese and salami."

There was no heaviness in the wine, or bitterness, common faults with Alsatian wines left too long in wood: "Light. A trace of that slate-y, earthy taste I don't like, like chewed gum. Light fruit. Fresh. Much better with food."

I asked about the gum taste. Parducci shook his head. "Maybe I'm too familiar with the wine. I can't detect it. And maybe it's the salt. Salt in anything detracts from the wine. That's why you need a wine with some sweetness before a meal."

There was logic there, but not for me. How about salt on melon, to bring out sweetness. Any strong and basic taste detracts from wine. A light sour, salt, sweet or bitter taste doesn't hurt. The Sylvaner was good with the slices of cheese and salami, and with a soufflé of tiny shrimp there was Chenin Blanc. The cheese and salami and bread were marvelous, the quality so good it almost made one willing to live in California. The soufflé was delicate, perfect with the fuller, rounder wine. The warmer vineyards certainly didn't bother Parducci. He was setting the style for Mendocino; how does he show his wines off at meals?

"We're like everybody else: the simpler the food the better. But we're especially lucky because of the lamb and the closeness of the sea and good vegetables and cheese and fruit. Most of our vegetables come from our own garden; lots of other things come from neighbors.

"I don't like White Riesling, a prejudice, so we use our Chenin Blanc for fish, any fish. One point five residual sugar, which is just right with fried fish or barbecues.

"Petite Sirah with a steak. Barbecued. Just salt and pepper and close to the flame for rare. A little further from the flame and a little longer on the heat for medium.

"Gamay Beaujolais for lamb. I barbecue rack or chops, George does short ribs. No marinade, just salt and pepper.

"Pinot Noir is for prime ribs in the oven.

"French Colombard for chicken and fish. George is the cook; he barbecues the best chicken."

When we had nearly finished lunch I asked why California Pinot Noir was so poor. John laughed, poked me in the ribs and after a tour of some

79

new aging tanks we went down to the big new warehouse and reception and into John's office, where he opened four bottles. I sniffed them. None of that nasty California flower, no sweetness. Here are my notes:

"'75—Clean, round, elegant. No cheap flower. No cooked smell. Good light taste, some cheese. Goût—fin. Heavy tannin, just bottled.

"'70—Clean, round, light bouquet. Vines 2 years old. Lovely dryness, development.

"'72—Real fruit, Elegant. No off tastes or smells. Clean, not too long, but constant. Tannin stays on.

"'69—Cedar nose! Elegant. ?????"

What's that cedar? That's like the old redwood taste.

"The '69 was never in wood. The wine fermented in a redwood vat of my father's; it must be a hundred years old and it's caked inside with tartrate crystals; redwood couldn't get through that. What you taste is from the bottle age and from the soil, not from wood."

I couldn't believe it. All that tannin couldn't come just from the grapes. He must leave some stalks in there; maybe there's some press wine; maybe the crushed grapes were kept cold for a time under carbon dioxide before fermentation was started; maybe he lets the fermentation get hot.

Parducci will explain the process. The stainless steel fermenters are chilled overnight; the Pinots are picked in the morning, so the fermentation starts slowly. (In Burgundy, cool September nights lead to a slow-starting fermentation; this heats up during the day. In the old days the fermenting shed doors were thrown open at night to cool down the must, leading Bordeaux winemakers to say that Burgundians cooked their wines.) It is allowed to go up to 90° and the last few hours of fermentation are allowed to reach 100°, allowing the heat to extract color and tannin from the skins. The wines mature in big vats. I saw some small cooperage. Parducci said a portion of the reds finish in small casks for special bottlings that go to those who want to hold the wines in a cellar for drinking a decade or so in the future. Regular bottlings see no small wood.

Wines are volatile; fermentation is a swiftly changing process. Winemakers do much of their controlling by instinct, just as a cook knows when a stew is done. Every batch of wine varies, almost infinitely. Winemaking skill makes the difference; Parducci is a master, so details scarcely matter—as long as what he does is right. Precisely how a winemaker decides when grapes are ready to be picked, then, just how they will be fermented, at what temperatures, for how long, when the fermentation will be stopped, how the wine will be cleared, how long it should stay in wood, what wood it should be aged in, how long it should be kept in bottle before it is ready for drinking—all these vary from vineyard to vineyard, variety to variety, vintage to vintage, winemaker to winemaker.

The '69 had the smell and stink of cedar and I didn't like it. The vines were only five years old, not old enough for good wines, to my mind. I liked the '72 and the '70, but the '75 best of all, because it was just bottled and tasted as if it came right from the cellar. Another time, tasting in another place, who knows? They were well-made wines, maybe best five years after the vintage. And they tasted like Pinot Noir, all except the '69, which tasted like California reds of the old days.

Parducci makes wines that bring out the character of the grapes, not augmented or modified by time in cooperage. Few wines are better than his.

A white wine cross between Gewürztraminer and Sémillon called Flora, developed at Davis, is in an experimental block at Parducci. Dry wines made from it have not impressed John and he has begun making a sweet wine from it. He also experiments with another grape of unknown origin, Green Hungarian, worth trying. (Burgess Cellars and Buena Vista also bottle this rather dull-tasting wine.)

My favorite Parducci wines are Zinfandel, Petite Sirah and Sylvaner, but all belong in comparative tastings.

Cresta Blanca. Guild is a giant cooperative of more than a thousand members, but its North Coast growers of premium varieties send their grapes to a fine old stone building in Ukiah that is now the Cresta Blanca winery. This was a famous old Livermore vineyard planted a century ago by a pioneer named Charles Wetmore from cuttings brought from Château d'Yquem and Château Margaux. Suburbs swept away the vineyard, whose name became the property of Guild in 1970. The winemaker at Cresta Blanca for thirty years was Roy Mineau, and he moved to Ukiah along with the name, to make the wines in the old ways. He modernized some, because there were grapes from almost sixty growers and more than 3,000 acres to handle. Moderately priced, the wines do well in comparative tastings.

The wines cover a wide range and are blends produced in substantial quantities. The Zinfandel and Petite Sirah are under $4 and stand out in tastings against wines costing twice as much. The Chardonnay, under $5, is a best buy.

Fetzer Vineyards. Bernard Fetzer was a lumberman in the Forties, when he bought a ranch snuggled into the folds of Redwood Valley and began planting vines. During the next couple of decades he sold his Sauvignons and Cabernets and Sémillons to amateur winemakers across the country, making wine of his own from grapes bought from Martini and Sebastiani. By the Seventies he was using his own grapes, from some hundred acres, and buying as much again, building to a production of 50,000 cases a year.

The wines are big, showing the character of mature grapes carefully fermented and aged for a time in oak, the reds for as much as eighteen months. One of their best buys they call Mendocino Premium Red, made from Carignane; the Premium White is a Colombard-Sémillon-Chenin blend. Tasters say they can recognize the typical character of Mendocino in Fetzer bottlings. Because they are well-made wines at reasonable prices (Carignane under $4) that do well in comparative tastings, they find a ready market. Tasted along with Parducci bottlings, they illustrate the range to be expected from Mendocino.

Weibel Champagne Vineyards. Squeezed out of their Alameda vineyards, descendants of a Swiss family of sparkling wine vintners began planting vineyards in Sonoma and Mendocino and established a winery in Ukiah, branching out into table wines. The firm makes sparkling wines for many private labels at the original winery in Warm Springs; that address on a private label, as well as Mission San Jose or Fremont, will identify a Weibel bottling. The range of good table wines is blended in Ukiah.

Edmeades Vineyards. Mendocino is full of valleys and as you cross the range from Ukiah toward the sea, there are young vineyards going in and many slopes where they could be. Before the final range, the blacktop cuts up through the Anderson Valley, the tops rarely more than a mile apart and mostly bare now, but with occasional redwood tufts. Stop near one about 10 miles from the sea and you will come on the nearly 40 acres at Edmeades, where planting began in the Sixties and will continue until there are more than 80 acres. The winery was once an apple dryer. Nearby is a small fermenting shed. Beyond a shade tree is a small bungalow. Beyond that is the vineyard. That's all there is.

Some people seek out the wines from small vineyards because they are rare and hard to get. The winemaking is usually amateurish, which means bad, or primitive, because such small operations cannot afford proper equipment, which means that the wines are uneven.

Edmeades represents neither of these, having a devoted owner in Deron Edmeades, and a skilled winemaker in Jed Steele, who worked around while going through Davis, particularly with Lee Stewart, over in Napa. He spent time around Burgundy and Bordeaux and elsewhere, to find out what the score was, or at least who was in the game. Efforts of both men pay off in carefully made, subtle wines.

But they are not to be taken too seriously, nor is it to be expected that aficionados will spend fruitless hours seeking the wines.

The '76 vintage produced three thousand cases. Deron and Jed hired a suite in a hotel down in LA, invited in a bunch of dealers, and Deron said, "This is it, gents, all of it has to be sold tonight."

They maintain a tasting room over on the coast, not so much to sell wines as to give them an excuse to get away. Gets lonely up there in the valley.

They have to do something to have fun on cold winter nights. One thing they do is make Edmeades Dry Apple '76, a judicious blend of Baldwin, Spitzenberg and Golden Delicious. (My notes do not show proportions, but it is 8% alcohol.) Then there's Mendocino Rain Wine '75, a nicely tart blend of Sauvignon Blanc, Colombard, Muscat and Johannisberg Riesling. Jed says it's good with fresh salmon or crab Louis. Deron says Dry Apple is good with roast pork stuffed with dates and figs and so forth.

They make another apple wine but I forgot to get the name. They could sell about ten times as much as they make, or a hundred times as much, because they are good. But winemaking leans them in other directions. You don't sit up there in the valley just to fool around with apples.

Then there's the White Zinfandel, not readily available. Deron says it is excellent with mussels steamed in a little beer, with saffron.

There is the '75 Chardonnay with a clean and fruity nose, good acid. A nice long taste with good tannin. Only $5.40, but all gone.

83

Their Zinfandel is perfectly balanced, with real flower in the nose, going to fruit. The taste carries on the same. Beautiful balance. Forget it.

The '75 Cabernet is aged in American oak, which Steele likes. The taste is clean, round, elegant.

Why mention such wines? Because maybe you can get some someday. You might find a bottle on a shelf, even be in Mendocino. Wines from good winemakers aren't that easy to find. If you see Edmeades, don't pass it by.

Across the valley on the bald east slope a 200-acre vineyard is going in, project of an insurance company. The land looks nice over there, good exposure. "Frosts come two weeks earlier over there," says Steele, "and there's wind. There was never frost in the old days before they cut the redwoods. Deron left that patch near the vineyard, and it helps. We don't get much frost."

If you get out that way, call to see if you could drop around. Maybe they could sell you a case, maybe even Dry Apple.

Tasting the apple wine reminded me of that chewing gum taste that had been coming out in white wines for the past few years.

"Bubble gum," said Steele. "They did some papers on that at Davis. Maybe it comes from too long a cold fermentation. If under sixty degrees F. for whites is good and under ninety is good for reds—most people go for under fifty-five and under eighty-five—then even colder is better. But maybe you lose more than you gain when you get too cold. The bubble gum comes in."

What about that resin taste from redwood?

"They claim the tartar coating in an old vat blocks it. Maybe it doesn't."

Winemakers work with what they've got—grapes, equipment, casks—with variations through every stage from vine to wine. Some believe in letting the grapes make the wine, others think every stage must be controlled. Nobody is ever quite sure. Much of the detailed literature is in French, a language unknown to most Californians. Local experience and native wit make most California wines.

Husch Vineyards. In the late Sixties a town planner escaped to the country—an old farm down the road from Edmeades that sloped to the Navarro River. The grapevine was straggling up from Sonoma and Tony Husch decided on twenty acres for independence to start—Chardonnay, Pinot

Noir and Gewürztraminer. In '71 he bonded an old granary as a winery, the first in the valley; wife Gretchen designed the label; and now there's a rosé of Pinot Noir as well as the red wine and the two whites, with more to come. More is needed because people like his wines—and the couple like the life.

* * *

Mendocino is the California wine world in miniature—sons of a bulk producer making premium wines at Parducci, a cooperative of growers whose grapes are marketed by Guild under the Cresta Blanca label, a transplanted maker of sparkling wines and others at Weibel, a master winemaker seeing what can be done with a small vineyard at Edmeades, a lumberman and town planner who have taken to country life at Fetzer and Husch. All of them make the best wines they can. Demand grows every year.

Lake County, east of Mendocino, has been supplying grapes to other wineries for years, but the aftermath of the wine boom of the Sixties was that a cooperative of more than thirty growers with six hundred acres formed Konocti Cellars. Optimum production may be fifty thousand cases, the first releases being five thousand cases of Cabernet and Riesling in 1976.

In a single generation, sons of grape growers and winemakers, skilled university graduates, capable managers, dedicated amateurs and hobbyists turned professional have begun making superior wines where only bulk production had been before. What has happened in Mendocino is happening in all of the California wine country—and in the rest of the nation as well.

Sonoma: An Old Region Reborn

"You won't know the place ten years from now. We take most of the grapes today, but the growers have seen what's been going on at Hanzell and Buena Vista, down south. It's like Burgundy over between Dry Creek and Dutcher Creek, and some small wineries are starting up. Won't be long."

That was just before Christmas, 1969, and Joe Vercelli, longtime manager at Italian Swiss had that gleam in his eye over a lunch of salami and cheese and steak and many bottles—all Sonoma—brought into the shiny restaurant in Geyserville, a wide spot in the road up at the top of the county. I made some notes, disbelieving, and Joe poured a foamy white wine without a label.

"You never tasted anything like this," said Joe, as we lifted glasses. Light and spicy perfume, exciting; light, clean, lingering sweetness, fresh and beguiling. Louis Martini's Moscato Amabile, fermented long and kept cool and sold only at the winery. Along with Myron Nightingale's Cresta Blanca Sauvignon and Wente's blend of the same with Sémillon, it was one of the three best sweet wines of California. "We'll do as well here pretty soon," said Joe. They have.

In 1970 Sonoma was planted mostly in heavy-bearing grapes sold to blenders, some 1,000 acres each of Colombard and Petite Sirah, 1,500 of Carignane and 3,000 of Zinfandel. There were almost 600 acres of Cabernet, about half as much Pinot, and plots totaling under 200 acres each of varieties like Sauvignon Blanc and Sémillon, Chardonnay and Chenin Blanc and Gamay. There were some 10,000 acres in all, the rest made up of small plantings. Acreage for heavy bearers shows little increase, but statistics for 1980 show 4,200 acres of Cabernet, 1,800 acres of Chardonnay, and so on. Acreage doubled, mostly in top varieties.*

The furthest outpost of the Spanish missions was in Sonoma. The last Mexican governor was Mariano Vallejo, who took over its vineyard when California declared independence in 1846, settling down to increase the acreage. His success with Sonoma Red and Sonoma White encouraged Haraszthy to establish Buena Vista.

The last outpost of Russian exploration was in the northern part of the county and while they planted no vineyards—nineteenth-century Bohemians did that—they left their name to a river and traces of their architecture. Jack London moved in to raise eucalyptus trees; orchards and hop farms spread all over the cleared lands; Luther Burbank carried on his plant breeding there; but today Sonoma is largely vineyard and vacation country, with vines on valley slopes and holidayers in the highland groves and along the beaches.

The Russian River tumbles down Mendocino's Ukiah Valley, flowing into Sonoma near Cloverdale, running south between Alexander Valley on the east, Dry Creek Valley on the west, then turning to the sea below Healdsburg. Both valleys form separate districts, while the benchlands

---

*Increases in quality plantings show how quickly supposedly conservative growers responded to demand:

	1970 acreage	1980 acreage (projected)
Pinot Noir	270+	2500+
Merlot	35+	560+
Gamay (Noir)	140+	320+
Gamay (Beaujolais)	—	470+
Johannisberg Riesling	80+	800+
Gewürztraminer	35	470+
Sylvaner	75+	90+
Pinot Blanc	60+	70+
Sauvignon Blanc	200+	260+
Sémillon	170+	180
Chenin Blanc	200+	300

and cleared draws along the Russian River are considered to be a third, although variations in soil and climate will lead to further divisions someday. California calculations rate them mostly Region Two, like Bordeaux, but cooler highlands along the river and along Dry Creek are rated Region One, like Burgundy, while somewhat warmer Alexander Valley has sections in Region Three, like the Rhône. The fourth district to the south, around the town of Sonoma and over east on Mayacamas slopes, is considered to be cooler because of the bay nearby; much of it is in Region One. There's plenty of variety, largely untested, and crafty experiment goes on every vintage.

Early growers were mostly Italian settlers who began arriving after the Civil War. When many of them became stranded in the fog and chill of San Francisco, a grocer turned builder and banker decided to establish a farm colony on 1,500 acres north of Geyserville. He called it Asti. Andrea Sbarboro wanted to attract countrymen from the Piedmont, Lombardy and Tuscany by offering them vineyard shares or wages in exchange for work. Most took wages instead of shares but the Italian Swiss Colony flourished by providing wines for immigrants crowding into the cities and factory towns of the Atlantic seaboard and the settlements along the railroads pushing west. Other wealthy San Franciscans established vineyards for themselves in the southern part of the county, using Italian workers, vast installations like Fountain Grove and Dunfillin, Tokay Vineyard and Madrone, including one of a chain of vineyards owned by Kohler & Frohling. Many were wiped out around the turn of the century by phylloxera, the louse that sucks the roots of the vines and infects them. Prohibition and then Depression wiped out more. Italian Swiss Colony and many others were absorbed by consolidation; growers formed cooperatives and sold their grapes or wines to the giants in the Great Central Valley. Many of the independents that survived—Martini and Prati, Foppiano, Cambiaso, Seghesio, Nervo, Rege—continue to do so, although several of these have replanted in premium varietals and offer wines to the public.

Sonoma drowsed, but early in the Forties a newspaperman named Frank Bartholomew bought 450 acres for a summer place, discovered that half-ruined stone buildings on the place were what remained of Haraszthy's Buena Vista and began replanting the vineyard. People liked Bartholomew's Green Hungarian, his Cabernet and a Sylvaner he called Vine Brook. A decade later, a wealthy ambassador named Zellerbach, who liked Burgundies, set up a model winery with vineyards and called it Hanzell. He brought in Burgundian oak casks for his wines, and his Pinot Noir and Chardonnay were a sensation.

August Sebastiani took over the bulk wine vineyard from his father in 1934, began selling wines under his own label, soon made a market for them. The Heck brothers, sons of an Alsatian winemaker, took over Korbel and began making sparkling wines from vineyards planted by those two Bohemians up on the Russian River.

Other sons took over, rebuilding vineyards. In the Fifties, Pedroncelli began offering wines; the old Rhinefarm vineyard was resurrected as Gundlach-Bundschu. The Bacchus wines of Wildwood Vineyard are now made by grandsons Robert and Fred Kunde; the old Zepponi winery is now ZD; the old Pagani winery is now Kenwood; Lamoine is now Grand Cru Vineyard. And more to come.

ALEXANDER VALLEY AND NORTHERN NEIGHBORS

The Alexander Valley lies east of the Russian River, running from above Geyserville down toward Healdsburg. It was once all orchard and vacation country with a few old vineyards here and there, but in the Seventies an oilman named Russ Green bought an old ranch on Hoot Owl Creek and began planting vines. Starting with 50 acres, he wound up with 250. These attracted attention. Widmer's of New York State put in 500 acres; Sonoma Vineyards put in Cabernets. Belle Terre supplies Chardonnay to Château Montelena and Château St. Jean; then there's Jordan; there's Alexander Valley Vineyards and Johnson's Alexander Valley Wines, a winery called Sausal and a host of grape growers. Then Green decided he needed a winery for his grapes and bought Simi.

Simi. Simi was founded by a couple of brothers from Tuscany who were caught up in the big gold rush of '49. To no avail, for they spent twenty years supplying San Francisco restaurants with vegetables, then bought some 100 acres of vineyard outside Healdsburg and began supplying wines to San Francisco's Italian community in North Beach. They prospered, the vineyard expanding tenfold, but Prohibition and Depression did them in. Bottling continued, but it was Green's looking for a home for his grapes that started Simi going again, with modern equipment.

90

By the mid-Seventies, winery and vineyards proved too much for one man, and Green sold Simi to a British firm that had a brewery among its holdings and needed wine for its chain of pubs. Tchelistcheff was hired as consultant, and a protégée of his, Mary Ann Graf, was hired as winemaker. American markets were needed, however, and Simi was taken over by Schieffelin, a major New York importer that felt it was time to get into the American wine business.

Alexander Valley grapes produce big wines, with an earthy taste, some say, so Graf and Tchelistcheff have worked out some variations to balance the wines. Press wine is fermented with free-run juice for red wines; they are fermented in open redwood vats so that the cap can be pushed down more easily. (The cap is the mass of pulp that rises to the top during fermentation; it inhibits action of the yeast and must be pushed down, or "pumped over," as it is called. Stainless steel fermenters are tall and narrow, making pumping over somewhat more difficult, and one view is that fermentation is more even in open vats.) A second fermentation in the wine reduces acidity by changing the harsh malic acid to mild lactic acid. It's called the malo-lactic fermentation and Tchelistcheff believes in inducing it so that it can be controlled; off-odors and off-tastes occur when it is not handled properly. Because many California wines lack acid, the secondary fermentation is often avoided. At Simi it is induced.

Details, details. But winemaking must be adapted to the grapes. Such variations make all the difference in the wine. Tchelistcheff, with his wide experience all along the coast, can make valuable suggestions about grapes from specific vineyards. A man with a small vineyard and a single grape variety can learn to make good wines in time. A winery with half a dozen or more grapes from various vineyards has almost too many problems to master. Simi buys its grapes, from Russ Green, among others. Graf concentrates on making the wines.

With so many variables, no wonder there is so much variation in the wines. It's all well and good to suggest that a seeker after wines find a particular variety that pleases, then explore those from different wineries. Alternately, when a wine from a particular winery pleases, it makes sense to try others from the same winery, hoping that there will be some consistency from one to another. This seems to be the case at Simi; the character of the grape is brought out and efforts are made to bring forth well-balanced wines with good acidity and medium body. The policy is clear.

A good wine to start with at Simi might be the Chenin Blanc, which is fresh and fruity, made from Alexander Valley grapes. Gewürztraminer, which is softer, and the Chardonnay, which is light, are also made from Alexander Valley grapes, as is the Cabernet that contains some 30% Merlot. When in doubt, there's always Zinfandel, nicely balanced and just the thing to serve with steak. Simi wines will give a good idea of what the Alexander Valley is producing these days.

Souverain of Alexander Valley. The Russian River plunges into Sonoma at Squaw's Leap, a gorge named after a lovelorn maiden who did the obvious, and not far down the road is Souverain of Alexander Valley, a vast installation now owned by a group of growers.

Hop kilns once dominated the countryside, square buildings with pyramidal roofs topped by a squared vent that repeats the shape of the base. The hops, too bitter and authoritative for the bland beers of today, were replaced by vineyards, and the kilns inspire the shape of several wineries. Souverain is the grandest, two great towers shaped like kilns, joined by a vast structure with a pitched roof that is the winery and storage rooms. One tower contains offices, the other a restaurant and lounges for the public, entered by wide flights of steps that lead up from a great parking lot in front of the building. Vineyards fall away before it.

The building was part of the well-laid plan of a flour company that decided it wanted to get into the wine business during the most recent boom in the early Seventies. They bought vineyards and planted them in noble vines; the new building won an architectural prize; then the accountants discovered the millions wouldn't pay off for decades, if ever, that money could make more money elsewhere; and the flour company pulled out. A cooperative, North Coast Grape Growers, stepped in, with plenty of help from banks, to take over an establishment somewhat more grandiose than was required. There's a summer theater in the courtyard, a gift shop, a winery sales room—that was badly needed—and the restaurant. Its manager trained in Europe, the cooks, in France. Here are wine suggestions for one of the dinner menus:

•Chardonnay with sautéed shrimp, with curry; or with creamed chicken breasts and grapes.

•Riesling with sautéed veal scallops finished with apples and cream; or with creamed filet of sole finished with mushrooms and white wine; or with grilled salmon and herb butter.

•Pinot Noir with skewered lamb, marinated and broiled with peppers, onion and bacon.

•Cabernet with halves of chicken stewed with Zinfandel, bacon and mushrooms; and with various steaks.

Menus are in French, like others across the country that offer paupiette de sole bonne femme, suprème de volaille véronique and tournedos, but here the wines are more carefully matched and most cost less than $4.00 (the Chardonnay is $4.50). Dinner dishes start at $6.50; lunches are half that, but don't include soup or salad. It's one of the best bargains in the country. Dinner with wines and a ticket to the concert cost $22.50, including tip and tax.

In the wine shop the wines are listed from dry to semi-dry: Green Hungarian and Chenin Blanc for less than $3, then the Chardonnay, followed by the Grey Riesling at the low price, the Johannisberg Riesling for under $4, then Colombard Blanc for less than $3.

The reds are listed from light to full: Gamay Beaujolais, Zinfandel and Petite Sirah are about $3; Pinot Noir is under $4, the Cabernet a little more.

You can order fruits and select from a cheese board for lunch, there are hamburgers with carrot and celery sticks for the youngsters, light eaters can order omelets and salads. They want to make it easy for you to enjoy the wines.

Trentadue. A new winery dominates the slope just below Souverain, vineyards stretching out into the valley. Leo Trentadue purchased the vineyards just before the Seventies began; it was then planted in blocks of Zinfandel, Petite Sirah and Carignane, since extended. The old way was to pick and ferment the grapes together, and he did this the first year with a special block that had been attacked by botrytis, the mold that causes the grapes to lose water and concentrate juice, the noble mold that produces Sauternes and the great sweet wines of the Rhine. The wine was 17.5% alcohol, full, fruity and deep, for once a wine that would stand up

93

to Roquefort. Since then, several winemakers have made wines from late-picked grapes, including Bruce, Ridge and Mayacamas. These Late Harvest wines have a special and limited appeal, particularly when made from red-wine grapes, and are examples of how much California winemakers are willing to experiment.

Trentadue puts a big 32 on his labels, making them easily identifiable, but production is small and mostly limited to California—wines to taste when you have a chance. His regular bottlings can be attractive wines.

There are some 140 acres of vineyard planted in more than a dozen varieties and most of the grapes are sold to other wineries (Ridge Geyserville Zinfandel is from Trentadue grapes). Wines are aged in small cooperage of American oak and most of the work is done by the family.

New Small Wineries. An organization called Bon Vin went into business in the early Seventies to market lots from small wineries and the firm did a good job of introducing wines like Trentadue in New York, Washington and other big cities. The process was costly and the firm was taken over by a Seattle winery, Ste. Michelle. Small wineries need such help. A new winery near Healdsburg with 65 acres of vines and optimum production of ten thousand cases, is Mill Creek, owned by the Kreck family. The first Cabernets and Chardonnays were released in 1975, followed by Pinot Noir and Merlot, early sales being limited to California. Further down the Russian River is Hop Kiln, with production of a few thousand cases. Marketing can only be done through some central facility that operates like an importer. A generation ago, wine buyers like Frank Schoonmaker used to traipse around Burgundy, tasting from casks belonging to vineyard owners who made such small batches that big importers with national markets were not interested in the wines, no matter how good. Schoonmaker would pick up odd lots and sometimes as much as a thousand cases from one grower—usually it was a hundred cases or so—then offer them to a few retailers in each major market. Much the same operation must be done by firms like Bon Vin. In no other way will we get to know the wines. (Lists of such small wineries appear in the back of the book.)

A spectacular winery and vineyard of some 240 acres has been established in the Alexander Valley by Thomas Jordan, a petroleum engineer based in Denver. Cabernet from the first crush in 1976, released in 1980, drinkable by 1985, may last long enough to welcome in the new century.

Clos du Bois, with a thousand acres, will market 20,000 cases, more under a secondary label, River Oaks.

When Russ Green began the plantings that eventually led to his acquisition of Simi, he involved a fellow oil executive in the development of 480 acres in the valley. Harry Wetzel III enrolled at Davis to be ready to make wines from his half when the contract to supply the grapes to Simi ended in 1975. His stainless fermenters and Limousin oak received the Riesling and Chardonnay of that vintage and were released two years later under the Alexander Valley Vineyards label. The Cabernet came along the following year.

J. Pedroncelli Winery. Roads wind east and west through the valleys around Geyserville, vineyards on many slopes, and the one to take west to Dry Creek is Canyon Road. Pedroncelli is on the north side, offering some of the best-made, most-straightforward wines of California, and at bargain prices.

It was once easy to pass over Sonoma wines—all those Italian names on wineries that sold to the big blenders. Any they sold themselves were imitation Chiantis, fair with spaghetti, bland, heavy with alcohol, full of that redwood taste. People began trying them when a few came east in the Sixties, noting that the redwood taste was disappearing, that there was some freshness from fruit acids, but still far below those from Napa and other counties south of the bay. But then Bercut-Vandervoort sent a shipment east and the Zinfandel became a favorite at tastings. It came from Pedroncelli.

Pedroncelli began bottling some of their own wines in 1955 when John and James took over the family winery. Henry Vandervoort, the San Francisco wine merchant and importer who was born in Bordeaux, became interested and asked the brothers to bottle some for his private labels. He noticed they were making a rosé of Zinfandel and talked them into saying so on the label, the first Zinfandel Rosé. Early in the Sixties, he tasted a special cask of their Cabernet Sauvignon, talked them into aging it long in wood and had them bottle it with his label, calling it An Importer's Choice. Encouraged, the boys began increasing the size of their vineyards—now more than 120 acres—and maturing wines in small oak casks, most of it Limousin, the oak of Burgundy. This worked fine for their Pinot Noir. Why not try some in Nevers, the oak of Bordeaux? This worked fine, too, giving the wine a special elegance. Why not use some Merlot to soften the Cabernet? The wine was light, soft, rounded.

Such experiment greatly increases the range of California wines—and makes good winemakers the envy of Europeans, who are bound by tradition and control laws that inhibit change. The Pedroncellis are not making changes just to make something new or spectacular. They use traditional and tested techniques—cool fermentation within limits, oak when needed, grapes picked when the acid-sugar balances are right even when the wines may be lighter in alcohol than others—but modified when necessary to suit their Sonoma grapes. They are not trying to make great Burgundy or Bordeaux, simply good Sonoma wines, fairly priced. The idea is that if you like one you will try the others—if you can find them.

Especially recommended: Zinfandel
 Pinot Noir
 Cabernet Sauvignon
 Zinfandel Rosé

Italian Swiss Colony. As part of the complex formed by Louis Petri, which includes some 1,800 members of Allied Grape Growers and the marketing arm of United Vintners, Italian Swiss Colony at Asti has a vast supply of North Coast grapes to call on. When Heublein took control of the group, keeping Beaulieu Vineyards as a separate company, but making Inglenook a brand for large blends of North Coast wines, Italian Swiss Colony continued as producer of low-priced bottlings and novelties like Annie Green Springs and T. J. Swann. The first includes Country Cherry-Berry Frost, Plum Hollow and Apricot Splash. The second has Easy Days and Mellow Nights, Stepping Out and After Hours. With the wines—from grapes—the Heublein assemblage produces a third of all California wines.

You might like to know more names of the wine-based fruit drinks. There's Fox Fire in Plum Velvet and Diamond Red flavors, and you might like to try Arriba, Swiss-Up or Bali Hai, the last with guava and other things. All of these are cheerful names, suggestive to the promoters who thought them up, appealing to those willing to pay less than two dollars a bottle for them. All the familiar names are there, too, at similar prices. You might want to try the Chardonnay or Cabernet.

Italian Swiss Colony, like Gallo and Guild and Franzia, has put out endless quantities of blends over the years, but the first wine that made an impression at tastings was their Zinfandel. When Gallo and other big producers took to putting out lines with grape names on the label toward the end of the Seventies, Italian Swiss brought out a line of varietals they called Colony, priced somewhat below the Inglenook line; both the lines sold well. A fierce competition exists for this market of wines with grape names, to be sold under $3.

The wines are meant to be sold in grocery stores, like beer or soft drinks. United Vintners, with its selling arm of Heublein, has a vast acreage of good grapes to call on, so their Colony and Inglenook lines should do well against those from the Guild cooperative, which is in a similar situation with their Winemasters and Cresta Blanca lines. The competition from vineyards to the south—and firms like Gallo, Bear Mountain and Monterey, among others—may keep prices down.

DRY CREEK

The long valley runs south, parallel to the Russian River, Dry Creek running into it as the river bends below Healdsburg. It is full of vines, most of the grapes going into blends of big wineries, but a few small ones like Viña Vista and Preston have begun offering a few wines. The only one with a certain volume—some 25,000 cases—is Dry Creek Vineyard.

Dry Creek Vineyard. David Stare graduated from Harvard as an engineer, then worked in Europe, where he became interested in wines. Early in the Seventies, after working around various wineries, he decided land prices were reasonable in Dry Creek, certainly more so than in Napa and other parts of Sonoma, so he began developing fifty acres and building a winery, with a long house on the hill above the vineyard. His first wines were made from quality grapes of growers round about, and they were so good that he is contemplating expansion beyond his original plans.

Stare likes dry wines; his Chenin Blanc is the driest you can find; his Sauvignon Blanc (called Fumé Blanc) is not far behind, nor is his Chardonnay. The preference is something more than a matter of style.

California's Mediterranean climate is invigorated by fog. Cool winds from the sea sweep up the valleys and the somewhat higher altitudes in the coastal ranges, but it is difficult for grapes to hold their acids and reach maturity without building up too much sugar. Wines have a tendency to be out of balance and soft, characteristics that are minimized by good winemakers. To make truly dry wines you have to stretch techniques, always chancy, and many hesitate to take the risks. Stare chooses to, successfully.

What's more, he thinks too much filtering of the wine takes out subtle tastes, so his wines sometimes cast a sediment or show suspended matter. This doesn't hurt the wine a bit, but makes buyers hesitant. This is a minor matter because there are enough wise buyers around to take all his production. Many of them are other winemakers; John Pedroncelli drops over regularly to pick up a few cases.

Stare also believes in judicious use of wood, putting his Chardonnay in small Limousin oak, for instance, to make a big wine, though dry. Those interested can read the technical details on his labels.

For people interested in comparative tastings, one might try a Dry Creek Gamay Beaujolais or Zinfandel and taste it along with those of Pedroncelli or some other Sonoma grower. The winemakers do this all the time, getting together for bread and cheese, salami and fruit, maybe a salad with steak from the barbecue—the simple foods that bring out the taste of the wines.

THE RUSSIAN RIVER

The river bends west, vineyards in its crook and along its length, making a geographical district of cool vineyards. Climates vary with breeze and height; winemakers find distinctions. Wineries have formed an association to guide visitors from one to another. Wine buffs must depend on taste to sort out the wines.

Geyser Peak. West off the freeway is an ancient winery named after the mount that presides over the area of thermal springs, Geyser Peak. Purchased by Schlitz Brewery in the early Seventies, it is a renovated complex built of native stone and wood that includes a new tasting room and shops around a flagged courtyard complete with fountain. The winery was modernized by Al Huntsinger, a shrewd winemaker who started out in Napa and then became involved with renovation of Almadén. Originally famous for its Four Monks vinegar, the 120 acres began producing wines for other wineries in the Sixties. The vineyards have been extended under Schlitz, and special lots of grapes are bought under long-term contract, several of them fermented separately and offered as Geyser Peak Limited Bottlings. Varieties without vintages are marketed under a Voltaire label; a Summit label identifies less-expensive blends.

Geyser Peak was fortunate in having Huntsinger and the crew he brought with him because he was involved with the expansion at Almadén, down into San Luis Obispo County, into Monterey and Livermore. He knows where the good grapes grow. All the new plantings in the early Seventies have forced down the prices of top varieties and he can buy fine grapes from mature vines at fair prices. He believes in letting the grapes make the wines, fussing with them as little as possible, so that what he bottles will be sound, with good fruit and body—available at reasonable prices.

Equally essential is a system for marketing the wines, provided by Schlitz through their familiarity with American drinking habits. Many good wines stay in California; distribution of those that are exported is often spotty; availabilities are spasmodic. Geyser Peak can offer a steady, gradually increasing supply. Optimum production is 250,000 cases.

The Limited Bottlings include a delicate Pinot Noir from a small vineyard in southern Sonoma owned by the Sangiacomo family. A full-bodied Cabernet is called Santa Maria, from a vineyard in Santa Barbara; a lighter Sonoma Cabernet comes from the Nervo vineyard down the road.

Geyser Peak has been instrumental in organizing the Russian River Wine Road, an association of wineries that pass visitors from one to another, and that are busy establishing the area in the popular mind as a distinct district. Various counties and districts have formed similar associations that publish maps and newsletters so that the welter of new names will be less confusing.

Davis Bynum Winery. A newspaperman with wine in his veins as well as ink, Davis Bynum came by it naturally. His father was officially a California historian and openly a wine buff, acting as a judge of wines at state fairs and at one time owner of a Napa vineyard. "You'll be making Barefoot Bynum Burgundy up there," said one of his friends, and when Davis could stand it no longer and began blending wines for faculty and friends near Berkeley, he gave the name to one of his wines, perpetuating the family joke. That was early in the Fifties, and as the wines became popular he began shipping them out of state. A broker liked the wines, but refused Barefoot Bynum on the grounds that sophisticated New Yorkers wouldn't go for a hick name. Wines were serious business. Retailers who were approached also liked the wines—but only if they could have Barefoot Bynum. The wine accounts for much of the winery sales, illustrating how well all channels of the trade understand their markets.

The offhand name belies the quality of the wines. Bynum bought special lots of grapes from Napa growers and others in the North Coast counties, and was thinking of getting the ink out of his veins and letting the wine flow free, when the wine boom struck. As the Seventies began his suppliers found that they needed all the grapes they could grow. There was nothing for it; Bynum had to open his own winery.

He bought an old hop kiln on some seventy acres where the Russian River curves west, below Healdsburg, and began turning it into a winery. Few newspapermen make enough to equip a winery, let alone start a vineyard or buy grapes, so Bynum sold shares—to growers. What was established is a free-enterprise co-op. Bynum makes the wines, his son assisting, production pegged at 25,000 cases. Just as well; on that scale, it's too much for one man to tend vineyards and make wines as well. The only alternative is a large staff or a conscientious group of growers.

Bynum likes light wines not heavy with wood or alcohol, and he prefers not to use oak for his white wines. He likes the fruity character of Russian River grapes and the occasional earthy taste in the reds, but the Zinfandel comes in from Dry Creek. Bynum uses open fermenters, feeling he gets more complexity from the fermentation and less heat to cope with because he can turn over the cap more easily. He likes to ferment reds below 80° F. and whites at lower temperatures, but not below 50° F., because when it is too cold the wines lack fruitiness.

Bynum is experimental with his wines, blending a Merlot with a third of Cabernet Sauvignon, for instance, or a low-acid Cabernet with some high-acid Ruby Cabernet, occasionally adding small proportions of other grapes to his Zinfandel. These are common practices in many wineries, sometimes spelled out on back labels, more often ignored. Only taste will tell if a wine made entirely from a single grape is better than one blended with another.

Bynum's wines are popular, not only because they are in the medium-price range, many under $4, but because they are not overpowering. Unassuming, you might say, although the fruitiness is there to attract attention.

Especially recommended: Sauvignon Blanc
                              French Colombard
                              Petite Sirah
                              Zinfandel

Korbel. Three Heck Brothers bought the Korbel winery down the Russian River near Guerneville in the Fifties. The winery was founded in 1886, built by a couple of Czech lumberjacks who used the redwoods they cleared to build the winery on a foundation of local stone and homemade bricks. The cleared land was planted from European cuttings and a sparkling wine was made, called Grand Pacific. Korbel descendants lost interest and the Hecks, who had learned sparkling winemaking from their father, who had made Cook's Imperial in Ohio, moved right in.

Fermentation was done in bottle and still is, and by the Sixties it had become known as one of the best California sparkling wines. There's Korbel Brut and Korbel Sec and Korbel Extra Dry, all of which are dry, Korbel Natural which is very dry, and Korbel Rosé, which isn't. The wines were so popular that they had to invent mechanical riddling racks to shake the sediment into the necks of the bottles. Shaking takes place three times a day, just before the winery opens, just after it closes and at the lunch break. The feeling is that nobody can stand all that jiggling during working hours. Everything else is automated, too, the upended bottles with necks full of sediment trundling along through a freezing bath, this plug then removed with a pop, the bottle refilled with similar wine and a dosage of sugar syrup so the wine has the desired dryness, then jiggled along to the capping and labeling machines. People love to watch it all.

Marketing was taken over by Jack Daniels, the Tennessee Sour Mash people, in the Sixties, and the brothers expanded the home vineyard to nearly 500 acres on various benchlands along the river. Present winemaker is the son of Al Huntsinger, the Souverain winemaker.

Perhaps the earliest success was Cabernet Sauvignon, clean, round, balanced, firm. There wasn't much around until the mid-Seventies, but Jack Daniels salesmen would take the odd bottle around to this or that retailer or restaurateur and customers began asking for the wine. Then there's the Pinot Noir and the Chardonnay and the others, large blends of good, reasonably priced wines. They make a couple of million bottles of sparkling wine, a quarter of a million cases of table wines. You can find their wines in most places and the wines are worth finding.

VALLEY OF THE MOONS

Sonoma is the big town in the south of the county it names, close to the flat stretches around the top of San Francisco Bay, backed by hilly country full of vineyards. Named by the Indians, who saw several moons dodging in and out between the peaks, the valley by day is as restless as it looks in moonlight. New vineyards and new wineries are getting wines to market.

Sonoma Vineyards. One way to get involved with wines is to have a grandfather with a German vineyard. Rodney Strong would stop off between tours of his dance troupe and help out in the winery. By the time he decided to fold up his Dance Quartet early in the Sixties he knew what his next show was going to be. He took over what was politely called a former boarding house in Tiburon, across the bay from San Francisco, and began bottling wines, blending them from stocks he had tasted in trips through Napa and Sonoma. He began selling wines with personalized labels by direct mail at the suggestion of a friend, Peter Friedman. This was so successful that the two leased a winery in Windsor, below the bend of the Russian River; as the business grew they saw the need for their own vineyards. By the end of the decade they had become involved with the planting of nearly 5,000 acres in a dozen plots on benchlands along the river and up in the Alexander Valley. These were sold to investors, with Strong signing management contracts and reserving the grapes.

The company went public to raise money to build a new winery, a large cross-shaped structure in the middle of a vineyard, with ramps leading over a reflecting pool to a central block containing tasting rooms and offices that look down into the winery and vat rooms. Steps lead down between two arms of the cross to a grassed enclosure where concerts and recitals are held and outdoor picnics and lawn parties can be set up. A kitchen provides catering services. By the mid-Seventies the new vineyards were in bearing and a New York importer, Renfield, bought a major share and took over marketing. Strong continues as winemaker and vineyard manager, his assistants including Mary Ann Graf, now at Simi, and Robert Underwood, now at Château St. Jean. Making wines with Strong at present is Forrest Tancer, trained in science, but drawn to wines.

"It's a passion, and most people drawn to making wines feel the same way," says Tancer. "There's constant experimenting, trying new ways to make wines better, lighter, more true to type, more reflective of the vineyards from which the grapes come. Last night I had a quiche of bacon and cheese with some Chardonnay from our Iron Horse vineyard and I can't wait to try that wine with one from Spring Mountain and Château Montelena and a Beaune Clos des Mouches, just to compare relative merits of the wines.

"The night before, I had some sauerkraut and knockwurst with one of our Rieslings, a nice light wine. I think twelve percent Riesling is almost a travesty. I'd like to make them about ten percent alcohol. I had a Cabernet with an apple and some Swiss cheese for dessert and was sorry not to have a different one to try with ours.

"Five years ago, you wouldn't want to have done that with Sonoma Cabernets, nor could you have found the wines. But we are now able to compare wines from same areas and vintages. There are a lot to choose from. With our vineyards in full growth we can now try making the same variety in different ways, to suit the grapes from different vineyards.

"Here's Chardonnay from one of the older vineyards, with much more tannin, but it slips right by because the fruit is there, in balance. This '73 is big, full of body, and the '74 is bigger. But still with delicacy.

"Many of our wines are big because of the grapes. Here is a '76 Gamay Beaujolais, big, full and fruity. Now taste this '71 Pinot Noir. The nose is still sharp from the Limousin oak. It's been three years in bottle and still so undeveloped. The wine will be perfect by 1980, and then it will be great with a cassoulet."

Press wine and a variety of blends are offered by mail under the Windsor Vineyards label. Several blends of top varietals are offered in magnums, vinified so that they can be drunk young. The first great wine from Sonoma was probably the '68 Cabernet Sauvignon from Alexander Valley grapes, but now there are several to choose from. Production exceeds 100,000 cases and as they get around the market, people will discover the new wines of Sonoma, thanks to men like Strong who put the show on the road back in the Sixties.

103

Especially recommended: Chenin Blanc
Cabernet Sauvignon
Chardonnay
Pinot Noir
Johannisberg Riesling
Gamay Beaujolais

Sebastiani Vineyards. If you left the hills of Tuscany before the turn of the century at the age of fourteen and headed for California, you couldn't expect to open a winery right away. You would work in a San Francisco vegetable garden for a while to get the lay of the land and then you would head for Sonoma, where the vines were, chopping wood, making cobblestones, until you had saved enough to buy a redwood tank and some grapes. It took Samuele Sebastiani eight years, but in 1904, at the age of twenty-two, he put up his sign. You can see the tank at the old winery today.

His son, August, began helping with the books while he was still in grade school, worked in the winery during high school and took over the running of the winery when he graduated from college in 1937. August's son, named after his grandfather, followed in his father's footsteps, helping supervise some 300 acres of vineyard and involving himself with the production of some million cases of wine a year.

This is larger than August had in mind, but in the mid-Seventies he found himself with tanks full of Cabernet and no place to put the new vintage, so he decided to put the wine out in jugs. "You'll ruin our image," said other winemakers, "Cabernet is noble, something grand in the public eye. You're making a chicken out of a peacock." Perhaps August could understand that, being a bird fancier; but he went ahead. Some of the grapes had cost him nearly a thousand dollars a ton; then, when supply outstripped demand the price dropped to four hundred dollars. Sebastiani figured he could replace the high-priced grapes at the lower price, sell the Cabernet as if it had been made from the less-costly grapes and make room for the new wines. He doubled his volume that year, delighting wine drinkers across the country and making up in publicity and new customers much more than he spent for the grapes. Other wineries are now putting the noble grapes in magnums and jugs. It's not the name, after all, but the wine, especially when the price is right.

Sebastiani was the first of the traditional Sonoma winemakers to break the pattern. He sold his wines in bulk. But he paid notice when Almadén began putting grape names on the label, watched the success of Napa vintners when they started calling their bottlings premium wines, admired Bartholomew's offerings from Buena Vista and noted the acclaim of Brad Webb's Hanzell bottlings.

One of Sebastiani's best wines was Barbera, dry, fruity and full. He began winning prizes with that. He saw that others were bringing out the fruitiness of the grapes, maybe too much so, that the wines were running high in alcohol, maybe too high, that there was a strong taste of wood, maybe too strong. Never too much, not even moderation, goes an old Roman saw, and Sebastiani began offering what had become known as the premium varietals at modest prices, without extremes of taste. Sound wines that just about anybody would like and could afford. In New York, prestigious Sherry Wines & Spirits, a store that had caught the imagination of eastern wine drinkers and earned their admiration by introducing scores of wines, put on a promotion of a dozen Sebastiani bottlings. This created interest among astute retailers in other cities and by the Seventies there were Sebastiani bottlings in all the major markets.

August Sebastiani likes making wines, but he likes wine drinkers even more. There was a fad for Beaujolais Nouveau, wines fermented as quickly as possible from grapes picked as soon as possible, then rushed to Paris and flown to New York so they could be drunk by Christmas. The trouble was that the new Beaujolais was usually sharp and raw. In Sonoma the vintage came a little earlier and the grapes were much fruitier. If wine drinkers were interested in fresh wines straight from the cask, why not bottle some Gamay Beaujolais Nouveau? Very successful.

Off and on through the years, there would be special lots of grapes that excelled, and Sebastiani began bottling these separately, at first for family drinking and gifts to friends. There was the Cabernet vineyard near his house, and some Pinot Noir that he especially liked, so August began giving them special treatment, putting them in small casks, letting them age in bottle. In 1977 the first of these Proprietor's Reserves were offered, including a special lot of Barbera, which is expected to live twenty years. The '71 Pinot Noir is expected to be good until the end of the century; the Cabernet Sauvignon of the same year should last as long. Aged in redwood, they are in the traditional California style, taking advantage of the

105

best of modern techniques, along with family secrets handed down from father to son.

August Sebastiani has always been fascinated by birds, maintaining an aviary of rare specimens and working to establish bird sanctuaries. Use of chemicals for pest control in the vineyards has been a worry because of potential harm to bird populations. This has led to a novel experiment, the ·releasing of ladybugs in the vineyards, which feed on thrips and other insects. The result may be a new method of insect control. If there's a new way of doing things, you can be sure the Sebastianis will try it.

Especially recommended: Barbera
Gamay Beaujolais Nouveau
Cabernet Sauvignon
Pinot Noir
Green Hungarian

Hanzell. When people become fascinated by wines they quickly find favorites, usually Burgundy or Bordeaux. For Ambassador James Zellerbach it was Burgundy. When he retired in the late Forties, he bought a hillside north of Sonoma, planted some twenty acres of Pinot Noir and Chardonnay, and built a winery with roof lines patterned after Clos de Vougeot. That Burgundy vineyard is so highly thought of that French troops are supposed to salute when they pass by. Some feel the same way about Hanzell.

Napa winemaker Brad Webb was hired to install a model winery. It was planned so that a day's crushing would fill a single vat, and everything else was geared to size. Burgundy methods were followed precisely, the wines were aged in Burgundy casks of Limousin oak. By the late Fifties Zellerbach could taste Sonoma wines that were hard to tell from those of the Côte d'Or.

Zellerbach died in the early Sixties but Douglas Day came along to carry on the tradition. Few people get the chance to taste the wines, but Zellerbach started a trend among small winemakers, who began using casks of European oak in which to age their wines. This was one of the most important developments in California winemaking, focusing attention on the fact that what happened to the wine in cask was as important as what happened to the grapes in the vineyard and in the fermenting vats. There is constant discussion today as to which oaks suit the various wines. Limousin oak imparts a somewhat vanillalike smell to the wine and is used for fairly light Chardonnays. Brad Webb, in his Freemark Abbey Chardonnays, uses the Nevers oak used in Bordeaux and the wines have a fuller character. Charles Krug has aged Chardonnays in Yugoslavian oak. At Beaulieu, Tchellistcheff's practice was to use very little oak and Wente uses none at all. Usually, the back label of the wine has a comment about cooperage. Attentive tasters can occasionally taste distinctions, but a good winemaker will mature his wines so judiciously that the wine will simply taste good and the way it should, the oak affecting the taste but not dominating it.

The upshot of such concerns is that there are many carefully made wines today, distinctive and pleasing to taste in pairs to see how they enhance a meal.

Hanzell is now owned by a firm called Hanzell Vineyards, Ltd., which is the property of a Canadian company called Eastern United Securities, the major shareholder of which is an Australian heiress said to be residing in France and whose name is given as Barbara Fane.

Buena Vista. Newspaperman Frank Bartholomew wanted a country place, so in the early Forties he bought at auction a run-down ranch of some 400 acres just east of the town of Sonoma, where the hills began to rise to the Mayacamas range. It was mostly a eucalyptus grove, but a brook ran through it near a couple of old stone buildings. There were some fields with a few gnarled vines. He asked the head of the Wine Institute, Leon Adams, if it might have been a winery once and was delighted to learn that it was Agoston Haraszthy's old vineyard.

He had a story. As he built his house in a vineyard near the brook, he rebuilt the winery buildings and began planting vines. By the Fifties he was offering a Cabernet and Chardonnay and many others, including the full Sylvaner he called Vine Brook. Some of his wines he sent over to a fellow who had set up shop in Napa to make sparkling wines, Hanns Kornell, and soon there was Sparkling Sonoma Pinot Chardonnay and Sparkling Cabernet Rosé. There was also a Rose Brook from Cabernet, a Zinfandel that might have come from Haraszthy's old vines, a Green Hungarian because Bartholomew liked the name.

Haraszthy had said it might take a hundred years for California to produce "as noble and generous a wine as any in Europe." Bartholomew's timing was perfect. In the Sixties he set up The Friends of Agoston Haraszthy to promote the wines. Then he sold the winery.

Young's Market of Los Angeles bought Buena Vista to supply their supermarkets, setting up a corporation to extend the vineyards and build a new winery on 700 acres up in the Mayacamas range on the Napa-Sonoma county line. Bartholomew retained his house and the home vineyard and bought 600 acres for new vineyards up in the hills behind it, calling it Hacienda Wine Cellars. You can taste wines from both in California and occasionally find some bottles east of the Rockies. Haraszthy's prophecy has come true.

Especially recommended:

BUENA VISTA	HACIENDA
Vine Brook	Chardonnay
Green Hungarian	Cabernet Sauvignon
Zinfandel	Pinot Noir

Other Small Wineries. On the road up to Santa Rosa from Sonoma there are several small wineries, Château St. Jean and Kenwood on the east, Grand Cru and Valley of the Moons on the west. The last sells most of its wines to blenders. Grand Cru is on a slope hidden behind a school and makes only a few wines from some 40 acres in a winery buried in the hill that used to be called Lamoine. Kenwood was once the old Pagani winery, noted for its Italian style, wines full of fruit, high in alcohol, long in wood, but a trio of new owners is trying modern ways.

Perhaps the most interesting of these, if only because its production is some 30,000 cases and therefore occasionally available outside of California, is Château St. Jean. The fanciful name was given to it by the three owners, growers with large holdings in the San Joaquin Valley, interested in seeing what could be done with North Coast grapes. Robert Arrowood, trained as a chemist, worked at Korbel during summers while at school, then with Joe Vercelli at Italian Swiss and then with Rod Strong at Sonoma Vineyards; he was hired away to get things going at St. Jean.

The long stuccoed villa actually looks like one of the so-called châteaux of Bordeaux, surrounded by 100 acres of vineyard with winery buildings back toward a hill. Fermentation is done in stainless steel tanks of one- two- and three-thousand-gallon sizes, there are some 500-gallon fermenters for even smaller batches. Arrowood made seven different Chardonnays in '75, for example, putting the fermenters to good use.

They had five batches of '75 Rieslings, covering each of the German styles: Kabinett from ripe grapes; Spätlese from late-picked grapes; and three batches affected by botrytis from selected bunches, and from selected berries that had raisinized. These were Auslesen, Beerenauslesen and Trockenbeerenauslesen, according to German nomenclature.

Fermentations take place under a blanket of carbon dioxide to keep air away from the wines, the action being completed in new oak barrels, and press wine is blended back with the free-run fermentation to get fullness. For the same reason, some stems ferment with the reds, on occasion, and even with some of the whites. Filtration is kept to a minimum, a centrifuge is used lightly to clear the wines for bottling. They use four kinds of French oak for the Chardonnays, including Tronçay and Alliers; Limousin and Nevers are used for the other whites. American oak is used for a Fumé Blanc, and no oak is used for the Rhine grapes and for a sweet Sauvignon. Complex records are kept to note differences, interesting to a drinker only when the wines are exceptional. One such is the Chardonnay from the nearby Wildwood Vineyard, whose volcanic soil brings out a full richness in the wines. One could compare this with the fruity Chardonnay made from Belle Terre vineyard grapes up in Alexander Valley— or with the five other Chardonnays they make, for that matter, or you could compare various years, or Chardonnays from other wineries . . .

Off from the road that goes over to Napa from Sonoma are two more small wineries that are beginning to make themselves known. The old Zepponi winery has been resurrected by a descendant named Gino, in partnership with Norman de Leuze. One of their best wines is a Pinot Noir from Carneros, over in Napa by the bay. The aim is to find growers with exceptional vines and make special batches of wines from them, in addition to the Cabernet and Pinot in their own vineyards. There is also a Riesling from Carneros that is sought after, but there is not much point looking outside California, at least until the Eighties.

Gundlach-Bundschu was a winery with some 400 acres, started before the Civil War by a San Francisco brewer and his son-in-law. They used Bacchus on their labels and started a Bacchus Club that held revels at vintage time in a glade on what they called their Rhine Farm. Prohibition did in the winery, and grapes were sold to other wineries. This seemed a shame, so great-grandchildren of the founders decided in 1970 to restore it. A third of the 300 acres left are contracted to Sebastiani, but there are enough remaining, along with new plantings, to reach 15,000 cases and

William E. Massee

more by the Eighties. There is Zinfandel, of course, and Cabernet, and a Sylvaner. But there is also Kleinberger, the California name for a Rhine grape called Elbling. It's also called Burger and not considered to be much of a grape. You can decide for yourself; it sells for about $3 a bottle.

The Small Wineries in Sonoma and Mendocino. There are half a hundred vineyards, new or rejuvenated, in the valleys of Sonoma and Mendocino counties, to join the score or more that have continued since Prohibition. Among them are a few that sell mostly in bulk—Fredson, Frei Bros., Seghesio, Cambiaso Sonoma County Cellars, Sonoma County Cooperative—but even the smallest now offer wines under their own labels, even if only at the winery or by mail. Here is a list of the smaller ones.

to 5,000 cases
Bandiera Wines
Dach Vineyards
Dehlinger Winery
Gundlach-Bundschu
Hacienda Wine Cellars
Hanzell Vineyards
Hop Kiln Winery
Husch Vineyards
Jade Mountain
Landmark Vineyards
Navarro Winery
Preston Winery
A. Rafanelli Winery
Russian River Vineyards
Sotoyome Winery
Joseph Swan Vineyards
Willowside Vineyards
Z-D Winery

to 15,000 cases
Alexander Valley Vineyards
Balverne Cellars
Davis Bynum Winery
Dry Creek Vineyard
Edmeades Vineyards
Grand Cru Vineyards
Johnson's of Alexander Valley
Lambert Bridge Winery
Mark West Vineyard
Mill Creek Vineyards
Trentadue Winery
Viña Vista Vineyards
Weibel Champagne Cellars

to 50,000 cases
BuenaVista Winery
Château St. Jean
Fetzer Vineyards
Jordan Vineyards
Kenwood Vineyards
Geyser Peak Winery
Kenwood Vineyards
Sausal Winery
Jordan Vineyards

NOTE: Around 100,000 cases are Cresta Blanca, Pedroncelli and Simi; Parducci, Sonoma Vineyards and Souverain Cellars produce twice as much.

Napa: One District Becoming Many

VIEWPOINT: MICROCLIMATES, MINI-DISTRICTS, WINEMASTERS

"Used to be easy for somebody to buy wines," said the retailer. "There was Burgundy and Bordeaux and the Rhine. Frank Schoonmaker or Wildman would come in with estate bottlings from small growers who made their own wines; there were the classed growths from Bordeaux. Then there were the wines from good shippers on the Rhône and Loire, from Alsace and Italy, a few odds and ends like the Swiss wines and Riojas. You could steer people from one to another, there were lots of good bottles under four dollars.

"Even California was easy, Cabernets from BV, Martini's Zinfandel, Wente's Sauvignon, Chardonnay or Riesling from one of the small wineries up in Napa, when you could get them. Then there was all that planting in the Sixties, all the new wineries of the Seventies. Look here."

He waved his hand at a wall of bottles, sectioned into nooks—Napa, Sonoma, Mendocino, Livermore, Monterey.

"I have more than a hundred wines arranged by region. Now I have to change it all. I'm going to arrange them by district—Carneros, Mayacamas, Silverado and the Wine Road for Napa—and that will help. It used to be easy to buy wines by geography."

He waved his hand at tables of wines in front of the sections.

111

"All the wineries out there make wines from the noble grapes, so on these tables I have them arranged by varieties—a dozen Chardonnays, or whatever—at different prices.

"Here are tables from top winemakers—Tchelistcheff, Heitz, Nightingale, Webb. You can taste the difference in styles."

He threw up his hands.

"Don't tell me it's too complicated. People come in and laugh, but they begin to get the idea. Try a couple of different bottles with dinner for the fun of it, not to see which is best. One guy looked around and said it was like a record shop. The big bands here, the combos over here, like big wineries and small ones. Then soloists like Ella and Sarah and Billie, they have styles the way winemasters do. The way Armstrong or Goodman or Basie plays standards is like the different grape varieties. That seemed to make things clear for him. Maybe it helps."

He looked around the shop.

"The sad thing is that this misses the point. Wines are meant to be enjoyed, not classified. We're having a veal stew tonight; there will be six of us. I'll take a couple of bottles of red and a couple of white, I'll pick up some cheese on the way home. And we'll have a bottle or two, maybe all four, to go along with the dinner. We'll pay attention to the wines but we won't go on and on about them. They'll taste good, the wines, and they will match the food, not the other way around. And if one doesn't, I'll recork it and have it another time. I do all this classifying so customers don't have to worry about it. What are you having tonight?"

Chicken, I told him, browned and simmered with herbs in white wine. He told me to pick out a couple of bottles and I picked a Heitz and a Webb, two Chardonnays. He picked up a BV Cabernet that Tchelistcheff had made.

"Get some goat cheese and save some of the white wine to have with it. Nobody tries white wine with cheese and it's so good. Then have the Cabernet. Going to be a good dinner."

We had some melon with prosciutto to start with. The Chardonnays were good with that. They were good with the chicken. They were good with the cheese, too, and so was the Cabernet. "What a nice dinner," said our guest, giving me a hug, and her husband patted me on the back, then kissed the cook. "That's the best chicken I've had in months," he said. We began cleaning up. "Weren't the wines good with the cheese," said my wife. I agreed.

112

* * *

My first trip to the Napa Valley, I got there in time for lunch.

"The winemakers get together every month to talk things over," said Ollie Goulet, the winemaker at Almadén. "They have to; nobody else will listen. Anybody comes who is free. It's not much of a lunch, cheese and stuff, but everybody brings bottles. It's in a beat-up old hotel in Rutherford, usually closed at noon, but they open up so they can get together. Shop talk, but you'll learn something. Maybe you'll be lucky and get a good group."

I was. It was one of the last of the lunches because the hotel closed down soon after, which was too bad. The room looked like an old-time barroom without the bar, push-up windows with small panes, closed tight against the dust, a pressed tin ceiling faded to mustard, beer ads on the ashtrays, ketchup bottles, paper napkins folded into glasses on small square tables. But some of these had been pushed in a row down the center of the room; a white cloth had been spread; and at each place were six stemmed wine glasses, big ones. Down the center were platters of cheese and salami and olives—a good antipasto—with loaves of French bread beside them. The classic winemaker's meal, it turns out, all over the world.

There were introductions and polite but curious glances, for Ollie had told them I was going to write about their wines, that I knew about French ones. Had been there, in fact. More than welcome, I was a new audience. There was quite a crowd.

Brother Timothy from The Christian Brothers, tall and lean in a black suit, wearing a clerical collar. The brotherhood was beginning to market table wines, a bold venture after so many years spent with fortified wines. They were changing labels, much to Brother Timothy's regret. He liked the cloistered arches and dark colors. I thought they were among the ugliest ever produced, but stayed silent.

John Daniel, from Inglenook, a big and friendly man in a tweed jacket, the only other one in the room. He had been responsible for starting a campaign devoted to premium wines only, those made mostly by the men in the room. He was the first to put grape names on the label, had inspired Almadén to do so. The premium wines had begun to appear in the good wine shops in the east, which pleased everybody there—a good beginning. The campaign died in the Sixties. An eager press agent had ar-

113

ranged a tasting at the Overseas Press Club for a visiting group of French winemakers, but the bottles had been mostly from the big blenders in the Great Central Valley. A reporter from the *Times* had wandered around asking the French what they thought of the wines. The polite French had talked about the weather, the big buildings in New York, anything at all to avoid comment, and the paper had printed a funny story about the tasting. The next day the press agent had been canned, and all promotion about any California wine stopped for a time.

Louis P. Martini, a big man in slacks and open shirt, was busy pulling corks. His father was still running the winery but Louis P. was making the wines. He was the first to make Zinfandel respectable, and he called his blends Mountain Red and Mountain White because many of the grapes came from vineyards up in the Mayacamas range. He was pricing his wines as low as possible, with the idea that everybody ought to be able to afford them.

Andre Tchelistcheff, short and slight and dark, in a white shirt, set out some bottles of his latest Cabernet Sauvignon, the best wine of Beaulieu Vineyards. Some people say his were the first really good Cabernets from California. And there were tall bottles of white wines he was experimenting with, Chardonnays and Rieslings that had not spent much time in wood.

There was Lee Stewart from Souverain, dapper in slacks and shirt, enthusiastic about a new Davis hybrid called Flora. One of the first amateur winemakers turned professional, he had cruised around the Napa hills one day in 1943, on his way to Mendocino to find a summer place, and had fallen for a chicken ranch on the side of Howell Mountain. There he had made Green Hungarian a wine to marvel over, and a wonderful Mountain Zinfandel.

Jovial Fred McCrea was setting out some of his Chardonnay as a treat, and some of his Riesling. Another amateur, an escapee from advertising, he had found his vineyard the same year that Stewart had, straight across the valley, 700 feet up in the Mayacamas range. Nobody argues when people say his Stony Hill Chardonnay was the first good one to come out of California.

Pete Mondavi, dark and shy, was setting out some of his new white wines. They were among the first dry ones made in California. Everybody crowded around to taste them. Bob Mondavi, as usual, was off on a trip, spreading the good word that there were great bottles coming.

This was the nucleus of Napa Valley winemakers in the early Fifties, and the wines they made opened the market for new wineries and influenced many of the older ones to change their ways. Other pioneers like the Wentes and Concannons dropped in whenever they had the chance; people from Almadén and Paul Masson appeared when they could. Winemakers from all the wineries, big or small, were welcome, which is the custom in wine country. Perhaps no group of men has been so influential. They gave heart to all those struggling to make good wines, to plant the best grapes, and by getting their wines into the marketplace they began to find those across the country who liked their wines.

It was after one when we moved away from the wines that had been set on tables against the walls and sat down to help ourselves from the cold plates. Everybody was hungry; now and then someone would jump up to get a bottle. People kept dropping in, James Nichelini with some Zinfandels, I remember, joking with Louis Martini, who regularly bought some of his wines, and there were some men from Davis, the wine college over near Sacramento. There was talk about the temperature ratings devised by Drs. Amerine and Winkler and how they had to be broken down now into smaller areas—microclimates.

This was a time for rebirth, after Prohibition, Depression, War and Recovery, this last having been difficult because of shortages, even of bottles and corks. As the cook passed around platters of steaks and bowls of hot potato salad, John Daniel gave me a quick history. Phylloxera had knocked out thousands of acres at the turn of the century. Sonoma had been a center, with more than fifty wineries; the few left produced only bulk wines. Napa had come along more slowly, the first few wineries mostly showplaces for San Francisco millionaires among the vineyards of bulk producers, most of whom had gone under during the Depression. There were scarcely a dozen premium wineries in the valley, most of them represented by the men in the room. They made good wines but they sold at not much more than two dollars a bottle, too little to gain respect from wine drinkers accustomed to spending twice as much for Burgundy and Bordeaux. And the Napa taste was different, more of the grape, and with an earthy taste.

"We call it Rutherford dust," said Tchelistcheff, "often pleasant, often too much."

I mentioned redwood, the smell of cedar or pine, the taste of resin. "We have lots of redwood," said Daniel. "We've found American oak too strong and European oak hard to handle." Tchelistcheff smiled, and Daniel changed the subject, starting to talk about new stainless steel fer-

115

menting tanks that were being introduced so no contaminants could get at the wine and temperatures could be controlled. Redwood wasn't a welcome subject.

During the next few days I found out why, going from one winery to another. John Daniel's big winery was full of redwood tanks and the old German winemaker insisted that they were splendid, so old that wines could not possibly pick up anything from the wood. He brought up old wines to taste from vintages as far back as the Twenties. The wines were dark and heavy, full of raisin and prune tastes, of spicy wood tastes not from oak. Somebody was wrong. Maybe it was me, because I was most used to tasting young wines from casks.

Only the smallest wineries seemed to be using oak. Tchelistcheff smiled when I tasted his Cabernets at Beaulieu. "We're getting away from redwood," he said gently, "but it takes time," and he had me taste some that had been aged in small barrels brought in from Bordeaux. That was more like it; my taste needed training.

But others complained, too. "That redwood taste," they'd say, and all through the Fifties the complaint continued whenever a bottle was opened.

Ten years later there was change everywhere. The redwood was disappearing, replaced by glass-lined fermenters and stainless steel. Cellars were full of oak. Vineyards were being replanted. Everybody was using grape names on labels. There was more variety in the wines, but still that heavy fruit and floweriness . . .

"Vintner's Row was a dusty two-lane ten miles long the last time you came out," said John Daniel. "It really started here at Rutherford and ended the other side of St. Helena. BV, Martini and Krug were on the east side. Inglenook, Beringer and The Christian Brothers were on the west side. Everybody else sold bulk. Even Beringer sold mostly in California. Then they widened the road."

New wineries were opening; new wines were coming from the young vines. There were new tastes, without strangeness.

By 1970, Napa was the prime grape-growing region outside Europe, with 12,000 acres in vines. Figures for 1980 show more than 21,000 acres.

The statistics on the following page show the great confidence that Napa Valley producers have shown in the country's interest in superior wines.

	1970 acreage	1980 acreage
Cabernet Sauvignon	1400−	5200+
Merlot	60+	680
Pinot Noir	40−	1100+
Gamay (Napa)	730+	1000+
Gamay (Beaujolais)	200−	600+
Zinfandel	680+	1300+
Petite Sirah	1040+	1130+
Barbera	30+	30+
Chardonnay	370+	2250
Pinot Blanc	40−	60+
Johannisberg Riesling	360+	1140+
Sylvaner	200−	200−
Gewürztraminer	110+	300
Sauvignon Blanc	275	530+
Semillon	180+	200−
Chenin Blanc	700	1250

VINTNER'S ROW BECOMES THE WINE ROAD

Vintner's Row of the Sixties ended above St. Helena at Greystone, the largest stone winery in the world when it was build in 1889 as a sort of cooperative. There, growers could age their own wines instead of selling them in bulk to San Francisco merchants. Phylloxera wiped out many of the vineyards before Greystone was finished and the grand plan never came to be. During the Depression it was sold for ten thousand dollars; parts of it were used for storage; then The Christian Brothers leased a wing, finally buying it in 1950. They installed sparkling wine facilities there and opened the building as a visiting center in 1955. A quarter of a million people come each year.

Visiting centers have become a part of California wineries, growing out of roadside stands set up in the first days of the automobile. As in most wine regions, there were few places to eat or stay, but the tasting rooms began attracting so many that the state wanted to put a highway through. This was squelched when the county named itself a greenbelt in 1968, cutting out developers by limiting land sales to plots of twenty acres or more pledged to farming. The state settled for repaving and widening old 29, by so doing converting it to Napa Wine Road. The town of

117

Napa began to spruce up for tourists, then an old stone winery called Vintage 1870 was opened up with craft shops and restaurants. Other buildings in what was practically a ghost town became antiques shops, book stores, a pastry shop called the Court of the Two Sisters, a restaurant called The French Laundry, a place for breakfast called The Diner. Vintage 1870 now boasts a vast wine shop with California and European vintages, a sausage store called The Wurst Place, even candle stores and organic juice bars. Tourist buses stop at The Grapevine Inn out on the highway; picnickers stock up at the Napa Valley Cheese Company just up the road.

A few miles farther along at the Oakville Cross, which runs over to the Silverado Trail, is the old outside and the fancy inside of the Oakville Grocery Co.; the Oakville Public House across the corner has an old jukebox and a young French chef. At the Oakville Grade, which runs up into the Mayacamas past the experimental vineyard of the wine college at Davis, is Pometta's Delicatessen serving pasta.

Beaulieu Vineyards built a fancy new visiting complex beside their winery at Rutherford, so the old buildings on the streets adjoining became Rutherford Square, boasting a couple of ice cream parlors, a bar, delicatessen and soup kitchen.

St. Helena has always been a center of sorts because of the hot springs and various institutions nearby, including the teetotal sanitarium of the Seventh Day Adventists. There are several refurbished inns, a French restaurant called La Belle Hélène and one at Freemark Abbey Gift and Gourmet, a complex that has a country store with cookware and cookbooks and a candle factory.

"This is going to be the Calistoga of Sarafonia," said the founder of the town by the hot springs, and the name stuck. There are still hot springs. Silverado Restaurant, on the main drag, is run by young hotel school graduates and features a Zinfandel Beef Buffet on Wednesday nights and more than a gross of valley wines. If all this palls you can run over to Pope Valley Parachute Ranch, fly up and leap out, or just watch the balloonists who soar aloft at any opportunity.

And lo, in a scant decade Napa Wine Road has become a full-scale tourist center, not tawdry and rarely tacky, but spaced out over thirty miles. The wineries have concerts during the summer; the library in St. Helena has a series of wine tastings; the Wild Horse Valley Ranch east of Napa has five square miles of riding trails; a good time can be had by all.

And now there are a couple of dozen new wineries, or ones renewed, along the Wine Road. A scant third distribute nationally, or ever will, but all of them signify that Napa is sailing along under its own banners, no longer selling most of its grapes outside the valley for the big blends of bulk shippers. The small wineries are there for the seeking; bread and cheese are to be had, shaded hillsides for picnics and the calm vineyards on every side.

Robert Mondavi Winery. Robert Mondavi has always been convinced that the Napa Valley could produce remarkable wines, but he has also been convinced that there was a lot to be learned from the great European regions. Probably nobody has traveled back and forth so frequently to find the best of both worlds. He was the first to experiment extensively with small cooperage, aging batches of Cabernet and Pinot, Chardonnay and Sauvignon in Nevers, Limousin, Yugoslavian and American oak. Their favorite is Nevers, particularly for Cabernet, with perhaps one barrel in four or five being American oak, then blending the wines from both. Now all premium wineries use small cooperage of one sort or another.

He has always wanted to make rounded, balanced wines, not so full that they would be overpowering or take decades to develop, but wines fermented to dryness that would invite another sip. Avoiding heaviness—from alcohol or oak or excessive fruitiness—his wines are generally of medium body. Son Michael and others involved in the winemaking share his convictions.

The winery is just below Oakville, a wide, low arch with a tower at the side and two wings angling out to enclose a grassy sweep where concerts and lawn parties can be held. One wing contains a visitors' lounge, tasting rooms, a dining room and catering facilities; the other, offices and laboratories backed by the winery. Based on elements from the old California mission style, the building is as light and graceful as the wines. It is shown on the label.

The winery is in an expanse of Cabernet. Martha's Vineyard, made into wine by Joe Heitz, is to the south; to the north are some vineyards of Freemark Abbey, Inglenook, and the Marquis de Pins #1 of Beaulieu; and stretching east across the highway to the Silverado Trail are the Cabernets of other premium producers. The Mondavi Cabernet may be the easiest of all to drink.

Mondavi solves problems. One of them is what to do with Sauvignon

119

Blanc, a fine wine with an unpopular name. He changed the name. The grape is known as the Fumé Blanc on the Loire, so he called his Blanc Fumé. Instantly popular. Half the wineries in the state now use the new name. Getting a fermenting wine over the cap of skins and pulp that forms is traditionally solved by pumping the wine over the cap or pushing the cap down into the wine. He mounted fermenting tanks on an axis, like a cement mixer, and they spin three times a day. Not for all grapes, of course, but whenever it seems called for. Traditional methods vary, as warranted by experiment. "We're beginning to pick up nuances that we never did before," says Mondavi.

Like all good winemakers, Mondavi tastes with his group every day, so that everybody knows what is happening in each cask. "There is no other way," said Mondavi. "You have to taste the wines as they develop. You learn only half of it when you drink only finished wines. That's the way I learned, by drinking. I think it is the only way."

Mondavi drinks a lot of wine, or rather, he tastes a lot. At dinner, there are usually four wines, two reds and two whites, often more "One is usually an import that is from the same grape, but that's to cultivate my palate, not just to rank them. Last night we had scampi, and the Krug Blanc Fumé was good with that, but I wanted to taste another. The restaurant didn't have one, so we tried Louis Martini's Chardonnay and that was good, too. One wine leads to another. If I find a certain characteristic in one, we might see if it's there in three or four others. You have to taste."

Wines from Mondavi are good wines to start on. To encourage the making of light and simple wines meant to be drunk as soon as bottled, he now has a wide enough distribution to market Mondavi Red Table Wine and White Table Wine. He makes them dry so there will be an alternative to the usual "mellow" wines in the low price range. The hope is that the Mondavi reputation will influence their purchase, even at the low price. There is a worry that the word "dry" on a label has been so abused that nobody will believe his are really dry. Maybe Mondavi can persuade buyers, thus filling that great gap in the range of American wines.

There are more than 600 acres in bearing and Mondavi manages some 300 acres more on long-term contracts, which account for two thirds of the grapes needed. The rest come from the Napa Valley. "We know them best," said Mondavi. "We're better off concentrating." Optimum production is around 200,000 cases of premium wines, which require plenty of concentration.

* * *

BV, Beaulieu Vineyard. The year of the century for California wines was 1883. Wente and Concannon started vineyards over in Livermore and Georges de Latour arrived from France to seek his fortune in the gold fields. He went broke there and wound up in Napa, scraping the bottom of the barrel. Literally, because he made a business of collecting the cream of tartar that coated the vats and selling this to be made into baking powder. In 1899 he bought his first land, and the new century found him in France, buying cuttings. The First World War found him buying a winery and expanding it. Prohibition found him selling altar wines with the support of the Archbishop of San Francisco, and the Golden Gate International Exposition of 1939 found him running off with the first prize out of one hundred of California's best reds. It was Beaulieu Burgundy, made out of Cabernet Sauvignon.

His greatest find was in 1937, when his French winemaker retired. Latour went to the National Institute of Agronomy in Paris and asked the professor of enology to find a good man. There was a Russian research assistant at the Institut Pasteur, who had been trained in Czechoslovakia and was being urged by one colleague to come to Chile and by another to come to China. Latour urged California. That year, the enologist had tasted Wente's Sémillon and Inglenook's Gewürztraminer at the International Exposition and he knew of the work of Bioletti, Winkler and Amerine at Davis. Andre Tchelistcheff came to Napa.

Beaulieu Vineyards had more than seven hundred acres by then—the home vineyard that extended below the Latour estate, more Cabernet down around Oakville and over toward the Silverado, another section down in Carneros. When Tchelistcheff tasted the wines he suggested that Latour forget the rest and concentrate on Cabernet. Latour needed a line of wines to sell and said he couldn't do that, but agreed to build a separate cellar for them and to get small cooperage. The wines were aged two years in wood and two in glass. Latour died in 1940, before they were ready.

His widow kept up the winery, and their daughter and her husband after that, but in 1969 all but the home vineyard and the villa Latour had built was sold to Heublein. BV was so popular by then that a large firm was needed to do the marketing.

Tchelistcheff had made the wine famous. His BV Cabernet is considered by many to be the first great red wine of California in modern times.

121

His experiments with Chardonnay and Riesling and the other noble vines raised their quality and encouraged others to experiment. His assistants went on to become winemakers elsewhere and several established their own wineries. In 1947 he established his Oenological Research Center in St. Helena to disseminate data about Napa wines and out of this came his consulting group, which now advises wineries all over the state, in the Pacific Northwest and in Mexico. No man has a wider familiarity with American wines or as beneficial an influence on them as Andre Tchelistcheff.

The sale of BV to Heublein shook the California wine world, a sign that more changes were coming, more business giants were moving in. The trouble was that nobody realized how good the wines were, how popular they would become. Except Andre, perhaps. And the man who was put in charge of BV by Heublein, Legh Knowles.

Knowles had been a trumpet player in the days of the big bands, a side man for Glenn Miller, among others, but after the Second World War he had joined Gallo as a marketing man. There was scarcely better experience, though hectic, and Knowles had been lured away by the growing young Wine Institute to be a regional ambassador. First in Washington, then in New England, he presented California wines to the trade, gave tastings and lectures to public groups, spreading the word that there were fine wines in California. There was much doubt. "You say they're as good as Burgundy or Bordeaux and they sell for two dollars?" a retailer would demand. "You want me to put them in and undersell my own wines and wreck my business?"

Knowles arrived at Beaulieu in the Fall of '69. "What's Beaulieu Vineyards Cabernet Sauvignon Special Reserve selling for?" he asked Tchelistcheff. "Three dollars," Andre told him. Knowles' first act at BV was to raise the price. To six dollars. Then he put the distributors on quota.

Uproar. The shock was greater than the BV sale had been. The only guy who charged a lot was Martin Ray down in Santa Rosa, but he had a dinky little winery, a boutique, for God's sake, and he made a couple of thousand cases and didn't like to sell them because he had no inventory. BV has a hundred thousand and they have to sell them. Crazy.

That was the sort of talk you heard when visiting wineries that year. Getting a rise out of winemakers was a lot of fun. They didn't know what they had.

They knew about the wines. Andre was growing Pinot and Chardonnay down in Carneros, calling their wines Beaumont and Beaufort to set them apart, the first with a light fragrance and the second with a taste almost like sage, that had never been noted before. They were from virus-free vines developed at Davis, perhaps imparting to the wine for the first time the true character from the grapes. Beauclair was from the new Riesling strains grown down around Oakville, with a unique and elegant fragrance. Selected lots of Cabernet, bottled as Special Reserve and given extra aging, were developing subtle secondary qualities. The wines were varying from year to year because of more or less sun, early or late picking, so vintages were put on the labels. Others were finding subtleties in their wines because of the new vines and new techniques.

They did not know about the market. The Kennedy White House had installed a California cellar; there was much grumbling when word went out to ambassadors that American wines should be served at state dinners. Sophisticated hostesses began serving Californian, from reverse snobbery or as a lark, perhaps. The best shops put in a few bottles, if only to show the breadth of their selections. Praise of native wines was considered the worst chauvinism, though, not in the best of taste, a way to get away with serving cheap wines. Most of the best bottles stayed in California.

Then Legh Knowles raised the prices.

Well, why not, the wines are worth it, said some of the winemakers, raising theirs. Californians used to snapping up bargains at the wineries protested, even refused to buy, but then the wineries had more to sell to their out-of-state mailing lists. California had a law that taxed wines held for aging, so wineries had been unloading wines as fast as they could; the law was repealed. Now wineries could build up reserves, sell wines only when they were ready to drink, hold wines until the market met their prices. And suddenly the prices of imports shot up.

When Tchelistcheff retired from BV in 1973, after thirty-five years, his wines were selling everywhere, and the prices were right. California can produce great wines, said Andre on his first day at BV; the Napa Valley is a great wine region, said Andre at a dinner in his honor given by Joe Heitz, one of his best students. And there are other regions to be heard from. The guests toasted him in one of his first wines, BV Cabernet Sauvignon '39. Then they toasted him in the wine that Knowles had raised to six dollars, BV Cabernet Sauvignon Special Reserve '64. Andre had plenty to be proud of—you could taste it there in the glasses. Then Joe opened his own Martha's Vineyard '69, which had just been bottled. You could taste it there, as well; the wine was selling for $35 a bottle in 1977. "Lots of things happened," said Andre, as he got up to make a speech, but then he never has been a man to exaggerate.

Inglenook Vineyards. Gustav Niebaum sailed through the Golden Gate with a cargo of Alaskan sealskins in 1867, the year of the Alaska purchase. The young Finn was 26; the cargo netted him half a million dollars; and he headed for Napa to start a vineyard. An unlikely idea for a seafarer, but as fashionable then as it is today, and by 1880 he was bossing a gang of coolies on a couple of square miles around a knoll that caught the early sun and had been named Inglenook by a Scot who was reminded of the snug firesides back home. Roads were cut in the soft stone, winding around the knoll and back into the hills; tunnels were dug; a stone channel was laid for a brook called the Navalle. The stone hardened when exposed to air and the dormered winery was built of it; soon clad in ivy, the building looked like something on a college campus with its tiled roof and central portico. To crown the knoll was a gingerbread house painted mustard with white trim and from its verandahs you could look down to the winery and the vineyards, planted in cuttings from Europe's finest vineyards. Europe took notice in 1889 when Inglenook wines won prizes at a Paris exposition.

"The roads were all cindered for neatness," said John Daniel, "and until the day he died he made inspections, wearing white gloves. The Bundschu clan from over in Sonoma made the wines until Prohibition, then I took over."

Daniel introduced new varieties, the Charbono of the Italian Piedmont, and a Red Pinot that the Christian Brothers called Saint George, and some of those developed at Davis. Captain Niebaum had installed big German ovals; Daniel brought in small French cooperage; but the wines continued to be fermented in redwood vats, giving them a flowery taste.

Daniel had no children, perhaps the reason he sold the winery in 1964 to United Vintners, the marketing arm of the cooperative called Allied Grape Growers, whose members own some 1,500 acres of Napa vineyards and many more elsewhere. Daniel kept back the house on the knoll and the vineyard, which was sold at his death in 1970 and is now owned by a film producer who makes no wines.

Allied Grape Growers do, though, marketing good jug wines and many others under the Inglenook banner. People always spoke well of the old Captain's wines, and of Daniel's, and they speak well of the Inglenook jugs today. The traditions were grand; Daniel led the way to premium wines of California. Under Heublein, Inglenook has kept up the tradition of special casks of Cabernet and their Red Pinot, marketing other jugs under the Navalle label.

To make them, they have built a big new winery in front of the old one.

Louis M. Martini. Louis M. Martini was a San Francisco clam digger working with his father at the turn of the century, but pollution in the bay was killing even the mussels, so they decided to branch out. They made a batch of wine in the backyard but the wine went bad. That was the year of the earthquake but they didn't blame it on that. Louis was sent back to Italy to learn how to do things right. He was nineteen and in a hurry, crammed three years of wine school into a semester and was back in time to make the vintage of '07, which turned out fine. Louis was in the wine business.

His first claim to fame was Forbidden Fruit, a concentrate he sold to home winemakers during Prohibition. With Repeal he began making bulk wines for his eastern customers and by 1940 he'd made enough to buy a vineyard, build a winery and age the wines. "Louis M. Martini" went on the labels; the bottles went on the market; and all his customers said they were the best wines that ever came out of California. They weren't far wrong.

The first vineyard was near the road, south of St. Helena. The second was to the west, running up to the Mayacamas foothills. The third was up on top, across on the Sonoma side, 300 acres he called Monte Rosso, because of the color of the soil. This gave him the idea of calling his blends Mountain Red and Mountain White, a name so appealing that it came to define a whole category of wines for those who wanted to use an American name on labels, not Burgundy or Chablis.

Up there are the red-wine grapes—Barbera, Zinfandel and Cabernet—and the first Folle Blanche marketed in this country, along with other white wine grapes. Chardonnay is planted over on the Russian River, along with small plots of other varieties, and on 350 acres in Carneros is Pinot Noir. Over east in the Chiles Valley are 100 acres of red wine varieties, which started out as mostly Petite Sirah. The hills there browned early but temperature readings showed it wasn't that warm so Cabernet and

125

Zinfandel went in and the acreage will double. Two thirds of the grapes come from Martini vines.

There is little acreage around the winery. San Francisco bedroom communities sprawled everywhere until the Sixties and Martini figured they would reach Napa sooner or later. A greenbelt law was passed, however, preserving the land for agriculture, so he needn't have worried. The result is that many of the vineyards are not in Napa and the wines are labeled "California Mountain."

Louis M.'s son grew up in the vineyards, but took his degree in food technology at Berkeley, not at all sure he wanted to work for so dynamic a father. The Davis courses were starting and so he spent a year there, out of interest, then came back to see how things might work out in the winery. The six-month trial ended with Pearl Harbor. After four years in the service, he came back to take charge of production.

The job was murder, only Louis P. will never say so. Louis M. was a tough old bird who would rather charm you or argue with you than drink his wines. For years a shed sat out in front of the winery by the highway, like the kind you see at a construction sight. Louis M. would collar you before you got into the winery and start bending your ear. How grand the wines were, how rich and full the tastes, how glorious the vineyards. He would spin you along for hours, good talk because he knew all there was to know, but maybe what you wanted to do was taste the wines, get your facts straight and push on. Ask a direct question and he'd shake his head, acting as if you were trying to get state secrets. "What do you want to know that for?" he would demand. "That's technical. Ask young Louis, he knows all the answers."

He did, too. And he was making marvelous wines. Young Louis expanded the winery—there was even a small tasting room by 1970—replanted vineyards, began making wines his way. Production had reached 300,000 gallons when Louis M. died in 1974, at 87. He had seen California wines come into their own and he had led the way. His son was doing the same again.

There's a chip off the old block managing the winery now, Louis P.'s daughter. A son is helping Louis P. make the wines, with others coming along. It's been a tough school.

Many Americans have learned about wines from the Martini bottlings, which have always been reasonably priced. Louis believes in large bottlings, not small batches, and while there are a dozen limited bottlings, these are sold mostly at the winery. His Cabernet still sells for less than five dollars; it is generally light and well-balanced, with lingering taste. The Gewürztraminer is one of the driest on the market; the Folle Blanche is light and fresh, so good that you wish there were dozens like it. Then there is Barbera, Zinfandel, Merlot—more than a score of others to choose from—always among the best buys on the market.

Beringer Vineyards. You could be in Mainz. Vintner's Row hugs the Mayacamas hills at St. Helena and into one of them the Beringer brothers had coolies cut deep tunnels. Then a crew of shipbuilders fronted them with the winery. The floors are timbers laid on edge, with a pitch, so that it can be hosed down like a deck. The brothers must have been homesick, or at least sentimental, because on the slope down to the road they built a replica of the family manse, a cut-stone block under steep slate roofs with timbered balconies and pointed dormers and arched windows. A monument to another time and place.

The home vineyard is across the road, in its center a low new building filled with row on row of small stainless steel tanks backed by larger ones, which are backed in turn by tanks still larger. You can ferment a score and more of thousand-gallon batches of wines, or five-thousand gallon batches, or larger ones. It is a monument of another sort, to the flexibility demanded by modern techniques and required by a master winemaker. It is the domain of Myron Nightingale.

Nightingale uses the old winery and its tunnels for barrel storage, hustling between the new and the old and around the countryside to the thousand acres of vineyards owned by Beringer, and others from which the grapes are bought. It's taken a decade to set things right.

The Beringer brothers made their first vintage in 1879 and descendants did the same through good times and bad, although distribution of even their most famous wine, Barenblut, gradually dwindled to a few California outlets. The firm was finally sold in 1970 to Nestlé, the Swiss giant, which had decided to enter the American wine market. It began rebuilding Beringer as its base. Nightingale, who had graduated from Davis with Louis Martini and had gone to Cresta Blanca in its heyday and stayed with it through many changes, was lured away to take charge of replanting the vineyards around St. Helena and others at Yountville, Knights Valley and in Carneros. As the vines came into bearing, Nestlé had a change of heart and Beringer was taken over by a Burgundian wine fami-

127

ly, the Labruyères of Macon. Nightingale began working his magic with the wines, whose optimum production is around 300,000 cases.

How old ways work with new in the hands of a man willing to experiment is shown by a report on a centennial bottling of Cabernet Sauvignon from the 1973 vintage. Grapes came from three small lots and about two thirds of them were vinified in classic Bordeaux style, fermenting twelve days at temperatures held below eighty degrees. Then the wine was pumped over the cap and rested on the skins for two weeks before storage in oak barrels, three quarters of them Nevers oak, the rest American.

Nightingale experimented with the remaining third of the grapes, waiting until they showed twenty-four degrees of sugar before having them picked by hand, fermenting them slowly for ten days at sixty degrees before putting them in wood. Merlot made up 11% of the blend and was fermented for five days at less than eighty degrees, then stored in redwood to preserve its fruitiness. The wines were blended in the spring of 1975, stored in thousand-gallon uprights of Nevers oak and bottled a year later. "Remarkable balance, a round soft flavor, magnificent bouquet," says the report. What about that redwood? Maybe California should leave redwood alone; maybe the wines are too fruity. They are too fruity for those who like European styles, in many cases. Perhaps not here.

And what about truly light wines for drinking young? Nightingale makes the big wines because he can, because there is a market, but he would also like to make 11% wines to be drunk within a year of the vintage. Maybe he'll make them some day.

When?

"When the people in the U.S. get to know that a wine doesn't have to be crystal clear to be good."

Filtering to clarity takes the guts out of a wine; the lower it is in alcohol, the less that is left in it when filtered to brilliancy. Something's wrong when a wine is cloudy—turgid—and such wines may simply be going through a change that may clear up in days or weeks. But a wine with motes in it, even specks, does not have anything wrong with it, necessarily. These often settle out, in any case, as sediment. Even red wines are clarified so much these days that few wines throw a sediment, even after ten years in bottle—and that is too bad. Winemakers dislike filtering wines too much, but if it is not done, even knowing wine buyers reject the wines.

Big wines high in alcohol, strong in fruit, can mask subtle dishes.

"When I want to show off a Cabernet I might just serve cheese and bread," says Nightingale, "for a Riesling, perhaps fruit and cheese. The old saw that wine and food go together needs repeating. The two are enhancing; we need lots of different wines. I like baked chicken and a big salad with our light Los Harmanos Chardonnay. Just rub the chicken with lemon, sprinkle it with pepper and baste it with white wine. Sometimes I just use Lowry's lemon pepper. But let's take a poll."

Nightingale's assistant, Ed Sbragia, grew up in his father's vineyard and said Chardonnay was fine with his mother's chicken cacciatore but he preferred his father's Zinfandel; he liked Chardonnay all by itself or a bone-dry Fumé Blanc before meals. With a cold salad of shrimp and rice, Riesling white or gray was very nice and Cabernet was fine with steaks. Nightingale laughed and helped himself from a platter of cold cuts. We were sitting on a terrace beside the old Rhine House, tasting recent bottlings, and Nancy Berghorn, who did winery publicity, said she liked an oaky Chardonnay with chicken and rosemary, which she baked in foil.

"I just wash and dry the pieces, rub them with garlic, sprinkle with salt and pepper, wrap a sprig of fresh rosemary with each piece and bake it for an hour at 350. And Myron's Zinfandel with veal marengo or paprikash, but I don't want to forget shashlik: take cubes from a leg of lamb, salt and pepper them, and marinate them overnight in red wine. Put them on skewers with slices of pepper, cherry tomatoes, mushroom caps and squares of bacon on each side of the lamb. Then you roll the skewer in a baste, barbecue it for ten minutes, roll in the baste again and barbecue for another ten minutes. Keep basting. You make the baste with a pint of sour cream, a stick of butter, a quarter-cup of brandy and two tablespoons of caraway seeds. Try that with your Fumé Blanc. Or Myron's Zinfandel."

Fumé Blanc, even Zinfandel, is hard to get in restaurants, California wines available being mostly the big three: Cabernet, Chardonnay and Riesling. It was agreed that with most restaurant fish dishes and luncheon salads Fumé Blanc was the best choice, but getting restaurants to suggest such wines was hard; just getting them listed was hard enough. California wines have a long way to go.

Nightingale has been moving things along for forty years. With the many small tanks and variety of cooperage he has the flexibility to make the big wines in demand and the lighter ones that are just coming to be. With optimum production of 300,000 cases he can meet the market; like so many of his peers, he's making it, as well.

Charles Krug Winery. Charles Krug came over from Sonoma one fine day in the September of 1858, taking time off from his job in Agoston Haraszthy's winery, and crushed a lot of grapes in a cider press for a St. Helena rancher. These were the first wines made in Napa, turning out so well that Krug married the daughter of the local mill owner in 1860, planted vines on the land she brought him as a dowry and built himself a winery. It was the first in the Napa Valley and part of it is still there at CK, just north of town. So is the old mill, now a landmark, and outside the tasting room is the old cider press for all to see.

They called him the wine king and his bottlings sold in Europe, but the phylloxera ruined his vineyards and Prohibition finished the winery. Meanwhile, over in Lodi, two sons of a bulk wine producer were growing up, and while they were in college at Stanford their father asked them what they wanted to do when they graduated. The wine business looked pretty good, since they had grown up in it, and Cesare Mondavi said they ought to see what they could find up in Napa because that's where the future was. In 1943, C. Mondavi & Sons took over Krug, Peter making the wines, Robert running the business, Father and the rest of the family handing out advice when needed. Peter was a good winemaker, though cautious, and Robert was a good manager, though daring, and between them they built the business to a quarter of a million cases. Bob thought a newsletter about the premium wines would help, so *Bottles & Bins* was published, the first of them all, edited from the beginning by Francis Gould, a founder of the California Wine & Food Society. Bob thought it was possible to make dry white wines in Napa and Pete began with Chenin Blanc, the first to do so. The two brothers saw the wine business different ways and in 1966 Bob accepted an offer to set up his own model winery, backed by the Rainier Brewing Company of Seattle. The family was not able to agree on what Bob's share of the winery should be and the courts ordered the sale of Charles Krug in 1977. Wines continue to be made, premium wines under Mondavi and Krug labels, popularly priced blends as CK.

Pete uses press wine in his Chardonnay and ages it in Yugoslavian oak, so the wine can take three years and more to develop into a soft rich wine.

The Cabernet is fermented with the skins for a time, in the Bordeaux manner, and also takes five years or more to develop, with tannin still be-

130

ing pronounced when the wines are ten years old. The Pinot Noir also may take five years to round out; there is Petite Sirah in the blend.

Freemark Abbey. A brace of growers and a consulting enologist decided they could market wines under their own label and not just provide the wherewithal for others, so they joined forces with a quartet of investors and bought the cellars of Freemark Abbey in 1965. It wasn't an abbey at all but a winery with a name made up out of those of previous owners, one called Abby, and the others Freeman and Mark. The winery was a fine old stone building, now a restaurant, candle factory and store, just north of St. Helena. Charles Carpy and Lawry Wood only needed the cellar to start and the skills of Brad Webb, who was the Hanzell winemaker. They bought the cellar. When optimum production neared 20,000 cases they built a laboratory, offices and a winery out in back. Visitors to the restaurant and shops stop off to taste the wines: Cabernet and Pinot, Chardonnay and Riesling, made in classic styles. Wood manages the York Creek vineyard up on Spring Mountain, among others, where a small plot of old Petite Sirah provides grapes for an occasional bottling. There is some Merlot for blending with the Cabernet, which comes from vineyards just north of Rutherford and produces the traditional Rutherford taste.

Webb has said he likes to control the environment of his wines—yeast, oak, temperature, and so forth—but let the wines make themselves. He also likes to make big, intense wines, liking grapes with 23 degrees of sugar, so that they will live a long time. The wines have been so successful that some of the partners bought Rutherford Hill, the winery built by a flour company on the Silverado Trail, which will be developed just as Freemark Abbey has been. Production from the two may reach 250,000 cases during the Eighties.

Sterling Vineyards. A trio of San Francisco papermakers felt the time was ripe in 1964 and put in more than 300 acres of vines just below a tall mount that pushes out into the valley south of Calistoga. On top they built a winery of white stucco with rounded corners and a belfry—it had a monastery look—reached by ski lift gondolas that rose out of the vineyards. These were planted mostly in Cabernet, but there was a big plot of Merlot because they knew they wanted to soften what was to be their

131

principal wine and also to bottle the softening wine separately. And there was to be a dry Chenin Blanc to go along with the Gewürztraminer and Sauvignon that would give a nice range, plus the grapes of Burgundy to provide a wider selection. They committed six million dollars for starters; an optimum production of 100,000 cases was planned. A winemaker with a new master's degree from Davis, Rick Foreman, was put in charge in 1968 to keep things going right. He managed well.

The winery was planned to be a great place to visit. There are ramps and catwalks through the winery where you can see the different processes, terraces to look at the view, a tasting lounge on top on different levels and more outside terraces. You can hold dinners there for as many as 150 or as few as 12 at a modest charge per head, including wines. There's an efficient staff, a list of valley caterers and sample menus with wine suggestions for dinners that range from steaks to whole spitted lamb—or you can have picnics on the terrace. San Francisco firms have taken to holding meetings and conferences at Sterling, with canapés on the terrace, served with Chenin Blanc and Cabernet Rosé. They go inside for salmon en papillote with Sauvignon Blanc. (For smoked or poached salmon, Riesling is the choice.) Two vintages of Cabernet are served with stuffed roast leg of lamb; Pinot Noir is served with the cheese, and old Port with pastry and coffee.

While the winery was being built, vintages were made in temporary sheds below the hill. To get just the right equipment, Forman, who had worked for Fred McCrea at Stony Hill and for Robert Mondavi, spent weeks in Europe touring wineries. He continues to make yearly trips. The design developed from this experience and the wines are made following European techniques to bring out the character of the Calistoga grapes. All but the Chardonnay is fermented in stainless steel, but Forman believes he gets more subtlety in his Chardonnay when it is fermented in small oak barrels. Sterling wines are in the classic styles, well-balanced wines that develop subtleness with age.

And now along the Wine Road are a couple of dozen new wineries or ones renewed. While scarcely a third of them are distributed nationally, or will be, all of them signify that Napa is waving its own banners, no longer selling most of its grapes outside the valley for the big blends of bulk shippers. The small wineries are there for the seeking, pennons in the breeze, bread and cheese to be had when the wines are found, and many a bough to shade you as the glasses fill.

NOTE: Three of the most distinguished of the recent wineries produce only sparkling wines—Hanns Kornell, Schramsberg and Chandon—to be covered in a separate chapter.

THE MAYACAMAS RANGE: MOUNT VEEDER, DIAMOND AND SPRING

Wineries up along the Redwood Road give a good idea of what Napa wines are like these days. The Christian Brothers are one of the oldest and make many good wines; Mount Veeder is a small new winery with a new vineyard where a prune orchard once was; Veedercrest is an old vineyard replanted; and Mayacamas is a small old winery taken over by a skilled young winemaker. The first you come to is Mont La Salle, 700 feet above the valley.

The Christian Brothers. The largest producer of Napa Valley wines is The Christian Brothers, who produce a wide range of moderately priced bottlings from a thousand acres of vineyard. The desire is to make superior wines that will be consistent from year to year as well as to reflect the distinctive characteristics of the grapes. This is done by blending one year with another—a sharp or light vintage being balanced with a soft or full one—so that the purchaser will know what to expect when he opens a bottle. The result is a collection of regional wines that shows what a major shipper can produce when concerned with quality, as do the Burgundies from Latour, the Bordeaux wines of Calvet, the Rhine wines of Sichel.

Their best wines come from Mont La Salle, some 200 acres of vineyard planted about half in white grapes and a red called Pinot St. Georges, which Brother Timothy likes. Expert opinion doesn't rate the red wine, tart and full, all that highly, but Brother Timothy made so many fine wines over more than forty years as winemaster, that Pinot St. Georges is always tasted as an example of what a great winemaker can do. Expert opinion is always questionable; Pinot St. Georges is the most popular red wine of The Christian Brothers.

The Brothers are a teaching order of the Catholic Church, who take vows of poverty, chastity and obedience. Not priests or clerics, they maintain schools throughout the world, those west of the Rockies supported by sale of wines. Brother Timothy was educated in one of their schools in Los Angeles, taught chemistry, and then was called to Mont La

133

Salle in 1935, when the first wines were being made. There he remained, and the American Society of Enologists chose him for their Merit Award in 1977.

The Brothers purchased Mont La Salle in 1930, building a novitiate there following the style of the stone winery. To pay for it, they began offering wines to the public and in 1938 they made an alliance with the firm of Fromm & Sichel to market their wines. The marketing firm, composed of members and friends of the Sichel clan and partly owned by Seagram, has been instrumental in placing The Brothers among the ten largest producers in the country, their storage capacity of around 28,000,000 gallons making them rank with the two other premium producers in the group, Paul Masson and Almadén.*

The Brothers buy about half their grapes for table wines, mostly from Napa growers, and have been a steadying influence on the valley economy, encouraging improvements in vineyard techniques that go beyond pruning to avoid excessive yields, or requiring sufficient acids in the grapes. They have encouraged innovation: fumigating soil to rid it of pests, planting vines that are certified to be free of virus, using wire trellises that allow air movement among the leaves, planting so that the grapes can be picked and moved quickly to the wineries. They built a fermenting station down in the valley, rings of tanks with an unloading platform and crushers, so that growers could deliver their grapes quickly at prime ripeness. In the old days, grapes could sit in trucks for hours, waiting their turn at the crushers.

Brother Timothy brought advances into the winery—handling wines so there would be minimum contact with air, aging in small cooperage and in bottles before marketing, cool fermentations to bring out grape tastes—influencing others to improve on traditional techniques or to eliminate poor practices. Their influence was felt in the Great Central Valley, where The Christian Brothers have a thousand vineyard acres and make sweet fortified wines and brandies. They bought the vast Greystone Cellars in

*Others in the top ten produce bulk wines under many labels at low prices and include United Vintners, Guild, Vie Del, Bear Mountain, Franzia, and the only one outside California, Taylor, in New York. Largest of all and largest in the world, is E. & J. Gallo, with 226,000,000 gallons of storage capacity. United Vintners ranks second and approaches 100,000,000 gallons, followed by Guild, approaching 60,000,000 gallons, the others having capacities around 30,000,000 gallons.

St. Helena, where a model sparkling wine facility was installed, as a showplace for visitors.

By keeping prices low they have introduced millions to Napa wines. With an extensive line of sweet wines like their Château La Salle and Pineau de la Loire and La Salle Rosé, they have attracted many not familiar with wines. Their Cabernets, Rieslings and Chardonnays have attracted others not willing to pay five dollars a bottle but who have become interested in dry table wines. Their brandy, XO, is one of the best made in this country and has the widest sale.

The public has an odd picture of their wines; perhaps because of their size they are classed with the bulk producers, and drinkers of those wines resist paying the dollar or so a bottle more that The Christian Brothers' wines cost. Those who buy premium wines pass up The Christian Brothers' bottlings because they cost less. Both groups of wine drinkers miss a good bet. Wines from the Christian Brothers are consistently among the best buys in both categories.

Especially recommended: Cabernet Sauvignon
Pinot St. George
Pinot Chardonnay
Johannisberg Riesling
Château La Salle
Pineau de la Loire

Mount Veeder Winery. A prune orchard above 1,000 feet on Mount Veeder Road, complete with log cabin on a fieldstone base, attracted lawyer Michael Bernstein and his wife early in the Sixties. First they tended the prune trees, planting a few vines in between, then they began pulling out the plums, until now there are twenty steep acres of vines, mostly Cabernet, but a third divided between Zinfandel and Chenin Blanc. Optimum production: 2,000 cases.

The Bernsteins sold part interest in the small winery in order to raise money to build it and so they could install the best equipment and set up a small laboratory. With vines in full production, the operation is in full swing, the family doing most of the work. The best way to get some of the wines is to call ahead and then go and pick them up. Bernstein has given up his city practice but the couple likes the life—and the wines.

* * *

Veedercrest. Veedercrest is a 300-acre vineyard further up the mountain that has been replanted in vines and is owned by a corporation run by winemaker Alfred Baxter. In the beginning, grapes were bought, and one of the first wines, a Chardonnay, ranked with a couple of estate-bottled Montrachets in a Paris tasting. This success gave the winery a market before it had the wines, a situation that anguished and delighted at the same time. Production of 20,000 cases by 1980 is planned. Meanwhile, the curious wait, the first wines being drunk mostly by other winemakers in the valley, who like to keep up on what the competition is doing.

Mayacamas Vineyards. A German pickle merchant built the stone winery and distillery of Mayacamas Vineyards at the end of the last century and a California storyteller named Idwal Jones wrote a book about it aptly called *The Vineyard.* The vineyard was mostly planted in Zinfandel. A fine home in the country, though much the worse for wear, thought Mary and John Taylor, when they bought it in the early Forties. The distillery they converted into a dwelling; their friends they turned into harvest hands and customers; and the winery they made into a corporation when new equipment was needed. The property was purchased by Robert Travers in 1968.

He worked summers on family farms while studying money and banking in college, reversing the process after graduation, working for a bank and looking for a winery on the side, studying nights. Books and courses weren't enough, so he went to work for Joe Heitz for a year and after looking over a hundred properties he found Mayacamas.

He decided to make only his three favorite wines and began planting his vineyard to Cabernet and Chardonnay, almost 45 acres. His first year, he made the first Late Harvest Zinfandel ever made because he was busy handling other grapes and told the grower to hold off for a while until he could make room. The Zinfandel came out at 17%, exciting many. He gets those grapes from the foothills of the Sierras over east, in Amador.

Travers doesn't have to worry about overbearing vines, his top yields being two tons and a half and sometimes half that. The soil is full of gravel, even rocky, and while they get sixty inches of rain, twice as much as down in the valley, the runoff can be classed as rapid, although snow can stay on the ground for a few days. He makes about 5,000 cases a year, the reds maturing in American oak tanks for a year or so. All the wines finish aging in small French oak cooperage.

The Traverses have marvelous wines to drink and to trade with other winemakers. Over a lunch, say, of cracked crab and Chardonnay, they might tell you of their market problems. If they limited sale at the winery to 1,000 cases and all of California to another 1,000 and kept 1,000 cases on reserve—which out-of-staters think is precisely what they should do—they could then supply twenty major markets with 100 cases each. In New York your friendly neighborhood store or favorite restaurant might end up with 12 bottles. Each year. One Californian tells lovingly of how an old Cabernet matched an old Bordeaux with a dinner of roast beef and Yorkshire Pudding. How nice.

Over dinner of roast lamb and a range of his Cabernets, Travers might point out that many a Burgundian or Bordelais produces only 1,000 cases for export, wines you might find in New York or Chicago. Half the Classed Growths of Bordeaux produce 20,000 cases a year; most of the rest produce 10,000 cases; and one or another can be found anywhere. And yet the demand for good California Cabernet is becoming as strong as the demand for claret. There's always Zinfandel; Travers produces twice as much of that as comes from Romanée-Conti, which makes 700 cases. The Late Harvest is delicious with pears and cheese.

Yverdon Vineyards. A love of wine may be in the blood. So may be the urge to pile up stone. Fred Aves' grandparents were wine growers in the Swiss hamlet of Yverdon, and while he made a living as a Los Angeles manufacturer, winemaking was a hobby that led to the purchase of an 80-acre vineyard at Calistoga. Lugging the grapes south was not the best way to handle them, so it was logical to sell out, buy an overgrown vineyard on Spring Mountain and start from scratch. That was 1970, and with the 10+ new acres on the mountain, production of some 25,000 cases by the end of the decade may encourage Aves to do more.

Production has been slowed by the building of a fieldstone winery with arched entries, and a stone house complete with the mansard roof and corner turret shown on the label. The buildings have a French aspect and so do the wines. All of it has been done by Aves and his son's family, and continues with the building of stone tunnels to store the wines, a kind of construction that hasn't been attempted since the last century. The grandparents would have been proud.

* * *

Spring Mountain Vineyards. Spring Mountain Road winds up into the Mayacamas from St. Helena, shadowed even at noon by oak and redwood. Hardscrabble roads angle off between outcroppings, showing glimpses of the terraced vineyards that have been called the most beautiful on earth. The largest of them is La Perla, several hundred acres owned by Jerome Draper, which made no wines and sold the grapes to valley wineries; his namesake plans to introduce a label by 1980. The vineyards were showplaces in the Gay Nineties but were devastated by phylloxera and Prohibition. The new wineries have only begun offering wines from the noble vines that began to be set out late in the Sixties.

Down where the road begins to climb is the grand Victorian pile called Miravalle, gabled and towered, its windows overlooking a pool, gardens and vineyards to the valley below. The view down the long slope between tall trees reminds people of Versailles, and when architects drew plans for new landscaping and the long new winery they marked the plans for the "Napa Sun King."

One of several ex-Navy men who have come to the valley is Michael Robbins, whose passions include Victorian mansions that need loving care. This is costly, but scarcely more so than vineyards or wineries, and with the three combined, Robbins has been busy using his training in law and engineering as a real estate developer around Los Angeles. Commuting back and forth could have killed him; perhaps his enthusiasm is what has made him thrive under the strain. He is famous as a master of detail, fundamental to both passion and profession.

Life in the wine country fascinated him during a tour of Europe; serving as a director of Mayacamas introduced him to the Napa Valley; and refurbishing a Victorian house with a few vines in St. Helena gave him a grasp of what was involved. He sold the St. Helena mansion, now St. Clement Vineyards, when he bought Miravalle. There are something more than 100 acres planted in Cabernet, Chardonnay and Pinot Noirien Petit, with optimum production around 20,000 cases. The Soda Creek ranch down east near the Silverado Country Club, planted in a Chardonnay that produces a light wine and in Pinot, is included in the production. Another 100 acres called Wildwood Ranch, on the Silverado Trail and running up to Conn Creek, are to become a separate winery.

Robbins came upon his special Pinot in a roundabout way. A friend called to say he had seen a picture of a Paul Masson vineyard that showed

138

bunches with sloping shoulders instead of the usual high-shouldered bunches of most Pinot strains. Robbins called Martin Ray, who had sold the vineyard to Paul Masson, first taking cuttings for his new vineyard, then giving some to the Davis experimental vineyard in Oakville. The vine had been given to the original Paul Masson by the Burgundian shipper, Louis Latour, who took the cuttings from his own Beaune vineyards. Or maybe from Romanée-Conti. The vines had been ripped out of the experimental plot, but cuttings had gone to Joseph Swann for his vineyards. Robbins obtained cuttings from there. The wine world is a small one, but complex.

Robbins is delighted with the winemaking life, which is satisfactorily sociable, for the clan is large and varied. There are the other Annapolis alumni, dedicated growers, escapees from business and industry and professions, skilled scientists, professors from the university, a stream of visitors from all over interested in wines. Because days are long and full, entertaining is mostly over dinner. Among the visitors are master chefs, people like James Beard or Jacques Pepin—and many Europeans—who step into the kitchen or even conduct classes for a few days each year. Not only the wives are dedicated cooks, for while there is help in the vineyard, help in the kitchen is usually limited to family. Robbins and his wife, like most of the other wine families, regularly have dinner parties that they try to limit to eight or ten.

Robbins likes to serve sparkling wines or light whites before dinner, ones that are not too sharp or too alcoholic. A light Riesling from Freemark Abbey, a Gewürztraminer, maybe a Chenin Blanc from Chappellet or somebody else, to see how that grape is coming along. The Chardonnays and Sauvignons are so big that they are usually served with a fish course. "I'm enjoying making quenelles at the moment," says Shirley Robbins, "of salmon for Sauvignon; of sole for Chardonnay. And soufflés are popular right now, of zucchini or watercress, sorrel or mushroom. Very good with a big Chardonnay or dry Riesling. In winter we do a lot of soups. Mike doesn't bring up his wines and say we'll have this or that. I do dinner and he finds the wines.

"We serve wines before the meal and have a first course because we like to try out wines. We've been able to do this since the early Seventies, because we've had the variety to choose from. But it may be into the Eighties before there is distribution around the country wide enough so that everybody can do so. Our wines are now so good that we serve them

139

right along with those from Europe. Ours mature more quickly and have more fruit, so what we've done is expand the range. For out-of-staters we usually serve California wines, often from other regions. For valley folks we serve French wines.''

"We do a lot of roasts, racks or crowns, and Pepin has a veal roast I like. We do a lot of chicken breasts, poaching them with stock and with vegetables. I like veal birds with a filling of ground veal and crumbs and various herbs. They change each time," Shirley said. "Sometimes I do them in stock after browning, sometimes in white wine—or red—or rosé.'' Mike Robbins likes to save Burgundy for the cheese. "It's encouragement, you know. Our Pinots are just coming along. There's a lot of competition.'' Mike has been quoted as saying that amateurs are turning winemaking into a competitive sport that brings out little differences so that there are many styles to choose from.

"Often enough, we have fruit for dessert, or maybe some pastry, to go with dessert wines. We like to serve sweet wines here in the valley because there is a good selection. And Sauternes are still cheap, good encouragement to the likes of Heitz and Martini and Mondavi.''

Ritchie Creek Vineyard. The smallest winery in Napa is a sod-roofed block tucked under the top of Spring Mountain, backed by four acres of Cabernet and a little Merlot. Peter Minor was a Berkeley dentist who built his stone-arched house above the vines on weekends, roofing it with barn boards on beams made of telephone poles. That done, Minor closed his practice and opened the winery, buying grapes to make Chardonnay and Riesling. Production of the three wines is less than a thousand cases. Minor may have to go back to dentistry to make a living, but he now has a new way of life, making wines in the French fashion.

Stony Hill Vineyard. On the brow of a hill between Spring Mountain and Diamond is the low-roofed house of Fred and Eleanor McCrea, surrounded by flagstone terraces. The view over the valley is to the east; in a swale to the south is the small stone winery overlooking a wide-decked swimming pool; and to the west the vineyards lift to evergreens on a higher hill. The vineyards slope around to the north, edged by a rocky road that bumps you up to one of the pleasantest spots along the Mayacamas.

McCrea used it as a retreat from his San Francisco job as an advertising executive, retiring there in the Fifties to tend his 30 acres of Chardonnay

140

and Riesling. "It's either goats or grapes," a friend said when he first saw the place. The McCreas decided on grapes after consulting with Davis professors and valley growers. The vineyard grew year by year, slower than the renown of his wines, which rarely amounted to more than a thousand cases. Most were drunk by friends and other growers, a few bottles occasionally escaping to Trader Vic's in San Francisco or the fabulous Imperial Dynasty run by the Wing family near Fresno, in the town of Hanford.

The wines are made in European style, fermented and aged in oak. McCrea added a few acres of Traminer, a little Pinot Blanc and some Sémillon, just to see what they might do, the last two so scant they are only for home consumption. But they all showed what could be done with white wines at a time when most growers had little confidence in them and they changed the planting pattern of the valley. McCrea died on New Year's Day 1977, but the winery continues, a memorial to a man who made history with his wines. People who get to taste them consider themselves fortunate and those who visit Stony Hill suddenly have a vivid picture of what is so alluring about a life involved with wine and vine.

Smith Vineyards. In a sod-topped winery built into the side of the hill, Stewart and Charles Smith plan a production of 6,000 cases from an old vineyard they began replanting in 1971 to Pinot and Cabernet, Chardonnay and Riesling.

Diamond Creek Vineyards. On the way up the next peak north of Spring Mountain, Alfred Brounstein began planting 20 acres of Cabernet and a little Merlot, the only wine he intends to make. Optimum production is 2,000 cases, but there will be three lots from vines grown in different soils; Gravelly Meadow, Volcanic Hill and Red Rock Terrace. The wines were first made in a stone winery on a neighboring ranch, but are now made in a cellar winery topped by living quarters. All wines are sold by mailing list and to winery visitors, who are invited to picnic on a nearby pond—and taste the wines.

Château Chevalier. The knight's castle of dressed stone, steep roofs and arched cellars is another Victorian fantasy surrounded by gardens and replanted vineyards, halfway up Spring Mountain. A partnership of Gregory Bissonette and Peter Hauschildt market Chardonnay and Cabernet under the Château Chevalier label, produced mostly by family labor. The 10,000-case winery markets, under a Mountainside Vineyards label, wines from purchased grapes, mostly for the California market.

THE SILVERADO TRAIL

The old coach road running up the east side of Napa Valley strings together a dozen small wineries tucked into the hills that form a district of themselves and make some of the best wines in the region. Where the trail begins at Napa is the Silverado Country Club, a resort built around an old mansion built by a Civil War general, now expanded to include several courtyards of two-story condominiums, rented by their owners through the club to those who can find an excuse to spend some time in the valley. It's a fine place to stay while visiting the wineries.

Clos du Val. Vineyards of Cabernet and Zinfandel run up the slope to a stuccoed winery with arched openings and a red-tiled roof against a background of low hills. Manager and one of the partners is Bernard Portet, from a family of French winemakers and a graduate of Montpellier, who made the first wines in 1972. They were made in an old stone winery nearby, the Occidental, a landmark built a century ago and leased for storage. Portet was attracted to the valley because of its vitality and its potential for producing fine wines. His is first of three French groups to set up operations. Optimum production is 15,000 cases limited to the two varieties, the best French and the best Californian. The wines are made following French techniques and modern innovations; they are drinkable when released after some two years in wood and one in glass, but continue to develop, perhaps for twice as long. Even the first bottlings from young vines are expected to live a decade.

Especially recommended: Cabernet Sauvignon
Zinfandel

Stag's Leap Wine Cellars. There is a pair of modest stuccoed buildings standing on a slope by the Silverado Trail, oak-shaded, a tarred road winding around them and up a knoll. On top, Warren Winiarski and family live in a low-roofed house which looks down the far side to some 40 acres of vineyard. The crags of Stag's Leap rise beyond, above a wide

142

vale. A University of Chicago professor choosing to change his life could scarcely have picked a better place to do so.

Winiarski came to Napa in 1964, wishing to apprentice himself to a fine winemaker, so he went to work for Lee Stewart at the old Souverain, then spent two years in Bob Mondavi's new winery. He became the managing partner of a group that bought the vineyards and planted new vines in them in 1970, Cabernet and some Merlot. He is also the managing partner of a group that built the winery, whose optimum production is 15,000 cases. Grapes are bought to make the Riesling, Chardonnay and Gamay Beaujolais, which also has Pinot Noir and Napa Gamay in its blend. The Riesling comes from Birkmeyer Vineyard in Wild Horse Valley, the Chardonnay from down toward the bay. The vineyards are stretching out into neighboring valleys and cool places around Napa and will continue to do so as long as the wines get better and demands grow.

His first Cabernet was made in 1973 and three years later placed high in a Paris tasting, where French judges ranked it slightly above three 1970 clarets from the châteaux of Mouton-Rothschild, Haut Brion and Montrose.

There was a furor. Such great clarets may take ten years to round out, a fact that sounds like a quibble. Winiarski's Cabernet tasted better at the time, even though still immature; it will begin to fade, perhaps by 1980, just as the clarets are coming into their primes. Such comparisons, however odious, clearly make the point that California Cabernets are excellent, and those from Stag's Leap are among the best. Cheers for the professor on his second time around.

Over lunch we ignored such comparisons, drinking his '75 Riesling, which had 12.6% alcohol. "Nice flower, fruit, there—good fruit," read my notes.

"There's less than point seventy-five of sweet reserve in there," said Winiarski. "It's a more beautiful wine when you have a touch of sweetness." Sweet reserve is called muté in French, referring to sweet grape juice, perhaps partially fermented, added to the wine. Sometimes the fermentation is stopped with brandy, occasionally grapes are dried on mats or allowed to stay longer on the vine to build up sugar, even raisinize, and are then used for sweetening a fermented wine. Less than one percent is very little.

Lunch showed off the wine. There was melon with a squeeze of lime juice, then mounds of small shrimp on slices of green pepper, the chilled shrimp bound with mayonnaise that was thinned a little with sour cream and a squeeze of lime. I had two helpings of the shrimp, which was especially good with the green pepper and even better with the wine. I said so. "I like to serve peppers with Cabernet," said Winiarski. "Lots of people say Cabernets have a green pepper taste, so it's nice to have the two together."

He began opening a bottle of his Gamay Beaujolais '75 and Barbara Winiarski set a plate of Granny Smith apples on the table with a tray of soft cheeses, Coulommiers and Cabochon. "This is much too cold," said Winiarski when he lifted his glass. While we waited for the wine to warm, Barbara talked about what she liked to serve.

"With the Gamay I always try to serve sautéed mushrooms because they taste so good. I just put some butter in the pan and swirl the mushrooms in them, with a little salt and pepper. I sprinkle on a little dried chicken bouillon and stir that in. And we like underdone beef with the Gamay. We barbecue a lot in nice weather. I make a marinade of two parts Gamay and one part olive oil. When I use a very dry wine I do it half and half. Then I add chopped parsley and chopped green onions or shallots and try to let it stand overnight or even longer. We have lots of herbs in the garden and I put in one or the other, never the same herb twice. Right now the rosemary is perfect, so I add a teaspoonful of that.

"We seem to be barbecuing butterflied lamb a lot. Usually I use white wine with the olive oil and always the rosemary. Chopped shallots or garlic go in with the chopped parsley and some marjoram. And some mint, along with the juice of half a lemon. Marvelous with the Cabernet."

What would she serve with that? "Pommes Anna are so good, and then cherry tomatoes and green pepper slices. Sometimes I sauté them a little. In the fall we love baked eggplant. I cut them lengthwise and scoop them out, then chop the pulp and sauté it in olive oil. Sometimes I stuff them with duxelles."

Families of winemakers are always deeply involved, children working around the vineyards or wineries until they rebel or become permanently involved. The wives do a little of everything, including bookkeeping and other paperwork, as well as entertaining visitors, handling publicity, maintaining mailing lists. Most important of all, they taste the wines—while they are being made, while they mature, when they are ready. Winiarski makes his wines in thousand-gallon tanks of Yugoslavian oak, then puts them into small barrels. These are then blended in various ways,

Winiarski trying various batches on a group of tasters: Barbara, of course, Dorothy and Andre Tchelistcheff—he is consultant to the winery—and others, until the desired proportions are determined. Merlot may represent five percent of the Cabernet, for example, or fifteen percent, or somewhere in between. The Merlot was so good in 1974 that a separate wine was made, with fifteen percent Cabernet. Every year is different.

"This soft cheese is just right with the Gamay," said Winiarski. "You don't want sharper cheese than that. But then I want Roquefort with Cabernet."

Roquefort is generally considered too strong for most wines. But then Winiarski makes a very big Cabernet.

Stag's Leap Winery. Stag's Leap Ranch, just below the peak that names it, was a wild resort during Prohibition, converted from a manor house to a bawdy one, complete with cabins out back, but it has come on better days again with the purchase by a corporation headed by Carl Doumani in 1970. He has three shareholders, several tumbledown stone buildings being repaired, and a name problem. Long before Prohibition there were wines from Stag's Leap Vineyard, but none when Warren Winiarski brought out his first wines, so dispute continues about who's really entitled to dub themselves after the giant stag seen leaping from peak to peak in the dream of an Indian maiden. She gave the peak the name, for luck. Not only wines are confusing.

The 100-acre vineyard, replanted in Chenin Blanc, Petite Sirah, Pinot Noir and Cabernet, has an optimum production of 10,000 cases. The first vintages were made nearby, but a rebuilt stone winery with a Moorish front and stone tunnels dug into a hill is the true home of what is called Stag's Leap Winery.

The old house had two floors of stone and a top one of wood, which Doumani took off, and now he has the perfect setting for a latter-day film about the Foreign Legion, battlements and all. Not many of the wines are expected to get out of California much before 1980.

Rutherford Hill. On a rise above the Silverado, just north of the Rutherford Cross, is a great wooden winery modeled after the early storage barns, the center for what was to be a group of vineyard estates. Sponsored by a flour company, the wealthy were to build posh vacation houses surrounded by vines meant to supply grapes to the winery. The scheme never developed, but a group of growers who were partners in Freemark Abbey, and others, took over the handsome building for their own wines.

Rutherford Hill thus started off with an excellent supply of noble grapes from mature vines. The growers are also members of a marketing group made up of several smaller wineries, with distributors around the country, so their wines were immediately available outside California. Such a marketing system was badly needed by producers of 25,000 cases or so who had no economical way of distributing nationally; now a neighborhood store can offer a selection of wines, working through a local distributor, in much the way a Bordeaux shipper will offer wines from several châteaux. A decade ago, Rutherford Hill might have been years getting the Cabernets and Chardonnays on the market.

Villa Mt. Eden. Mount Eden looks across the valley to Oakville, and down on the Silverado Trail to the vineyards that have taken the name. The nineteenth-century vineyard was bought in 1970 by James and Anne McWilliams, from the world of banking, and replanted for them by the scion of a wine-importing family, Nils Venge. There are almost 90 acres of Gewürztraminer and Chenin Blanc, Pinot and Chardonnay, Merlot and Cabernet, and Napa Gamay. The Gewürztraminers of the early Seventies were bottled by Joe Heitz, but are now part of the Villa's offerings, whose optimum output can reach 15,000 cases.

Venge has presided over the refurbishing of the tile-roofed building complex that includes the winery where he made its first wines. A Davis graduate, he was involved in the planting of 400 acres for Charles Krug in the Carneros district and in vineyard management for Sterling, then worked in the Heitz Wine Cellars. When the vineyard celebrates its centennial in 1981, the wines will be in national distribution.

Caymus Vineyards. When you come from a family of Alsatian wine growers and you have bought 70 acres of Rutherford vineyard in 1941, tending them for thirty years, and are not always pleased with what others do to your grapes, the itch to market your own wines calls for scratching. Especially when you have Pinot Noir, which nobody is doing right by. Nothing fancy, just the bottles and good equipment and a couple of sheds for it. Charles Wagner put them up in 1972, near where Conn Creek crosses the Silverado and flows through the valley.

Many of the new wineries represent an extraordinary investment in capital, perhaps $100,000 for a winery and $10,000 an acre for a mature vineyard. Wagner's was an investment of a lifetime spent growing fine grapes. Maybe his son had something to do with it, for they had made batches of wines through the years and his namesake had grown as enthusiastic as anybody in the valley. Their first Pinot Noir was the '73, and there was a Pinot Noir Blanc—just to show how well it could be done—a Riesling and a Cabernet.

Other growers roundabout had patches of incredible Zinfandel. Wagner knew of some over in Sonoma, a bit down in Dry Creek, more over in Amador in the Sierra foothills and some from Lodi. A blending of Zinfandels can be better than a wine made from a single plot, argues Wagner, and he has the wine to prove it, which may take ten years to develop. Everything else is from the home vineyard; optimum production can reach 10,000 cases, some of which eludes greedy San Franciscans, for a perceptive New York distributor has latched on to a quota. Having found a bottle of Caymus Pinot, you can taste what the grape can become in good hands.

Heitz Wine Cellars. "Go see Joe Heitz if you want to taste some good wines," said the network engineer. "He was stationed in California during the war and got the bug, so he went to Davis, got his degree, worked around, then became Tchelistcheff's understudy at BV in '51. He was pulled away to set up the enology department at Fresno State but Napa was where he wanted to be, so he and Alice borrowed five thousand dollars and bought a little Grignolino vineyard on the highway near Louis Martini. There's a story there; the banks wouldn't lend him the money because he had no collateral. Everybody knew he was one of the best winemakers around, and finally one of the vineyard owners who had credit up to here said lend the man the two dollars and they did. Maybe it's the best thing that ever happened in Napa because his success made it possible for the others. Go see Joe."

The old Brendel vineyard had less than a dozen acres, so they produced a wine called Only One, because that was all they had. The winery was a shed the size of a garage, made into a tasting room in 1961, with a little sign that said "Heitz Wine Cellars." A smiling fellow with a crewcut offered a couple of samples—Grignolino, Zinfandel—and when he heard I was writing a book, he said, "Come on up to the house. We bought it in

147

sixty-four and have been five years fixing it up. There's a great old stone winery, not very big but big enough for now, and that's where I make the wines. We buy grapes from growers around, then I also buy wines and bring 'em up right. It's hard to run a vineyard and make wines, too, and I like to make wines.''

We drove over to Silverado and back up a little lane to the end, where an old farmhouse sat under a tree across from a tall stone block pushed back into a slope. There were new stainless fermenters, racks of small barrels, a chicken wire cage stacked with bottles. Joe picked up a few and a lady with a worried look came up to meet us. "Take him into the living room," said Alice. "I'm canning." She bustled us into what once was the parlor, Joe set down the bottles and snapped his fingers. "There's the new Chardonnay I want you to taste," he said. "I'll get it. Alice, you get glasses." He hustled off and Alice grabbed my arm.

"He's not supposed to be here. We had it all set up for him to stay in the tasting room until six. It's his fiftieth birthday and we're having a surprise party. Now you'll have to keep him in here for an hour, until everybody comes. Don't let him get out for anything." She poked me in the ribs, hurried off for glasses and had them set out by the time Joe got back.

It was quite a tasting. There were four Chardonnays and we started with the one still in cask. Big fruit, lots of tannin, but mostly from the grapes, already coming into balance, real elegance. "Plenty of tannin there," I said. You can always say that, and then the winemaker tells you whether it comes from the grapes or from the cask and how long it was fermented and how long it stayed in wood; this takes a good ten minutes. "It's mostly from the grapes," said Joe, starting off. A car drew up. "Who's that, Alice?" Joe shouted. "Just somebody delivering canning jars, I'll take care of it," Alice shouted back. Joe turned to me.

"Good acid," I said. You can always say that, and the winemaker tells you it was point eight four, or whatever, and the Brix was twenty-two, and how it fermented out to twelve point something, all of which takes ten minutes, at least. Joe opened the second wine. "We need more glasses," he said, getting up. "I'll get them," said a voice from the door and Joe looked surprised. "First time he's ever done that, hard to get them to do anything," he said, as a boy came in with a fistful of stemware. Another car pulled up. "I'll take care of it," said the boy, darting out. Joe shook his head.

"There's something funny in there," said I, tasting the second wine.

You can always say that, and if you frown a little or shake your head, the winemaker will spend several minutes telling you how the wine is perfect, elegant, fruity, balanced, just coming together, and really not ready to drink for a couple of years but you can taste what it is going to be. You could, too. Cars kept coming up, heads kept popping up, shouting, "I'll take care of it," and Joe kept sitting down again.

"There's a taste of sage in here," I said after Joe had poured the third bottle. You can always say something like that, which was what Tschelistcheff had told me that morning about one of his wines. Joe spent fifteen minutes telling me how the new generation of vines would make wines like none anybody had tasted for a hundred years. I nodded a lot and finally he poured the fourth bottle.

Usually you taste in the cellar, spitting out the wines. If you sit around drinking bottled wine, you sometimes drink too much. Joe was obviously delighted to have gotten away from the tasting room early, and question and comment had encouraged sipping. We were feeling fine. Cars kept pulling up. Joe would get up. "I'll get it," somebody would shout. Joe would sit down again. "It's like Grand Central Station around here," he said, lifting a glass.

I lifted mine. Lovely. "You don't charge enough for your wines," I said. You can always say that, and the winemaker will take a lot of time explaining how he wants to charge as little as possible because he wants people to be able to afford his wines, but how everything costs more these days, and do you have any idea what corks are selling for. "All you people have inferiority complexes," I said. "You're afraid to charge what the wines are worth." Indirect compliments framed as accusations are always good for ten minutes. Joe was declaring how his complex was as superior as anybody's when Alice threw open the door and shouted, "Surprise." He was surprised, and also a bit tight. So was I.

"You did fine," said Alice. "Now you have to stay for dinner."

"How did you like Joe Heitz?" asked the engineer. Dandy, just dandy, I told him, and Alice is great, too.

That was a fine way to find out about Heitz Chardonnay. In '73, when I was out for a visit to revise a book, Alice had a dinner celebrating Tchelistcheff's retirement from BV, with a procession of Cabernets. Another fine learning session. There was a handsome new winery, a compact hexagon across from the old one, that cost many times the original loan, but Joe had no trouble getting the money for it. His Martha's Vineyard Cabernet and the more than a dozen other wines he was making were now famous. In '77, I drove up on a summer evening to see how things were going. Joe was watering a pine tree that had got little attention while he and Alice were away at an enologists' convention in San Diego. I had invited myself to dinner and there was to be fish Joe had caught while playing hooky from the meeting. To round out the group, there was a smiling couple from Los Angeles, among the first to distribute Joe's wines.

We sat on the terrace with four vintages of the Chardonnay, sipping the wines, nibbling on salted nuts. Here are my notes:

" '75 clean, fruit. '74 fresh, full. 'Elegant,' says Joe. '73 rich nose. 'My favorite,' says Joe. '72 Perfect.''

The greater the wine, the less need be said about it. Heitz wines are never overpowering and are characterized by full flower and fruit from the grape, perfect balance and great finesse, wine words that are used to denote exellence.

We had the same wines with a mélange of fish filets sautéed in butter, each tasting slightly different, and bringing out various qualities of the wines. The elder son, now grown up and busy in the winery, barbecued a sirloin to go with the Cabernets. "I'm glad you're here; we don't often get the chance to taste so many from Martha's Vineyard at once," said Joe. Here are my notes:

" '72 big nose. '70 flower more than fruit. Earth taste. 'More Frenchy,' says Joe. '69 fat. 'More classic California, like the '68,' says Joe. '68 full. 'Makes your nose just want to laugh,' says Alice.''

Joe opened the wines as we sat down. All of them were enclosed at first. My notes read, "Like a bunch of disgruntled bells, clanging hard notes until they wake up." First one was good, then another. We sniffed them, then drank the one that tasted best. The bouquets jogged up and down, quickly changing; by the time cheese was served all of them had opened up. We enjoyed catching them as they released bouquet, closed up, finally expanding. "That's why it's no fair to taste wines; you must drink them," said Joe.

The Grignolino had been grafted over to Chardonnay; there were some seventeen acres now around the winery, much of it Chardonnay. That day, Joe had bought a small plot. "I want to plant it in Louis Martini's Chardonnay, the one he got from the experimental station. It's planted in a lot of different places and I'm going to follow it around to see where I

150

want to get cuttings." In spite of himself, Joe is tending vineyard. The youngsters are grown up to help.

I asked Alice what she likes best with the Chardonnay. "Fresh salmon," she was quick to answer. And the Cabernet? "Filet of beef or rib roast," she said. Filet doesn't have taste, it's mostly just tender, was the comment. "I wrap it for a few hours in a cloth soaked in brandy, then oven roast it fast," she said. Alice is a famous cook, but she likes to do simple dishes with the best wines, letting the wines show off.

Optimum production for Heitz is about 40,000 cases. Then he'll have to build another hexagon. He doesn't anticipate any problem with the bank.

Joseph Phelps Vineyards. When you've built bridges and such all your life, maybe it's natural to want to own a vineyard, but Joseph Phelps is one of the few construction engineers to do so. He bought a little more than a square mile of rolling country just off the Silverado, put a little lake in a low spot and a winery up the hill, then set out 120 acres of vines. That was in 1972, behind a ridge that pushes out into Napa, off the road that leads to Joe Heitz. There's a timber structure at the entrance and a paved track curls through the vines and around a knoll of oaks to an entrance court shadowed by a larger timber structure, a trestle becoming grape arbor.

The winery is two blocks—one is the fermenting room, and the other barrel storage and bottling—connected by a bridge that contains offices overlooking the vines and the lake. The grand scene is pictured on the labels.

Walter Schug, from a German wine family and trained at Geisenheim, with California experience since 1959, supervised the installation and made the first wines, assisted by chemist Bruce Neyers, also manager of marketing.

Rhinelanders have been in California vineyards since the early days and the new generation is determined to make outstanding Rieslings. Some of the most spectacular are Schug's Late Harvest Rieslings, light in alcohol and lingering in taste, with a fruity tang to remind you of Spätlesen of a sunny year. Wines from late-picked grapes that develop the noble rot can be less than 11% alcohol, their sweetness making them appealing. They are often served with creamed dishes and smoked or spicy meats, but perhaps they are best drunk by themselves, as Rhinelanders do, or as

151

dessert with pears or apples and soft cheeses. The Gewürztraminers are usually under 12% alcohol, soft and spicy, the Fumé Blanc not much more but strongly fruity. The trend is to make wines on the light side, but fruity.

Phelps buys grapes from the Stanton ranch in Yountville, and others, often bottling them separately, but using some to augment those from their own vineyards. A small plot of Syrah was found below St. Helena and cuttings were planted in the home vineyard, making Phelps the first winery to offer bottlings of the noble Rhône grape. Original plantings were set out in 1935 in the Davis experimental plot at Oakville but yield was so small that growers preferred the Duriff and called it Petite Sirah. Now that yields are not the first thing considered by growers, the true Syrah may be coming into its own, thanks to Phelps. Optimum production is around 25,000 cases, with emphasis on national distribution and sale of three-bottle packs to a growing mailing list.

Chappellet Vineyards. A good road, State 128, cuts across the Silverado Trail and winds east, up past man-made Lake Hennessy on the left and the rise of Pritchard Hill on the right, eventually joining the road that swings down through the Chiles Valley. Donn Chappellet stopped looking when he saw Pritchard. There was a wide-eaved house on top, built around a court, with windows looking across the lake and far beyond into the valley. And all around the hill were slopes for vineyards, nearly 100 acres of them, between sheltering rises of fir and oak. This was it; friends and neighbors put in three more plots totaling 70 acres to add to his own grapes.

He came to the hill in 1967, after some twenty years running food-vending operations around Los Angeles. With a partner, he bought a coffee machine to get started, another, and then there were thousands. This wasn't what Chappellet had in mind. Wine was what he had in mind, a winery, and ten years later he had both.

The winery is spectacular, made of triangles that could represent the three lives of wine—on the vine, in cask and in bottle—but doesn't. A friend of Chappellet's had the idea of hiding the winery under a pyramid of earth and Richard Keith, who has designed many of the new wineries, including Heitz, Sonoma and Clos du Val, drew up the plans. Buttressed concrete walls more than 200 feet long were laid out in a triangle, then equilateral triangles of ribbed steel were pitched over these. Nobody could figure the stresses for bearing the earth loads, so Cor-Ten was used, which quickly rusts to the color of old brick. The pyramid rises modestly above the olive green foliage of the trees. Dirt was bulldozed against the concrete and sodded. The symbolic shape, still not defined, appears on the labels.

The triangles are pulled apart at the corners, forming entrances to the pyramid, where all winery activity takes place. A cantilevered stairway leads to the peak where a six-sided room opens out to a terrace and the view. You can look down into the winery and see the winemaking process at a glance—where the grapes come in, where the juice is fermented and where the wines are stored in casks.

What does the architecture of the winery have to do with the wines? Where people choose to build, and what, shows something of the character of the winemaker, surely expressed in what he bottles. Chappellet presents his wines with starkly simple labels; the winery is inconspicuous on the land. What is inside is astonishing.

One of the state's driest Chenin Blancs comes from Chappellet—he doesn't like sweetness in table wines—and his Cabernet has a lightness and finesse that sets it apart from others, many of which are heavy with alcohol and oak. The Chardonnay also has a certain delicacy, for he doesn't like to make table wines of great body and fullness. His Rieslings and other whites are fermented very cold, in the low forties, because he likes the results. Press wines go into lower-priced wines marketed as Pritchard Hill, although some of the Chardonnay and Riesling are reserved for the Chenin Blanc. Optimum production is about 25,000 cases.

Chappellet thinks his hill vineyards and their small yields of perhaps three tons an acre produce better wines than those on flatlands. There is support for this from comparative tastings, where his Cabernet always ranks high. Only four wines are made, allowing for a certain concentration of effort and care. The elegance of his wines matches the tastes of delicate dishes; the wines are distinctly French in character, one would say, having in mind those that are noted for delicacy, like the Musignys of Burgundy or the Margaux of Bordeaux. Chappellet might be pleased with the comparison, but he would leave it to you to say so.

Nichelini Vineyards. In the rumple of hills to the east lies Chiles Valley and in an oak grove near a canyon, excavated for the wine, is the cellar and a terrace. On top of this a Swiss homesteader built his house before

153

the turn of the century. His name was Nichelini and his descendants tend 50 acres of the vine up in the valley, making fresh and simple wines like those you might find in the Beaujolais or Savoie. The best wine is surely fruity Zinfandel, meant to be drunk young, but just as popular are a rosé made from that grape and two well-made whites, Chenin Blanc and Sauvignon Vert. The vineyards are nine hundred feet above sea level and do so well that Louis Martini put in a vineyard above Nichelini's and others have planted vines in Pope Valley to the north.

Jim Nichelini is much too carefree, content to sell his wines around the Bay Area and to passersby on their way to the resort area around Lake Berryessa over east, not especially interested in wider distribution nor in the serious intent portrayed by the millions newly invested over in Napa. When winemakers get together at their frequent tastings, Nichelini has been known to throw a ringer—a bottle picked out of a bargain bin or somebody's homemade wonder—just to confuse the experts. On the terrace where people taste his wines there is an old Roman winepress—it's shown on the label—and Nichelini has been known to say that's what he uses, though even his grandfather kept it mostly for show. He twiddles the accordion for visitors when the spirit moves him, even playing requests. One of them might be "Clementine."

Cuvaison Cellars. The Silverado winds up to Calistoga, but before it gets there, a long, low Spanish-looking building of stucco and stone, with arches and tiled roofs, ranges above a vineyard and below the wooded hills. Cuvaison was begun by a couple of engineers enthusiastic about wines. Their enthusiasm waned and a New Yorker took over the property, placing in charge the winemaker who had started out with Chappellet, Philip Togni. Togni trained in Bordeaux, worked in Algeria and Chile, then at Gallo before making wines on Pritchard Hill, beginning a new program in 1975.

Grapes are purchased from hillside growers, those from the 30 or so acres in front of the winery being considered as valley grapes and so sold to other wineries. Production of some 20,000 cases is limited to three wines: 8,000 Chardonnay and Cabernet, the rest Zinfandel. Wines from particular vineyards are occasionally identified on the label when a lot seems extra grand.

* * *

Château Montelena. The century-old winery just beyond the end of the Silverado Trail at the foot of Mount St. Helena became the property of Lee Pasich and friend in 1972. Built in the crenellated style then fashionable in France, the stone walls push into the hill, with living quarters back above the left facade. The winery looks down on a lake built by subsequent owners in the Chinese fashion, with arched bridges joining small islands and willows drooping over. It's a nice place to taste wines, out there in the red pavilions, particularly the Chardonnay, which has starred in many tastings.

A Croatian winemaker trained in Yugoslavia, Mike Grgich, made the early wines of the new regime in the European style. They are constantly being compared with French bottlings but the owners insist they simply want to make good wines meant to be enjoyed. Optimum production is about 20,000 cases.

The Cabernet is good with steak. The Chardonnay is good with chicken sautéed in Chardonnay. The chicken is rubbed with tarragon, stuffed with celery, onions, carrots and parsley, browned in a little butter, then cooked covered for less than an hour with perhaps a quarter-cup of the wine. (You have to prick the chicken with a fork until the juice runs clear.) With that, green fettucini goes well. Beat an egg yolk into a cup of cream, add three-quarters of a cup of grated Parmesan, stir in a cup of half-and-half and fold into the cooked fettucini. Salt and pepper to taste. Serve with a green salad with an oil and vinegar dressing and some fresh dill.

A second label, Silverado Cellars, is used for small lots of wines. Some of the wine goes beyond California but bottles are hard to come by. Planned production will not be much more than 20,000 cases, the wines beginning to be available in California by 1980, perhaps elsewhere later on.

NEWCOMERS—CARNEROS TO CALISTOGA

Wines are a new frontier to most Americans, fascinating as the sea or wilderness, and present-day pioneers are renewing all the old vineyards ruined by phylloxera, Prohibition and Depression. This time the vines are better suited to land and weather, but like yachtsmen or horse breeders, winemakers pursue the ultimate. Whether or not we need a multitude of costly fine wines is beside the point, nor does it seem to matter that we

155

want many good wines at low prices. Newcomers are aiming only for the best, partly because they can do so, partly because the vine and wine represent the highest form of agriculture and a way of living on the land, away from cities, offices, commuting. So the newcomers labor at their craft for those who can afford them.

Carneros Creek Winery. Ten acres of early-ripening Pinot Noir and other grapes from neighbors on slopes near the bay—Chardonnay, Cabernet, Zinfandel—will supply an optimum 10,000 cases from the furthest south of Napa wineries. The project by a couple in the importing business was put into operation by an amateur winemaker who worked with them, Francis Mahoney, who planted the vines and operates the winery.

Tulocay Winery. Optimum production of 1,000 cases of wine from the same grapes as Carneros will come from this small winery east of Napa, with the first wine offered in 1978.

Trefethen Vineyards. Oak Knoll is on the north edge of Napa, the biggest winery in the town. The old timbered building is the last one left of the old wooden wineries, now restored by Gene Trefethen, its 600 acres replanted under the management of his son, John. Optimum production can reach 100,000 cases in the Eighties.

Napa Wine Cellars. Charles Woods was a Montana construction engineer and amateur winemaker who sold out in 1972 and bought a boat, with plans to sail around the world with his wife. Winter caught them in San Francisco and Woods began going to Napa for grapes, making wine while waiting for spring. A small plot north of Yountville was on the market, and Woods sold his boat and began building a winery—a dome joined to a canted block with a flat top which is the fermenting room. He had always wanted to build a dome, which makes a good space for barrel storage and for a small tasting section. From the three acres of Chardonnay, Woods made his first wine in 1975, and he plans an optimum production of 10,000 cases from purchased grapes.

Cakebread Cellars. John Cakebread is an Oakland photographer who became interested in wineries by taking pictures of them. At the end of a long lane north of Oakville, near a pond and some twenty acres of vineyard, the Cakebread family and friends built a wooden winery with a shed roof and a roofed fermenting pad patterned after early California barns. The whole family is involved, one son going to Davis, the other majoring in business administration, to make the most of an optimum production of some 3,000 cases.

Silver Oak Cellars. Storage for an optimum production of 4,000 cases is back from the Oakville Cross, in a winery devoted to a single wine, Cabernet Sauvignon. Owners are Justin Meyer and Raymond Duncan, who ferment the wine at their Franciscan Winery on the highway. First vintage was in 1972.

Franciscan Winery. Just above Beaulieu Vineyards at Rutherford is the redwood Franciscan Winery, set up by a group of California businessmen as a major entry into the wine world. The enterprise foundered and the winery and a thousand acres of vineyard were taken over by Justin Meyer and Raymond Duncan. Meyer is a Davis graduate who worked with Brother Timothy at The Christian Brothers for nearly a decade and he is helped in the winemaking by Leonard Berg, a Davis graduate whose uncle is Harold Berg, the Davis professor and expert on grapes. When long-term contracts for the grapes have run out, the winery's production from their own vines will increase, perhaps reaching 200,000 cases by 1980.

Rutherford Vintners. Bernard Skoda, who worked with Louis Martini for years, has set up his own winery across the road from Franciscan, releasing his first wine, a Cabernet Sauvignon, in 1977. A few wines from premium varieties will be made from purchased grapes, the amount depending on market response.

Raymond Vineyards & Cellar. The Raymond family is part of the Beringer clan and when Beringer was sold in 1970 they determined to start their own winery. Zinfandel Lane crosses to the Silverado from the Wine Road above Rutherford and they bought a 90-acre vineyard on the south side of the road. Two sons, one trained in farm management, the other in enology at Davis, have worked on the land from the beginning, preparing the soil, planting the vines, planning the winery, making the wines, with optimum production of 20,000 cases by 1980.

* * *

Grgich-Hills Cellar. At Rutherford is the new winery of Miljenko Grgich, the winemaker who made Château Montelena's Chardonnay, the one that did so well in Paris tastings against French peers. There are 20 acres at the winery and 140 more belonging to Austin Hills, scion of the coffee family. The two have formed Grgich-Hills Cellar, starting with Chardonnay and Riesling, with plans for an optimum production of 10,000 cases. The name, though memorable, may be changed.

V. Sattui Winery. A winery nearly a century old that languished during Prohibition has been reestablished by a great-grandson of the founder, Daryl Sattui. The low, stuccoed winery of heavy timbers and arched openings is set in an old walnut grove just north of Zinfandel Lane. There's a picnic area with tables made from old wine barrels, a cheese shop, and a tasting room in a corner near the rows of German ovals and willow-bound Burgundy barrels. Some wines are made there; others are bought for aging and blending; but sales are presently limited to winery visitors and California outlets.

Sutter Home Winery. This had long been a bulk winery, named for a relative of the man who discovered gold and started the gold rush, but owned since the Forties by the Trinchero family, when the younger generation decided to establish their own label in the Seventies. They found a plot of old Zinfandel in the Sierra foothills, over east in the Shenandoah Valley, and the wine they made from it was exceptional, big and at its best when aged. Their best wine and others are made from purchased grapes, with optimum production of some 20,000 cases.

Spottswoode Cellars. An old St. Helena winery, once called Lindenhurst and renamed by a lady named Spotts, had some 70 acres of vineyards remaining in the Sixties, offering wines locally under the Montebello label. New owners prefer the odd name, planning an optimum production of 15,000 cases with initial California distribution.

Conn Creek Vineyards. When Annapolis classmates began buying vineyards and wineries in the valley, Bill Collins thought he would, too. With almost 300 acres in bearing by the mid-Seventies, it was time to consider making his own wines from his Conn Creek grapes. He and partner Bill Beaver leased an old stone building north of St. Helena, hired Brad Webb as consultant, and installed John Henderson as winemaker. Henderson had learned his craft at Souverain with Lee Stewart; he now runs the winery while Collins runs his electronics business and Beaver teaches at Stanford. Optimum production of prime varieties is perhaps 15,000 cases, with plans for national distribution by 1980.

St. Clement Vineyards. A steepled Victorian frame house is on a rise above the highway south of St. Helena, terraced vines making a front lawn, all of it restored by Mike Collins. Eye doctor William Casey and his wife spotted it when Collins put it on the market, preparatory to moving up Spring Mountain, and bought it in 1976. The name comes from a Maryland island where Casey's forebears settled—it has a nice ring, they decided—and with Brad Webb as consultant, they began making their wines with the help of Jon Axhelm, who started out with Collins. Production is 1,000 cases, mostly for friends.

Stonegate Winery. Even newspapermen are drawn to the world of wines, particularly when they have grown up in their father's Michigan vineyard; so when James Spaulding began teaching journalism at Berkeley the sensible thing seemed to be to buy some Napa vineyards. There are more than a dozen acres of vineyard on a steep hillside west of Calistoga and about as many on the winery property south of town on the slope leading up to Sterling. The family winery has an optimum production of 5,000 cases of premium wines, mostly from their own vineyards, with sales pretty well limited to visitors.

The Small Wineries. Wineries producing less than 50,000 cases a year have been lumped together rather condescendingly as "boutique wineries," having limited sales. If the phrase still signifies what it did originally—small specialty shops concerned with excellence—the term fits. Fine wine shops around the country stock many of their wines or can can get them. A family winery with 40 acres of vineyard may produce 8,000 cases. A small winery producing 15,000 cases or so may represent an investment of a million dollars and more.

* * *

159

Really small wineries	Small wineries	Family wineries
2,000–5,000 cases	5,000–10,000 cases	12,000–20,000 cases
Mayacamas	Caymus	Burgess
Stony Hill	Nichelini	Clos du Val
St. Clement	Chateau Chevalier	Raymond
Stonegate	Carneros Creek	Spring Mountain
Cakebread	Pope Valley	Villa Mount Eden
Mt. Veeder	Napa Wine Cellars	Veedercrest
Silver Oaks	Stag's Leap Winery	Stag's Leap Wine Cellars
Tulocay	Spottswoode	Yverdon
Stewart Smith	Rutherford Vintners	Conn Creek

NOTE: There are other wineries in the valley which sell in bulk, notably the Napa Valley Cooperative, whose production goes to Gallo, and the Sunny St. Helena Winery, whose production goes to Krug. For many growers, though, there is a steady urge to own one's own label, so there are always new ones to look for.

Santa Clara: The Big Move South and Those Who Stayed

Santa Clara Valley runs south from San Francisco Bay much as the Napa Valley runs north, with a few vineyards and wineries on its western flank, facing the morning sun. The valley itself is now filled with inhabitants, who have long since forced out the extensive plantings of Paul Masson, Mirassou and Almadén, which now get their grapes from Monterey and other locations well beyond the bedroom towns. The largest and most widely distributed of the Santa Clara wineries, these three are really representative of Monterey. For wines typical of the valley you must seek out small producers like Ridge or Bruce.

Well below the bay to the south, beginning near Morgan Hill, is a cluster of old wineries, most of them Italian, whose production is mostly bulk wines and whose sale is mostly limited to California. Exceptions are Rapazzini and Pedrizetti and Gemello, whose wines sometimes leave the state. San Martin is also in national distribution but most of its vineyards are in Monterey. A group near Gilroy have names like Live Oaks, Conrotto, Bertero, Fortino, Hecker Pass, Thomas Kruse, Kirigin Cellars, Giretti; wines to sample when you see a label.

Up in the Santa Cruz mountains on the west are renewed remnants of old vineyards that can be considered part of the Santa Clara region. The smallest of these is the family winery of a salesman of building materials, Robert Mullen, in Woodside. Grapes come from small plots of the old La

161

Questa vineyard, whose wines commanded the highest prices, and a few more from vineyards around the winery and neighbors' plots, but production amounts to little more than 600 cases a year. The wines are light because the vineyards are high and cool, well suited to Chardonnay and Pinot, although the light and fragrant Cabernet made the Woodside Vineyards reputation. Family and friends rally round to make the wines—and drink much of it. The best way to get to taste them may be to go to communion at the Village Church, which uses the reds as altar wines.

Amateurs have revolutionized California wines in little more than a generation, although considered opinion has it that enthusiasts make dreadful messes. Most of them start by crushing berries and fruits, graduating to concentrates and essences, to which they add sugar and yeast and acids, letting this bubble away in demijohns until the cloudy murk stops working; the result usually tastes like sugar water with moldy bread in it. When grapes are used, they are usually the wrong grapes; air has usually got at the ferment and oxidized it, making acetic acid, and the result tastes like a mild vinegar that would ruin a salad. Results infuriate the amateur with an artistic bent or a scientific one, especially those who are determined or hate to fail, and the persistent may produce something better than your average jug wine. This is a spur to greater effort, and by using the best grapes, keeping air away from the ferment and being as meticulously clean as a surgeon in an operating room, an enthusiast can make wines that are better than good. The most influential of amateurs was Martin Ray.

In 1936 Ray bought the languishing Paul Masson vineyard, 60 acres of grapes. He made his money in real estate, and made his first wine in 1935. Beginner's luck—it was so good, Ray felt he had a calling. If you did everything right and let the wines make themselves, you couldn't go wrong. Julian Street, just about the only acknowledged American wine expert in those days, wired Ray that his '36 Pinot Noir was the "first American red wine I ever drank with entire pleasure." There was no stopping Ray, who proceeded to make wines for the next forty years.

All that time he was a gadfly to the industry, inveighing against use of any but noble grapes, doing anything to interfere with the natural process of fermentation, particularly anything chemical or mechanical, adding anything like acid or sugar to the fermenting grape juice. He thought it a crime to borrow European names—that was really robbery—and insisted wines should be sold bearing the names of the grapes they were made from, 100% pure and unadulterated. He was scorned as a purist, reviled as an eccentric, condemned as a nuisance—and finally respected as a fine winemaker, if only because he charged so much for his bottlings and got what he asked for.

He sold Paul Masson in 1943 when the big distillers were buying vineyards to insure a supply of alcohol, planting a vineyard on Mount Eden, two thousand feet above the valley. His Martin Ray Vineyard continues to make wines with his son as winemaker, and the nearby Mount Eden Vineyards, owned by a group of investors he brought together, makes more. Production from both amounts to only a few thousand cases, mostly available in California.

David Bruce Winery. David Bruce lives 2,000 feet up in the Santa Cruz, above Los Gatos, his vineyards on the slope in front of his house. He passes them every day on his way to work. He is a dermatologist with offices in San Jose, but when he is not practicing he is in his 25 acres of vineyard or in the winery. Now much more than a hobby, winemaking is a second career and his wines are some of the biggest and fullest made. He spends three days a week at each profession, taking Sundays off when possible. He produces about 5,000 cases a year, with one person to help him in the vineyard and one to help him in the winery.

Bruce likes Burgundy, so Pinot and Chardonnay are in the home vineyard with Cabernet and a few Riesling vines. Grapes for other wines are bought, the Zinfandel from the Sierra foothills, but most of the grapes come from Santa Cruz vineyards. He handles the wines as little as possible, aging them in small barrels hung on the walls of the winery, where they are easy to get at.

Bruce wines are a surprise—because of their fullness and intensity—to those used to European wines or familiar with premium California wines that are widely marketed. Too much wood, they say of the white wines, comparing them to the lighter wines of Napa. Too much tannin, they say of the reds, ignoring the fact that the wines may need a decade to reach maturity. They are models of their kind, though, perhaps the true successors to the wines of Martin Ray. They are made the way Dr. Bruce likes to make them; their popularity around the country shows that many share his tastes.

163

* * *

Ridge. When you can make your own wines it's only logical to think of buying a small vineyard and David Bennion did so in 1960, talking a trio of his fellow scientists at Stanford Research Institute into sharing costs. Ridge is 2,300 feet up on Monte Bello Road in the Santa Cruz Mountains with a few acres of vines, mostly Cabernet and Zinfandel, augmented by grapes from hillside vineyards in other regions. By 1970, Bennion was supervising the vineyards, and winemaking was in the hands of Paul Draper, who became interested in winemaking while working in Europe and spending all his spare time visiting friends in the wine business in northern Italy and Bordeaux. Subsequently, Draper made wines in Chile for three years, using Bordeaux techniques. On joining Ridge, a search began for hillside plots and a range of full-bodied reds are made from these, the source and methods used being spelled out on the labels. Some Chardonnay and Riesling are made, sold mostly at the winery. Optimum production is around 25,000 cases.

Gemello Winery. Soon after Repeal, John Gemello began making Zinfandel from high mountain vineyards above his Mountain View winery, big and fruity wines high in acid in the European style. Forty years later there were several of them: some aged in Limousin oak might remind one of Burgundy; others aged in Nevers oak recall Bordeaux; and there is a full, intense Zinfandel from grapes in an old vineyard in the Sierra foothills, to be compared with those of Ridge and the Sutter Home Winery in Napa. Success with these has led to producing a range of Cabernets from Santa Clara grapes, high in alcohol, slow to develop. There are several other wines, notably those from new vineyards in the Carmel Valley of Monterey, which include a Gamay Beaujolais from the same cuttings that produce the Pinot Noir of Stonegate Winery in Napa. Sales of all are mostly limited to California.

Vine Hill Vineyard. Two small vineyards in Santa Cruz supply grapes for Vine Hill, whose president is Richard Smothers of the television comedy team. Production: 4,000 cases.

Novitiate of Los Gatos. Let us make altar wines, said the fourteen novices who set out vineyards on a foothill of the Santa Cruz that pushed down to Los Gatos. That was in 1888 and they continued to do so, unlike

164

The Christian Brothers, for eighty years. There were always a few wines for townspeople who came to the Jesuit novitiate for them, but when it became necessary to sell some of the vineyards for subdivisions, it was decided to plant new plots in noble vines and market a few wines—10,000 cases to start. There are now some 600 acres in bearing, more than 100 of them behind the big stone building, which is now a residence. The novices return each fall to harvest the grapes. Perhaps the most unusual wine is one made from muscat grapes and sold as Black Muscat, and there are several other blends of fortified wines as well as those marketed with grape names. National sales are still pretty much limited to altar wines.

Almadén. You might say Almadén revolutionized the California wine business twice, or maybe three times. The second time was 1941, when Louis Benoist bought the fine old house surrounded by vines for a weekend retreat and then wondered what to do with the winery. Frank Schoonmaker had begun selling a few of California's best bottlings when war had cut off his European vintages and Benoist asked him for ideas. The first thing was to get a winemaker and Schoonmaker lined up Ollie Goulet, who had been making wines for Martin Ray and wanted to make a change. The next step was to do something about the wines: Schoonmaker noticed some Grenache in the vineyard, the vine responsible for the best rosé of France, Tavel, and showed Goulet how to make the wine. Bearing the grape name on the label, it was the popular hit of the Forties and paved the way for many others marketed with grape names, which were popularized as a new class called varietal wines.

The first revolution began when news of the Gold Rush reached Bordeaux and young Etienne Thée sailed off to get some. He found none in the goldfields, but had better luck when he bought the knoll in Los Gatos and began planting cuttings from Bordeaux and Burgundy. His son-in-law, Charles Le Franc, carried on the good work, and his son-in-law did the same, finally breaking away to establish his own vineyard, Paul Masson. Pestilence, war and hard times wrecked Almadén until Benoist came along with Schoonmaker, Goulet and Grenache Rosé.

You could hear the third revolution happening if you sat on the terrace at Almadén any sunny morning in the Fifties. Over coffee and croissants on your breakfast tray—bright with silver, flowered Limoges porcelain and linen napkins—you could hear the hammering of carpenters from beyond the vineyards. Driving down the lane and through the gates you passed row after row of new houses. There were no greenbelt laws for Santa Clara county as there were for Napa and the land was being taxed as subdivision, not as farm acreage. All that remain of Almadén are the fine old house, the winery and 40 acres of vineyard.

Schoonmaker began looking south on the advice of Davis scientists. Professor Bioletti, before the war, Professors Amerine and Winkler after it, saw a great future in the highlands of San Benito county, adjoining Santa Clara but beyond the reach of developers. Vines were first planted there in 1797 by Franciscans at their mission, San Juan Bautista; many later went into Cienaga Valley and the Paicenes region to the south. Benoist bought these, eventually owning some 4,000 acres, the largest holding of premium vines in the world. He built a storage warehouse covering 4 acres at Cienaga, rebuilt the winery there, which straddles the San Andreas fault—that was for red wines—and built a new winery for white wines at Paicenes. By 1967, investment had been so enormous that he sold it all to National Distillers. The plantings started the movement south that led to the development in Monterey, the third of the revolutions begun by Almadén.

National Distillers continued the planting, adding another 4,000 acres in Monterey and east of the bay in Alameda County. Investment is enormous, but Almadén needs it all for the thirty-plus wines they market, some nine million cases, from Mountain Red jug wines to special bottlings of Vintage Brut, one of California's better sparkling wines.

Paul Masson. Paul Masson was a carefree young Burgundian who came to Santa Clara in the Eighteen Seventies to help a friend who had inherited a vineyard near Los Gatos. Things worked out fine and in the Eighties he bought a Santa Cruz mountainside above the town of Saratoga and set forth his vineyard. His wines quickly made him famous and his joviality made his parties a legend, even in convivial San Francisco. His sparkling wines were most popular of all—Anna Held bathed in a tubful at one of his parties—and he traveled the continent spreading their good name. One year in Paris he entered a national wine judging contest and won—to the consternation of Parisians who immediately changed the rules so that only Frenchmen could compete. When he sold the winery to Martin Ray in 1936 it was said he did so because he could no longer taste so well and had lost interest; he died soon after.

166

When Seagram took over the firm in 1943, management was turned over to descendants of two Rhineland families, Alfred Fromm of the fifth generation, and Franz Sichel of the seventh, both of whom bought shares; the two subsequently set up the separate marketing firm in conjunction with Seagram that today distributes wines of The Christian Brothers. On Franz Sichel's death, Otto Meyer, who had married into the clan, took over the holding and ran the company until Seagram made Paul Masson a subsidiary of their import house in 1971.

Like the founder, Meyer was an exceptional taster and presided over the expansion of the company. The vineyard in the sky continued to function, its wines made in the old winery that had been built from stones of a twelfth-century Romanesque church front, brought around the Horn to front a San Jose church that had been demolished. The flagged space before the winery was used as the site for chamber music concerts. "Music in the Vineyard" became so popular that the concerts continue, now a tradition, to be held every summer. Seven vineyards now present summer concerts and up in Sonoma, Souverain has a summer theater.

The terraced residence on the rim of the hill was turned into a guesthouse. For tourists, a new winery of arched bays was built where the winemaking process could be watched from a high gallery. It is entered by a ramp that winds up over a pool full of water jets so that you feel like a bubble rising in a giant glass of sparkling wine.

Meyer's greatest contribution was the establishment of vineyards in Monterey to replace those being overrun by subdivisions. Professors at Davis had suggested that the Salinas valley would be ideal for grapes because breezes from Monterey Bay cooled it during the afternoon. Meyer put in 5,000 acres of vineyard and built a vast new winery there. Water was obtained from the great underground river flowing beneath the valley, the expense of drilling being offset by the growing demand for premium wines.

Because the management group had been long involved with the international world of wines, Paul Masson began sending its wines abroad, to markets in Asia and Africa, but also to Europe and South America. They brought in young winemakers from abroad, men like Ed Friedrich, who had graduated from the wine college in Trier on the Moselle, and Guy Baldwin, who had begun making wines in Canada. Paul Masson paved the way for other modern American wines to venture into world markets.

And Meyer introduced new wines, from new grapes. Several promising crosses had been developed at Davis after thirty years of trying, vines that produced soft and pleasant wines from vines that produced heavily and retained fruit acids even in warm vineyards. They had been developed for the giant producers in the hot Central Valley, but Meyer planted them in cooler locations and produced some surprising wines. To identify them clearly, they were given brand names suggestive of their qualities. Beginning wine drinkers like white wines because they are served cold, like more-familiar drinks; so Paul Masson presented Emerald Dry, a blend based on Emerald Riesling. A soft red, light in acid, is called Rubion, a blend based on the Ruby Cabernet. A somewhat fuller red is a blend called Baroque. Less bland than the "mellow" wines in jugs, more winelike than concoctions like Cold Duck, they are meant to introduce people to the realm of table wines instead of being an alcoholic substitute for soda pop.

Because Paul Masson is so large, about the size of its peers, The Christian Brothers or Inglenook, the wines are often put in the same class as the bulk producers in the Great Central Valley. They should be more aptly compared with the big European shippers of France, Italy and the Rhine.

Mirassou Vineyards. The French that came to Santa Clara ran to daughters. When they married, the sons-in-law came into the businesses, taking over in the fullness of time, with what feelings of anguish and satisfaction one can only guess. Pierre Pellier brought the first cuttings of Folle Blanche and Colombard, among others, to his brother's nursery in San Jose in 1858. They were drying up by the time he reached Panama, so he bought a cargo of potatoes, and stuck the tips into slits to keep them alive the rest of the way.

Three years later he took cuttings to the east, in what is called the Evergreen district, setting out some 300 acres over the years. Pierre's son was named Peter and he had a daughter who married a Mirassou, taking over the vineyard and giving it his name. They had two sons, Edmund and Norbert, who had four. Also a daughter, who married Don Alexander, who became a winemaker. Between the five, they have about a score in the sixth generation. Surely some of them will go into the business.

Ed and Norb sold in bulk, but made a few wines for the family and friends, winning prizes with them at state fairs. The children picked up pocket money working in the vineyards, scrubbing butts, helping with the wines. In the Sixties, they approached their fathers with a scheme—how about setting up a marketing company and selling their own wines? Ed and Norb put up the money, charging them the same interest as the bank would. As the subdivisions crowded in, another company was set up to plant new vineyards down in Monterey, now 600 acres. Ed and Norb backed that, too, keeping it all in the family. The fifth generation owns the label, the cooperage and the new vineyards. The sixth will work in there, somewhere.

When Almadén started planting down in San Benito, the Mirassous realized they had to find new land and began looking—up in Mendocino, north of Sacramento, over in the Sierra foothills, even in Southern California. Ed and Norb found an old Davis report that said the Salinas valley running south from Monterey Bay between the coast range and the Pinnacles should be good for grapes, cooled by winds off the bay. Son Pete, who had begun taking over vineyard management, went down for a look. Masson was looking there as well, and Otto Meyer hired Pete to put in 1,000 acres. The Mirassous put in 300, later trebling it. Then the Wente Brothers of Livermore put in 550 acres. Many more followed.

The Mirassous sold 3,000 cases under their own label in 1966, increasing it sixty times in a decade, perhaps reaching 250,000 cases early in the Eighties. The Mirassous have been particularly successful with their white wines, a fruity, full Chenin Blanc with some sweetness, a big and spicy Gewürztraminer and a nicely balanced Sylvaner sold as "Riesling," which is the California practice. Three of the brothers own a small vineyard in the southern part of Santa Clara at Gilroy from which a Late Harvest Zinfandel is made. There is a delicious sweet dessert white called Fleurie; they call a light wine made from Petite Sirah Petite Rosé. Almost a score of wines are made, including a sparkling wine that is fruity and well-liked, mostly Pinot Blanc and Chenin Blanc, with some Colombard, perhaps to honor the founder. There is, though, no Folle Blanche.

Tepusquet Cellars. Lee Stewart's growing fascination with orchids was one of the influences that led him to sell Souverain, and the name began moving around the North Coast. The flour company that bought it put the name on the new winery built near Rutherford on the Silverado Trail and on the new winery built in northern Sonoma to handle grapes from Alexander Valley vineyards. The name stuck there and Souverain of Alexander Valley became the property of a group of Sonoma growers. Rutherford Hill became the name of the winery on the Silverado Trail, owned by

169

Napa growers. The original became Burgess Cellars, owned by an airline pilot of that name.

Lee Stewart turned his attention to Tepusquet Cellars, down in San Luis Obispo. The new winery, starting out with production of 80,000 cases has some 2,800 acres in the county and roundabout to draw on. First vintage was 1976.

Felton-Empire Vineyards. Grapes from the famous old Hallcrest vineyard in Santa Cruz went to Concannon during the first half of the Seventies. The twenty-odd acres produced remarkable Cabernets and Rieslings, and this acreage became the nucleus of Felton-Empire, which is offering remarkable wines. Their White Riesling for 1976, as an example, indicates on the label that the grapes came from three vineyards—52% Hallcrest, 33% Vine Hill, 15% Beauregard—where there was some botrytis, and that the alcoholic content is only 10%. That's a lot of information to get on a label, but this is a growing trend. A label on a bottle from a premium winery may well have to describe the wines in winemaker terms to gain popular acceptance, an early sign that advertising jargon and helpful hints for the hopeless may be on the wane.

A shrewd buyer reads labels, not necessarily put off by poor graphics or empty words, but certainly attracted to good design and precise information. Felton-Empire White Riesling rewarded attention—a light and elegant wine of subtlety. Their others command similar attention.

Livermore: Gravel, Gravel, Everywhere

Livermore Valley is a spread of gravel half an hour across the Bay Bridge, just beyond the Alameda sprawl, a clutter of bedrooms that goes from Berkeley clear down to San Jose. It should be farther away.

Charles Wetmore noticed a slash of limestone above his vineyard, long since gone, so he called it Cresta Blanca. The label is now attached to Mendocino wines. At the near end of Livermore is Pleasanton, where Ruby Hill makes fine reds and whites, sold in bulk. But there is also Villa Armando, owned by a New York company that sends all its wine east; among them is just about the best Italianesque wine to be found, called either Barberone or Rubinello or Vino Rustico. Lately, Villa Armando has been selling vintaged bottlings from premium grapes, which retail for less than four dollars; seek out Mountain Zinfandel, Barbera and Pinot Blanc. They are mostly available in New York City, which is a nice change. Almadén has plantings down in Sunol, and grapes from other vineyards go into blends of the big wineries.

The prizes are a little farther east, protected by greenbelt laws.

Wente Bros. A wine called Valle d'Oro Sauvignon Blanc won the prize for the best white wine at the Golden Gate Exposition of 1939. "Who made it?" asked Frank Schoonmaker, in California, scouting for wines to replace the European bottlings being cut off by war. Herman Wente, he was told, and after tasting them all he bought six more, dubbed them Schoonmaker Selections, put the Wente Bros. name on the label and introduced them to New York. Production is now over 350,000 cases and the wines are better than ever.

Carl Wente came from Germany in 1880, learned winemaking from Charles Krug in Napa and bought a small Livermore vineyard in 1883. He had three sons: a namesake who was advised to take up bookkeeping and did so successfully, becoming the president of the Bank of America; middle son Ernest was the farmer of the lot, took his agricultural degree at Davis and became the best viticulturist in the state; youngest son Herman went to Berkeley to study enology and became the most respected winemaker of his generation. It pays to listen to your father.

During Prohibition they made some altar wine for Beaulieu Vineyards but wound up raising feed for their hogs, cattle and sheep. With Repeal, the vineyards were replanted but the wines were sold in bulk until Schoonmaker found them.

Ernest expanded the Livermore holdings to 850 acres and then added 550 more in Monterey, his son Karl taking over the winemaking when Herman died in 1961. Karl did his uncle proud, making big, balanced Sauvignons and rounded Petite Sirah from Livermore grapes; superb, flowery Rieslings and dry Pinot Blancs from Monterey.

The Monterey vineyard is to the south in what is called Arroyo Seco, which runs down into the Carmel Valley and lies near a cut in the western range that pours cool air into the vineyard. There was no phylloxera in the Salinas Valley and the soil was sandy, which inhibits the infecting louse, so most growers put vines in the ground without grafting. Ernest felt that yield could be kept down by grafting, so the Wentes put in grafted stock; he was right, for the vines produce a modest four tons or less an acre. Acid is satisfactorily high, the vineyard being cooler than expected, so Pinot, Cabernet and Zinfandel produce superior grapes. Because the vineyard is best-known for white wines, the reds are often passed over. Pinot Noir does particularly well in Arroyo Seco, the Cabernets are light and balanced. Wente buys about a quarter of its grapes, including some Mendocino Grey Riesling to add to what is grown in Livermore. Grey Riesling is a grape of small repute, producing bland wines that are popular in San Francisco; it is the best-selling of all Wente wines.

Karl Wente was also the prime mover in developing the modern winery and a new tasting room early in the decade. Even the drop in the wine market in the early Seventies seemed to have little effect on the growing popularity of his wines. His sons were taking over aspects of the business when Karl died suddenly in 1977 of a heart attack at the age of 49. Like his uncle, he was one of the outstanding winemakers of his generation; his sons have a great tradition to carry on.

Concannon Vineyard. Petite Sirah makes a sturdy, balanced red wine with a lingering taste when grown in Livermore gravel and the Concannons were persuaded to bottle some, not to use it all for blending. There are those who insist that it is the best in the state. Other Concannon wines have adherents just as enthusiastic about the light and elegant Cabernets, the fruity and rounded Sémillon, the golden Sauvignon. All these come from the home vineyard of 250 acres; the Zinfandel comes from Amador in the Sierra foothills—a rosé is also made from that—while Chardonnay and Riesling come from various contract vineyards. And there is Rkatsiteli, as well, supposed to be the best of the Russian grapes, which Jim is making into a tart, flowery wine. Joe runs the vineyards. The two brothers and their two sisters inherited Concannon, and there is another generation coming along to carry on the good work and keep the flag flying on the tallest flagpole in California.

The father of them all was Captain Joe, who served with Pershing's cavalry but had to come back to run the winery when his nine brothers and sisters would have none of it. He put up the flagpole to remind him of the grand career he'd given up. Grandfather James had arrived in Boston from Ireland as the Civil War was ending and headed for Maine, where he hopped bells in a hotel, worked his way up to manager, and then decided to head west. The first archbishop of San Francisco took a shine to him and suggested a likely lad could do well by selling a new invention to the many businesses starting up, all of which could use rubber stamps. James ranged as far as Mexico City with his stamps, and there he saw the need of a street-cleaning company. He got this going, sold out to some Frenchmen at a goodly profit and went back to San Francisco to regale the archbishop with his adventures. The archbishop suggested it might be time to settle down; why didn't he buy a ranch and make altar wines? Concannon bought 300 acres of Livermore gravel in 1883, got vines from France, and soon the archbishop was drinking Concannon wines. Sale of altar wines saw the Concannon winery through Prohibition, making it one of the few wineries to survive without letup from the last century.

Concannon still makes an altar wine out of Muscat de Frontignan and another sweet wine they call Château Concannon, made from a blend of Sauvignon and Sémillon from vines that originally came from Château d'Yquem. Some of the Cabernet is supposed to be from cuttings taken from Château Margaux in the Bordeaux Médoc. And there is a foundation block—vines grown to provide cuttings. The Riesling comes from the mother block at Davis, which was started from a single bud, or clone, taken from Schloss Johannisberg in the Rheingau. Cuttings from the mother block are used to start a foundation block in the various regions around the state, and the cuttings are used to establish vineyards. These are certified vines—certified to be free of virus—and such stocks have provided all the vines that have been planted in the past decade or so. With much of the planting in California completed, these certified vines are now being used for replanting vineyards around the world. Clonal selection is carried on at wine colleges around the world and may produce a collection of super-vines from noble varieties that will raise quality and yield wherever they are grown. California is the first major wine-producing area to grow them in quantity, so wines produced from them are attracting attention—and gaining favor—around the world. With their foundation blocks, skilled growers like Concannon may be ushering in a golden age of wines.

Both families live in a compound of houses and winery at the vineyard, but they do get away now and then, especially for duck hunting. They have a famous marinade for roast duck—equal parts of soy sauce, vermouth and red wine, preferably Petite Sirah—the same wine they serve with the duck. Because the families are large and friends numerous, the Concannons occasionally do special bottlings in magnums, a few of which get out to the trade. Optimum production is around 50,000 cases of about a dozen wines, with no plans for expansion.

Monterey: New Fields to Conquer

Plantings during the Seventies by wineries based elsewhere made Monterey a major district. New plantings may make it the biggest premium wine producer in California. The largest of them with headquarters in the valley is Monterey Vineyards.

Monterey Vineyards. Ten thousand acres of noble vines were set out early in the Seventies, variously owned by individuals and companies who agreed to supply the new winery with grapes. It was soon discovered that there were too many grapes for the new winery, so a large portion of the yield is now sold to others. The winery, a separate company, is under the direction of Dr. Richard Peterson, who got his doctorate at Davis, worked several years at Gallo, then took over the winemaking at Beaulieu Vineyards as Andre Tschelistcheff neared retirement. The challenge of a new region was great and Peterson couldn't resist.

As the grapes have come to bearing, they have built up a following. The whites have been well-made; the reds have been light, as can be expected from young grapes. This is appealing because they can be drunk young and are simple in taste. The problem is that there are so many of them. A major effort is being made to widen the market. If pressure to sell is strong enough, the prices may continue low.

Chalone. Some of the most interesting wines of Monterey come from vineyards on a limestone outcropping two thousand feet up in the Gavilan mountains east of Soledad near the Pinnacles. Soil has eroded in the national monument, leaving towers and twists of rock that was once a bandit hideout and is now a playground for rock climbers. Chalone Vineyards is making exceptional Pinot Noir and Chardonnay in a climate warmer than the valley. Three of the brothers Graff, in partnership with Philip Woodward and John McQueen, produce some 10,000 cases of wines from 125 acres of vineyard planted in Burgundy grapes and Chenin Blanc, plus purchases of French Colombard and some others. Whites are fermented in small cooperage, which helps their French Colombard to be one of the best California wines at around three dollars; their Pinot Noir is easily California's best although cost is around ten dollars and competition will come from maturing Monterey Pinots early in the Eighties.

Richard Graff believes the soil and the milder climate make the difference in Chalone wines, as do the traditional practices that follow those of Burgundy. Even though the milder climate requires addition of acids to the fermenting juice, shorter days mean variations in grape development; such changes, and others, make the wines easily distinguishable from Burgundies. Chalone makes good wines in their circumstances, as do others elsewhere; Burgundians have had more practice and a longer experience to draw on, good winemakers there producing wines of greater subtlety than most of those from California. Price for price, comparisons find bottles of similar excellence in both areas. And so goes the judgment, grape variety by grape variety.

Callaway Vineyards. Southern California has been full of grapes since the earliest days, the largest plantings being in the Cucamonga Valley, a desert east of Los Angeles where an Italian from the Piedmont, Secondo Guasti, found underground water and started things off by planting eight square miles of grapes in a hundred varieties. His company was IVC, the Italian Vineyard Company, headquartered in a town he named Guasti, and he attracted Captain Paul Garrett, who planted 2,000 acres for his Virginia Dare. Others went into neighboring counties, San Bernardino and the rest, but the main survivor was Brookside Vineyard Company in Guasti, owned by the Biane family, which produced bulk wines and inexpensive ones, and became part of Beatrice Foods of Chicago in the Seventies. Scions of the Biane family turned further east, to Rancho California.

176

Temecula is a high mesa in southeast Riverside County, a development of sixty square miles divided into ranches around a man-made lake, some developed for cattle, horses and sheep, others for avocado and citrus groves—and grapes. Another section, even larger, awaits development.

Still further east is the Salton Sea, surrounded by a desert whose hot updrafts pull Pacific winds across the mesa. Indians called it the land where sun shines through, and the misty air is cool at night, not too sweltering during the day. Ely Callaway took over 135 acres of vineyard at the suggestion of the Bianes, who had planted several 40-acre and larger plots for themselves and others.

Callaway, the retired president of Burlington Mills, proceeded to establish a model winery that could set grapes to ferment scarcely an hour after picking. Five years after the plantings he put three whites of his '74 vintage on the market, subsequently offering Cabernet, Zinfandel and Petite Sirah. The early vintages were made by Karl Werner, the former winemaster of Schloss Vollrads in the Rheingau, using German yeasts, and the Riesling, Sauvignon and Chenin Blanc caused a sensation. The fact that they were balanced and more-than-drinkable, from an area once considered too hot for noble vines, was enough to open the New York market. The wines are generally soft and light.

177

Valley of the Giants: The Sacramento and San Joaquin

California wines are good because the Great Central Valley is so hot. The sun beats down on the four hundred miles of flatland between the Sierras and the coast ranges, forming updrafts that pull cool Pacific air through the Golden Gate and through coastal valleys, tempering them. Some tempering occurs in the middle of the great valley, where the Sacramento flowing south meets the San Joaquin flowing north; their joining forms a delta maze that empties into the top of San Francisco Bay.

Streams that feed the rivers fail to water the land enough, but a vast irrigation system fed by Sierra melt turns it into some of the richest land on earth. Vast orchards share ground with fields of flowers grown for seed, vegetables, vineyards. Two bottles of every three California wines come from the Great Central Valley.

Sacramento and adjoining counties in the upper half of the valley do not attract the giants because vineyards in the Sierra foothills must go into small pockets of land in the Mother Lode country. Wineries like Torre and Gold Hill and D'Agostini may be sending bottles around in the Eighties, but most of the grapes go to other wineries. In the delta country over west a few thousand acres of good grapes do the same.

The main center of interest is west of Sacramento at Davis, where the wine college has been training winemakers and experimenting with vines ever since it was moved from Berkeley after Repeal.

179

The Davis campus of the University of California has its own winery and distillery, as well as a 140-acre vineyard planted with a thousand of the named-grape varieties and a hundred thousand crosses produced from them in an experimental program begun by Dr. Harold Olmo in 1933. Promising crosses are tested in experimental vineyards in Napa and Fresno.

Much effort has been spent producing noble vines free of disease, starting with a single bud, or clone. These are grown in a heated environment for a few weeks, growth proceeding faster than any viruses that may be in the plant; cuttings certified to be free of disease are then planted in a foundation block in the college vineyard. Cuttings from these vines are then planted in mother blocks in the experimental vineyards and cuttings from them go into increase blocks at private vineyards like Louis Martini's and Concannon's and into nurseries. Vineyards are planted with cuttings from the increase blocks.

Cuttings and clones are exchanged with other wine colleges around the world, Geisenheim and Montpellier, for example. Students are exchanged, as well, widening the fraternity of winemakers and vine growers.

The program of certification began early in the Seventies. Demand could not be met. A system of hastening growth by planting cuttings in moist atmospheres in greenhouses began. Called mist propagation, a million cuttings from a single vine could be produced in a year. First sales were limited to California, but by the end of the decade they were going around the world.

Professor Eugene Hilgard, who set up the original wine college at Berkeley, hired an Englishman named Frederic Bioletti to carry on his wine studies. When the enologists moved to Davis to join the viticulturists, Albert Winkler succeeded him, followed by two of his most famous students, Maynard Joslyn and Maynard Amerine. The problem was simple: find out what makes wine taste bad. Oh yes, and while they were at it, find the best locations for noble vines, and good grapes for hot climates.

Winkler-Amerine charts eventually divided the state into five regions, based on degree-days. (Multiply the number of degrees over 50° F. each day, by the number of days in the growing season, for degree-days.) The charts guided the plantings of the Sixties and led to development of new areas like Monterey and Santa Barbara.

Joslyn-Amerine studies of controlled fermentation and maturation of wines in vat, cask and bottle changed winemaking everywhere and had the two men rushing around the world to explain their findings and coordinate them with those of Montpellier, Geisenheim, Conegliano and others.

Research was carried on mostly for the benefit of that half of the valley south of Sacramento, the San Joaquin. There giants dwelled, growers slowest to change because of enormous investment in what they had. The wine boom stirred them.

With the Seventies, so-called mid-varietals went in. Ruby Cabernet, Barbera and Petite Sirah joined Grenache and Zinfandel, which doubled. Emerald Riesling and French Colombard, even Chenin Blanc and Sémillon, were planted. There must be two hundred square miles of the new grapes, with another hundred to be ready by the Eighties, at least partly because replantings can be designed for mechanical harvesting. Wine grapes account for a third of those grown.

The least hot area of the San Joaquin is in the northern part of the county that takes its name, centered around Lodi, which is surrounded by fifty square miles of vineyard extending north to the state capital and down to Elk Grove. Lodi-Sacramento is a region to itself, dominated by the Flame Tokay and Guild, a cooperative with a thousand members. Flame Tokay is a handsome grape that reddens in local vineyards but not elsewhere. A reddish fortified wine called Tokay is no relation, usually being a blend of California sherry and port. There are thirty square miles of Flame Tokay and twenty of wine grapes, more of Zinfandel and Carignane than anywhere. More than a score of wineries and a dozen distilleries make brandies and fortified wines and the rest, but most of it goes to the giants.

Guild. There was much consolidation among the wineries after Repeal. Guild operates six wineries, including a vast new one in Lodi, with a tasting center that boasts a walkabout plot where samples of most California vines are planted. Labels include Roma, Cribari, and their famous Vino da Tavola, first of the mellow wines. Their most prestigious line is Cresta Blanca, a separate company that crushes grapes of its North Coast members in the Mendocino winery.

Of the small wineries offering wines, one is famous for vinegar. Barengo Vineyards was bought by Dino Barengo from the Mondavis when they moved to Charles Krug. It was called Acampo; Barengo made a popular

Ruby Cabernet. He sold the place to Winkler/Scheid Vineyards, who own five square miles in Monterey, contracted to Almadén. W/S sold it to an entrepreneur with a square mile of grapes near Fresno. His name is Kirkorian. Barengo stayed on to make the wines. Thus are wineries shuffled around, not to mention grapes.

The East-Side Winery on the east side of town is a cooperative with some four score members, offering wines with grape names under its Royal Host label.

The Escalon-Modesto section below Lodi is predominately planted in Grenache, along with other recommended warm-weather grapes. Wineries like Sam-Jasper, with its Delicato Cellar; Bella Napoli, founded by a Neapolitan who changed his name from Antonio Cappello to Tony Hat; and Cadlolo all market some wines but sell mostly to the giants. So do smaller wineries like Oakdale and Pirrone.

The area is dominated by Franzia, now owned by Coca Cola Bottlers of New York, which markets low-priced wines under many labels, which can be identified by their mailing address of Ripon. Family members continue the operation of the firm. Three of the Franzia clan, Fred, Joseph and John, Jr., have set up a new winery, Bronco Wine Company, with various labels, most of them on inexpensive wines.

Near Franzia is the United Vintners complex consolidated by Louis Petri, which included such well-known firms as Mission Bell, Gambarelli & Davitto (marketed as G & D), and Italian Swiss Colony. He combined this with the giant Allied Grape Growers cooperative, making United Vintners the selling arm, and then sold the lot, including all the labels, to Heublein. The courts stepped in, claiming that this was in the nature of a monopoly or restraint of trade, or what not, and the case may be in the courts for years. With Gallo in Modesto looming large, there is room for argument.

E. & J. Gallo Winery. Gallo has been the strongest influence on wines since Pasteur or perhaps the phylloxera, take your choice. It is the largest winery on earth, and the best, in a country where consumption is low. One bottle of every three we drink comes from Gallo. Gallo is a family winery.

The two brothers made their first batch of wine right after Repeal in a rented warehouse in Modesto and by 1935 had their first winery—on Dry

Creek. They made the cheap reds and fortified sweets common to the valley, getting rid of the woodiness and off-tastes as they went along, obviously supplying exactly what people wanted because they grew and grew and grew.

Ernest was outside, in the market, Julio was outside, in the vineyards, and their children fitted in wherever needed. They were quoted as saying they wanted to be the Campbell's Soup of the wine industry, but obviously they intended to be Heinz and General Foods as well. They trained the toughest and shrewdest salesmen around, graduates who are running half the wineries today, and sometimes it seems that every winemaker in the business passed through Gallo somewhere along the way. The laboratory is the best there is; scarcely a wine made anywhere is not tested by Gallo, and research into taste and techniques is as intense as in any three wine colleges you care to name. None of this hampers the Gallos, who may not fly by the seat of their pants, but depend on what they taste in the glass and their sense of what people want in a bottle. After all, the only thing they really have to do is look at their sales charts. Nobody else can. Nobody else really knows how many carloads Gallo sells of how many different brands in how many markets. It's a private company, strictly a family affair.

They own 10,000 acres of vineyards, it is said, and probably more. They buy all the production of the two largest Napa Valley cooperatives and other large ones throughout the North coast counties, and probably process more North Coast wine than anybody. All the production comes from more than 150 square miles of vineyard. When their apple wines took off, it was said that they were the world's largest users of apples. Legends are as large as sales.

There was a question whether green or brown glass bottles were best for wine. Gallo tests showed a brown-green glass was best. When nobody would produce it they built their own glass works. Just as well. Louis Petri had built a tankship so wines could be sailed to Atlantic ports for bottling, saving enough on shipping to give him a few cents' edge on every bottle. Gallo blunted this by devising a lightweight bottle.

Aperitifs were a segment of the market nobody paid much attention to, leaving it to the likes of Dubonnet and the Italian vermouth firms. Gallo started with Thunderbird in 1957, progressed to one with soda pop bubbles in 1960. They called it Ripple. These first pop wines gave way to Cold Duck, which put Gallo into Concords and experiment with other native grapes and hybrids. These are labeled American, not California, wines because grapes from other states are used; but if the label says it comes from Modesto you can be sure it comes from Gallo.

Alcohol did not seem to matter so much in pop wines so the Gallos tried some at 11%. There was Spañada, to horn in on the Sangria craze, and Boone's Farm apple wine for those who maybe didn't like Concord or even wine but liked a little fizz.

That worked, so maybe 9% was better. Along came Strawberry Hill, apple wine with strawberry, and Wild Mountain, of Concord. Wine has to be 10% in California to be legal, so the Gallos didn't even bother calling it wine. At one point, there was Pear Ripple and Pagan Pink, tasty with passion fruit, at 10%, along with Red Ripple at 11%. We have noted what they did with rosé.

The effect of this was worldwide. Sangria had taken off from the Spanish Pavillion at New York's world fair in the early Sixties, pushed along in Gallo fashion by the Feinberg brothers and their importing firm, Monsieur Henri. (This is now owned by Pepsico who bought it to get Pepsi-Cola into Russia in exchange for marketing Russian wines here.) Portuguese rosé had a good start but Gallo's launching of pop wines gave it a further push. Italy came in with Lambrusco. Liebfraumilch followed Gallo into radio and TV advertising and sales soared. Gallo had no intention of pointing the way, but there is no doubt they did; Europe's pop wines amount to 80% of imports.

The only wines Gallo has never bothered about were the high-priced premiums. This offended drinkers of traditional table wines, who had the odd idea that only good table wines—and maybe a little Champagne, Sherry and Port—were all that counted. They scorned Gallo, perhaps upset at being ignored. Gallo used North Coast wines for blends, practically a crime, and sold millions of gallons of Chablis, even Pink Chablis (holy cats, what next?), Burgundy, Rhine and something called Sauterne (without the *s*, you notice!), and don't even mention Red Rose. Then they came along with Hearty Burgundy, which fooled just about everybody in blind tastings, which scarcely seemed fair. Oh, yes, you got tired of it after a few jugs, but what else could you get for $1.69? What Gallo made was simply not table wine. Summer of 1977 arrived and so did Ernest & Julio Gallo Varietals. Barbera was the prize of the lot of eight, at $1.99 in New York.

What will happen when all the giant producers, perhaps none of them as dedicated as Gallo because they are corporations, begin marketing Chardonnay and Cabernet and the rest? Many of them have been planted in the San Joaquin, where they don't belong. An innocent getting the word that Cabernet is good may buy a bottle from valley grapes and find it poor. All the grape names, taught to the public at vast expense for decades, are they all to be bastardized?

Maybe. Then you have to do what the Gallos do. Taste the wine in the glass and use good sense. That's what wine is all about. Ernest and Julio are educating palates all over the world, which was not what they had in mind at all. They had the simple idea of selling wines.

Whoever said that fine wine was just for the table, with Sherry before the meal and Port after, with Champagne for celebration? Whoever said simple country wines from the oak were the perfect drinks, with or without bread and cheese? That was only part of the drinking world. Wines had entered the world of thirst with vermouths and aperitifs. What about the beer world? Beer companies began making fruit wines to compete with Gallo. When Gallo entered the soda-pop universe, soft-drink makers entered the wine world. What about the hamburg–hot-dog–fast-fry stratum, the bar and cocktail crowds? Wine was everything to a few. Why shouldn't wines be something to all? The Gallos don't put fences around their wines, which are for anybody, anywhere, anytime. The English made the old worlds of wine because they were the market. Gallo is making a new one for every market. Let the carloads roll.

* * *

Fresno is the center of what Californians call agribusiness, headquarters of farming corporations that measure plantings in miles. Counties to the south—Kings, Tulare and Kern—form a district with Fresno and Madera to the north, and here the only fine wine is Ficklin Port.

Fresno State, once devoted mostly to wine business but now with full programs in vine tending and winemaking, trains students who will add to the list. One of them, Dale Landis, bought the best grapes of fellow students and made good Ruby Cabernet and Zinfandel, but for this, as for the other twenty-odd wineries, bottlings are available when you are there.

Down in Tulare, California Growers Winery bottles a range of wines from the new plantings. In Kern, California Wine Association bottles many labels, including Eleven Cellars wines and two famous brandies, Aristocrat and A. R. Morrow. CWA was once a huge conglomerate that eventually dwindled, the brands becoming property of Perelli-Minetti. Sons of the founder run the firm. They are marketing wine from a patented grape developed by Antonio Perelli, who liked to wander around vineyards and take seeds from grapes that looked promising. His "101" is planted on half a square mile and the firm refuses to sell cuttings from it, preferring to have the varietal exclusively.

Further south is the Bear Mountain Winery, a cooperative of one hundred growers with many noble varieties and others. Their main brand is M. Lamont, and like many other valley firms they bottle for private labels of distributors and wholesalers. Wines from them can be identified by the postal addresses of Arvin or Lamont.

There are new vineyards and replantings everywhere in the San Joaquin and there are certain to be new labels. The wines have yet to prove themselves of more than casual interest, and that only because of price. The wines are mostly bland and lightly sweet, but bottles of a new breed are appearing on the market, fairly dry, pleasant enough. Let's see, wines light in alcohol are already being made. Now if they were higher in acid and fresh, made to be drunk within weeks of the making . . .

You may be sure that the wines of the future are going to be of the sort that sell. All of them will be, likely, imitations of Gallo. But maybe not.

Part III:
Native Vines and Country Wines

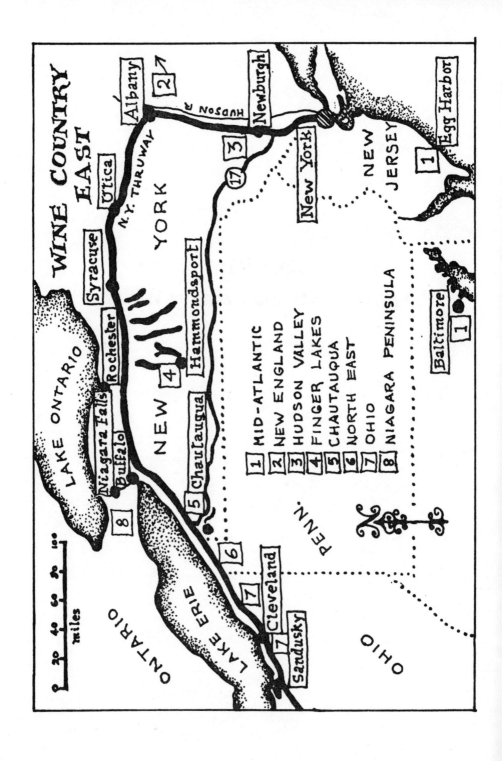

WINE COUNTRY EAST

ONTARIO

LAKE ONTARIO

LAKE ERIE

OHIO

NEW YORK

PENN.

NEW JERSEY

Sandusky
Cleveland
Niagara Falls
Buffalo
Rochester
Syracuse
Utica
Albany
Newburgh
New York
Hammondsport
Chautauqua
Baltimore
Egg Harbor

HUDSON R.

N.Y. THRUWAY

miles
20 40 60 80 100

17

7
7
8
4
5
6
3
2
1
1

1 MID-ATLANTIC
2 NEW ENGLAND
3 HUDSON VALLEY
4 FINGER LAKES
5 CHAUTAUQUA
6 NORTH EAST
7 OHIO
8 NIAGARA PENINSULA

The East and Elsewhere

"The problem is marketing," declared the chairman of the board. "Your average wine shop has room for five or six premium American brands. There's Paul Masson in California, The Christian Brothers and Almadén. There's Taylor here in New York and Widmer's. Then there are the medium-sized premium producers like Beaulieu Vineyards, Louis Martini, Robert Mondavi in Napa; Sebastiani, Korbel, Geyser Peak in Sonoma; and you might add Monterey or Mirassou from south of San Francisco—all seeking that sixth place. And think of some of the fairly large wineries like Souverain or Parducci or San Martin, or Ste. Michelle in Washington. These wines have to fight for shelf space with imports and with the giant California wineries who are beginning to market wines with premium names. If you can't get on the shelves you can't sell."

There was Pillsbury Flour that moved in and out, Coca Cola running Taylor, Sterling and Monterey, the various brewers and importers and conglomerates that had taken over wineries and vineyards.

"There are a hundred small wineries getting their wines around. A retailer may put in a few, the way he puts in Burgundy or Bordeaux or Rhine wines. If they don't move he stops buying. And who can keep track? How many will take a chance on a high-priced Cabernet or Char-

189

donnay or Riesling that's never been heard of? How many Zinfandels can a store stock? Maybe the Europeans have lost the market to the little wineries because importers are concentrating on novelties that can be marketed all over the country. How many importers are going to bother with a few thousand cases of eight-dollar Burgundies or Bordeaux regionals like St. Emilion or Médoc? They're going to disappear.''

Maybe the cold hand of marketing is going to shrink the number of wines available, squeezing out the small and good.

NATIVE GRAPES: LABRUSCA AND COMPANIONS

Nature held things back in the past. There were plenty of grapes growing wild.

There was *riparia,* which grew on the banks of the Saint Lawrence and along rivers into the deep south. There was *labrusca,* called the fox grape because of its taste, with the same range, and there was the sand grape of the lower Mississippi basin, *rupestris,* reaching north to Illinois and west to central Texas. There was the summer grape, *aestivalis,* along the Atlantic seaboard, and a larger version, the Post Oak grape, in the southwest, and the Spanish grape of Texas, *berlandieri.* There were the Muscadines of the South, the most spectacular being the Scuppernong. None of them made good wines.

The grapes of Europe were brought in, all of the species *vinifera.* Scientists say this originated in the Caucasus; others insist it was in the Garden of Eden. It wouldn't grow in the New World. Not until the middle of this century was a way found to make it survive eastern winters, and at the same time, crosses of *vinifera* with native grapes began to produce good wines. The French call these crosses American hybrids and Americans call them French hybrids, and to evade the issue they are called French-American vines. With luck, and a chance at the market, they will replace Concords.

New York: Concords, Kosher and Hybrids

The best wines of New York's three main wine regions come from some of its smallest wineries; Benmarl Vineyards on the Hudson, Bully Hill Vineyards and Vinifera Wine Cellars in the Finger Lakes region in the center of the state, and Johnson Vineyards Winery in Chautauqua, the western county bordering Lake Erie. There is another region being heard from, the eastern end of Long Island, where Hargrave Vineyard markets Cabernet Sauvignon and Pinot Noir, Chardonnay and Sauvignon Blanc. There are others coming up.

Wines have been made along the Atlantic seaboard for a thousand years, starting with Lief Ericson's crew. Vines have grown there ever since the glaciers receded. Wine was made in all the early settlements and all of it had a strong, musky taste—like the reek of a startled skunk, the stench of fox. European vines died off when planted, but crosses made with native vines grew, producing wines with less of what was called a foxy taste, although still strange. There were dozens of them; perhaps the best was Delaware, which makes a perfumed white wine, good for blending. Whites like Dutchess, Isabella, Missouri Riesling, Niagara and Noah are still useful in blends, as are reds like Ives, Cynthiana and Delicatessen. Then there's Catawba and Concord.

The Catawba takes its name from a river in North Carolina's Buncombe County, on whose banks it was discovered in 1802. The county

191

gave its name to high-flown tall talk because a Congressman indulged in it to impress his constituency. Sparkling Catawba inspired Longfellow to write the worst verse on wine in English, after tasting a bottle sent him by Nicholas Longworth, the Ohio millionaire who made it:

> Very good in its way
> Is the Verzenay,
> Or the Sillery, soft and creamy;
> But Catawba wine
> Has a taste more divine,
> More dulcet, delicious, and dreamy.

The verse has the same treacly fascination as the wine, cloying and feral, which even a few misguided Londoners ranked above Champagne. Today's Catawbas are less startling, being blended.

The most popular grape of all was Concord, named after the town near Boston where Ephraim Bull selected it from a group of Labrusca seeds he had planted. Grape seeds do not breed true, for grapes are self-pollinating, their flowers containing both male and female components. Vine cuttings are needed to produce grapes true to those from the parent vine and Bull offered his at five dollars per cutting. Nurserymen produced their own and he died in the Concord poorhouse in 1895. His epitaph reads, "He sowed, but others reaped."

What others reaped is awesome. Concords dominate vineyard regions in the Northeast, the Northwest and most places in between. A prohibitionistic dentist named Welch read Pasteur's experiments about heating wine and it occurred to him that you could heat grape juice before it became wine and make a non-alcholic beverage, wholesome enough for babes. He founded Vineland near Atlantic City in New Jersey in 1868 and two years later he and his son Charles offered "Dr. Welch's Unfermented Wine" to churches for communion. The grapes died, so he moved to the New York Finger Lakes and set out Concords, moving on to Chautauqua to do the same, then south to Pennsylvania, north to Michigan and west to Washington. The Welches set up plants everywhere, eventually selling out to the National Grape Cooperative, also known as Welch Foods. For generations, children have known the taste of grape juice as that of Welch's, and the taste of Welch is Concord.

Perhaps thinking along those lines, a New York bottler named Leo

Star, who had founded Monarch Wine Company to make fortified wines, devised a syrupy kosher wine from Concords for Passover. He called it Mount Zebo and sold some in 1934, but much of it was returned after Passover. The following year, he refused to take returns and what was left over sold quickly to non-Jewish buyers. Star then decided the fact that the wine was kosher accounted for its appeal. In the Jewish religion, *kosher* means that the product is clean, natural and unadulterated, made under the supervision of a rabbi. He went to a maker of kosher foods with the idea of using its name on the label; a licensing agreement was worked out; and Manischewitz Kosher Wine was born.

A Chicago bottler, Wine Corporation of America, had a similar Passover wine they called Mogen David, meaning the shield of David, and when something went bad with their other stocks, they decided to concentrate on their sweet kosher blend, calling it "the wine like Grandma used to make."

The success of Manischewitz and Mogen David caused everybody to start pushing sweet Concord, producing a new category the trade called kosher wine. This caused confusion; the public thought all kosher wine was sweet Concord, when the fact is that any wine made naturally and without adulteration can be certified as kosher by a rabbi, as are the Cabernets and Sauvignons from Israel, marketed here under the Carmel label.

The next great spurt for Concord came when a Michigan restaurateur carbonated some lightly sweet Concord wine and called it Cold Duck. This had a great vogue in the Sixties, now waning, although there are still dozens of versions on the market.

The trouble with Concord was that it made poor table wine, strongly foxy when made to be dry. It was as bad, if not worse, than any of those made from native grapes. The native grapes, by the twentieth century, were all crosses of various native stocks, of little interest to anybody used to European bottlings. Something else was needed.

This was provided by an editor for the *Baltimore Sun*, who made wines and repaired violins for hobbies. He didn't like wines from Labrusca and in the Thirties he began planting French hybrids. These were vinifera varieties crossed with American vines.

The noble vines are tender plants, susceptible to cold and disease. They are also shy bearers, at their best when only a few bunches come from each vine. To produce hardier vines with bigger yields the French imported American vines and began experimenting with them. These vines bore on their roots a louse that did not affect them but destroyed vinifera. It was the phylloxera, which devastated all the European vineyards. The only cure was grafting, and in Europe today all vines are grafted to American root stocks.

Crosses of vinifera and American vines—thousands were made—rarely produce superior wines by themselves, but some of them make wines good for blending. Philip M. Wagner began planting all he could find in his Boordy Vineyard in the Maryland suburbs. One after another proved to be better than the native vines. Discerning growers began putting them in eastern vineyards, replacing Concords and the other native grapes. They will be dominant in eastern vineyards by the Eighties.

Experiment continues with French-American crosses at the Enological Experiment Station in Geneva, north of the Finger Lakes.

"We can make white wines as good as any in the country," says Robert M. Pool, who graduated from Davis, got his doctorate at Cornell, and is in charge of grape breeding. "The hybrids lend themselves to blending. The varietal concept has been oversold. I've got the best job in the world. It's exciting. We're making new wines."

Marvels can be made. Early hybrids were crosses of two varieties, like Müller-Thurgau, which is named after the man who crossed Riesling with Sylvaner to produce a soft wine low in acid that can be dull but quite refreshing when drunk soon after the vintage. Crosses may emphasize bad characteristics—these are discarded—and years can pass before a good one is found. The good ones are crossed with others—each is numbered and named after the man who did the crossing—and after decades exciting wines are being made. One of these is Cayuga White, which was a hit at a tasting for the press of all New York wines, held in 1976. It was light, crisp, well-balanced, with a delicate aroma and fruity taste. "We've got bigger and better wines than that," declares Pool.

Even though trained in California, Pool is really not concerned with bigger—only better. Geneva Station issued a twenty-five-year summary in 1976, covering vineyard and cellar notes through 1973, and the vines and wines since then are proving better. Not until the Eighties, though, will people become convinced that hybrid blends can rank with California Chardonnays and Sauvignons.

"Marketing is the problem," says director W. B. Robinson. "The world glut of wines in the first half of the Seventies made it hard for our growers to sell their hybrids to the wineries. It is temporary, but how can we urge growers to plant more hybrids when the market is slow for those they have? Cayuga White has to compete with all the other whites and nobody knows about it."

What about the foxy taste? Nobody knows what it is. For years it was taken to be methyl anthranilate, but by using chromatography a young winemaker trained at Davis named Richard Nelson has found that grapes without the compound produce foxy wines. Hot after it, Nelson is sure they can find out what makes a wine foxy and eliminate it, any year now. When they do, grape growing around the world will be revolutionized— again.

As for the vines, the trick is to get a good one on a root stock that will produce enough bunches and no more. A vine producing too many bunches results in poor wines. Geneva research associate Keith Kimball claims to have the best vineyard in the state, but all six acres are in root stocks, dozens of them, to find just the right one for every grape variety to suit every soil in which they may be planted. "Not enough work has been done on root stocks," says Kimball firmly. Quite likely.

A vine takes three years to bear—you cannot expect to get really good grapes until the vine is twice as old—and then you have to make wines over two or three years to get your fermentation right; and then the wine may need a year or so to age, maybe longer. A decade may be needed. Before that, of course, you would have had to find the right vine and match it to the right root stock. Experiment in hybrids really began in the first decades of this century, was interrupted by depression and war, finally brought results in the last couple of decades. The marvels are to come.

Already there is the root stock called Couderc 3309. And there is a list of hybrids in the hundreds, some thirty of which have been given names. Of these, the ones to look for are

WHITES

AURORA: Fresh, distinctive bouquet, ranging from soft to tart, but clean and fruity. Originally Seibel 5279.

CAYUGA WHITE: Clean and fruity, light perfume, often tart and fine. Developed at Geneva by crossing a Seyval with Schuyler, numbered NY 33403 GW 3.

RAVAT BLANC: Once considered the best of whites, this Chardonnay cross has a light aroma, high acid and occasional harshness. Originally Ravat 6.

SEYVAL: Fruity with good bouquet and body, considered to have superior sugar-acid balance. Originally Seyve-Villard 5-276.

VALERIEN: Fruity and well-balanced, with good body. Originally Seyve-Villard 23-410.

NOTE: The New York cross of Pinot Blanc and Aurore, numbered 44968, has good body, high acid and ranges from fruity to flowery. There are at least a dozen others, seeming to indicate that white wines will and should predominate in New York and neighboring states. Pool has high hopes for Vidal 256, which is a cross from Ugni Blanc, Ravat 34 and Ravat 51, which is a Pinot cross called Vignobles.

REDS

BACO NOIR: A fresh, light wine, the first of the crosses to be bottled; its claretlike quality has a distinctive spicy aroma. Derived from Folle Blanche, it has good acidity and develops some with age. Originally called Baco Number 1.

MARECHAL FOCH: Straightforward wine with a fruity smell and taste, tart but generally well balanced with good tannin. A cross of Pinot Noir and Gamay developed in Alsace, it ripens early. Originally Kuhlmann 188-2.

CHANCELLOR: A dark, full-bodied wine, tending to be low in acid, sound and simple. Heavy producer planted widely in southern France. Originally Seibel 7053.

DE CHAUNAC: Dark in color, full in body because of tannin, but lightly fruity. Originally Seibel 9549.

CHELOIS: A berry smell and taste, light but tart. Originally Seibel 10878.

NOTE: There are more than 150 crosses detailed in the report from Geneva Station, and good ones seem to be: Seyve-Villard 19-307, full-bodied and fruity; Seibel 14117, which is similar but more tart; and tannic Seibel 8355. Pool says ones to look for are Castel 19637, Leon Millot, Seibel Nero and Landot 4511.

All the grand bottles glisten in the imagination, fragrant young whites with new tastes, not strange ones. It's California in the Fifties, all over again. Amateurs did it in California, wine lovers, for the fun of it. The East needs more amateurs.

The wild wines from native grapes still hold a fascination. Their tastes suit native dishes—clambakes and chowders, country hams and farmer's sausage, gumbos and crab cakes—and recipes from the old country changed by settlers in a new land— corned beef and pastrami, finnan haddie, curries, sweet and sours, boiled lobster, smoked salmon. The new wines will suit them, too, widening the range.

Marketing may wipe them out, with the big companies making blends like the old ones, leaving no room for new wines appealing to a new generation. But big companies are slow. Long ago, a winemaker would hang a bush above his door to signify that the new vintage was ready. The saying was that good wines need no bush. Maybe customers will find the new wines before they are lost in the big blends.

THE HUDSON VALLEY

The Dutch planted grapes almost as soon as they bought Manhattan but their hearts weren't in it. They even turned away from pohickory, which the Indians made by mashing the hickory nuts on Governors Island and letting them ferment. What they liked was the product of the Staten Island distillery set up by the director of the colony, Wilhelm Kieft, in 1640, where corn and rye were mashed and boiled to make whiskey, the first in the New World. There was rum; later there was gin; and it wasn't until the Huguenots settled on the Hudson highlands in the 1660s that much wine was made. The French Protestants were not happy with their first wines from the native grapes, but it was better than whistle-belly-vengeance, made by boiling beer with molasses and throwing in bread crumbs; or bogus, which was rum and beer mixed.

The French persevered around New Palz. In the second quarter of the nineteenth century one Jean Jacques made wine good enough to sell to his

197

church in Washingtonville. He called his vineyard Blooming Grove, and when a cult called the Brotherhood of the New Life started a vineyard in Amenia, two brothers named Emerson who were New York wine merchants blended the wines and developed a substantial market. Eventually, they bought both establishments, which continue today as Brotherhood Winery, making mostly sweet wines and some dry ones from native grapes and hybrids. It is the oldest winery in the country. One of the Emerson brothers, Edward R., wrote several books about wine; one, a laborious and hilarious claptrap of drink called *Beverages Past and Present*, compiled from earlier random sources, was published in 1908 and can still be found in libraries and secondhand bookstores.

The first commercial winery was in Westchester, at Croton Point, established by a New York doctor infatuated with wine, Richard Underhill, in 1829. The winery languished when young members of the family went west—to the Finger Lakes.

The first modern winery to become known was High Tor, started in the Fifties by a transplanted California playwright named Everett Crosby. Friends used to help pick the grapes, the first from hybrids available in New York, where they had a vogue. Crosby sold the small vineyard in 1971 to Richard Voigt, who owns a chain of Peppermill Restaurants in Connecticut, the only places where the wines are now available. The wines were from old vines, skillfully made by an Episcopalian priest, Father Thomas Lee Hayes. The hybrids are now blended with a few vinifera grapes planted at High Tor.

The most distinguished winery on the Hudson is Benmarl, in a hilltop vineyard above the town of Marlboro, planted after the Civil War by Andrew J. Caywood, who developed the Dutchess grape. Mark Miller pulled out the few that were left when he found the vineyard in 1956, replanting in hybrids and test plots of vinifera, especially Chardonnay. Miller is a skilled illustrator who moved to Burgundy after the war to be near the expanding market for magazine illustrations in Europe, at a time when American magazines were turning to photography, and there he became hopelessly enamored of wines and learned how to make them. He came back to New York to find a vineyard, and after he had planted a dozen acres, he realized he would need help. He thought of the idea of selling vine rights to individuals: by becoming a member of his Societé des Vignerons, you would be entitled to the production from two vines—a case or so—and you could help with the vintage and picnic on the winery

198

grounds, drinking your own wine and gazing down at the majestic Hudson, looking for all the world like some of the better sections of the Rhine.

The wines were different, though, as beguiling, if not so grand. His Baco Noir may be the best in the state—others opt for the Chardonnay and Seyval Blanc—but consistently attractive are his Blanc Domaine, Rouge Domaine and Rose Domaine.

Also in the area is the Hudson Valley Wine Company, bought by members of the Feinberg family when they sold Monsieur Henri to Pepsico. There were 200 acres of old vines, and replanting to hybrids and vinifera began, mostly to improve the blends of the low-priced wines.

There are some kosher wine producers, Royal Wine Corporation and Marlboro Industries; Mandia Champagne Cellars produces some table wines, as do the others.

Cascade Mountain Vineyards offers a quickly fermented red from Leon Millot. Others are starting operation.

There are several amateur growers, among them Tom Clarke, who began with a plot of Chardonnay in Connecticut. In Marlboro he has enough Riesling, Chardonnay and hybrids to open his own winery, but he prefers to make wine for himself and friends and to sell some grapes to other amateurs.

THE FINGER LAKES

Boats used to be the only way to travel on the long lakes gouged by glaciers in the center of the state—on a map they look like the clawing of the bears that once roamed there. Some of the old landings and docks can still be seen where the pickle boats chugged in with supplies for cottagers and farmers, where excursion steamers landed vacationers at gingerbread hotels. Varnished launches carried picnickers; cargo boats hauled grain and lumber, fruit and wines to the towns that spread out into the rolling farm country at each end. Steep slopes, practically mountains, thick with trees and brush, noisy with brooks, hemmed in the lakes, many of them scarcely a mile wide. Vines went into the high meadows after the first cuttings flourished in the rectory garden in Hammondsport. Reverend Bostwick got his vines from the Hudson Valley, figuring the lake would hold off frost and temper winter cold. That was in 1829 and when the Civil War ended, several wineries began to make sparkling wines from the native

199

grapes. The first of these was the Pleasant Valley Wine Company, which blended Delaware with Catawba, the result being so pleasing that a Bostonian claimed it would be the greatest in the west, the west being anything beyond the Hudson. The wine was dubbed Great Western; the company changed its name to that of the wine; and in 1873 Great Western became the first American sparkling wine to win a European gold medal—at the Vienna Exposition. The wine was called Champagne, of course, and a post office called Rheims was set up in the winery to further the deception. This was a departure, because New Yorkers preferred to give their towns Greek or Roman names, like Naples on Keuka Lake, or Ithaca at the foot of Cayuga Lake. But, then, there was Geneva at the head of Seneca Lake, to honor the Swiss settlers, so Rheims was a name worth taking. Great Western was taken over by Taylor Winery in 1961 and the name has since been used on its premium wines, particularly those sold under grape names and not with names of European regions.

Taylor Wine Company. Half a century after the first vines went in there was need for a cooper and Walter Taylor came out from the east with his bride. He bought a farm on Bully Hill, planted Ives and Delaware because they were the most popular at the time, installed his parents to help out, raised five children and watched them grow with the vines. When Prohibition came, he bought an old stone winery with a mansard roof that is now a visitor center, weathered the lull by making juice and jelly, then began the expansion that made it the largest winery outside California. The children took over the winery, and when the family bought Great Western as a Christmas present for themselves in 1961, nearly 300 growers were supplying Taylor with grapes, from as far away as Chautauqua, over on Lake Erie. The 1,000 acres of home vineyard were being replanted in hybrids and contract growers were encouraged to do the same, so that there are now more than 5,000 acres, a third hybrids, to draw from. Taylor went public to finance expansion, the first winery to do so, and grew to become the sixth largest in the land. Two of the most popular blends are Lake Country Red and White, but there are a multitude of others, including the several hybrids and sparkling wines produced under the Great Western label. The parent company of Coca Cola in Atlanta bought control in 1977, then added Sterling and Monterey Vineyards later in the year; with Manischewitz in New York and giant Franzia in the Great Central Valley of California controlled by Coca Cola Bottlers of New York, the soda-pop world combined with the wine world.

Bully Hill Vineyards. Scion of the family and namesake of the founder, Walter S. Taylor struck out for himself in 1970, setting up the family vineyard as a winery to show the world how great the wines of the Finger Lakes can be. Squabbles about natural wine had severed his relations with the parent company, for he burned with purist fever.

Walter wants to squeeze grapes and step back, declared others. Not so, said Walter, but you fool around as little as possible. Wines should be made without adding sugar to build up alcohol, or water to mute the acid taste, or wine from outside the region to change them, or chemicals to improve them. No chaptalization, amelioration, adulteration or sophistication was his creed. No misrepresentation without vexation seemed to be his motto, as he proceeded to supply the latter by declaring the various standard practices were dishonest, though legal. For a symbol on his labels he showed a woodcut of a hand raised as if signaling, STOP. It was the left hand, showing the palm, with vines growing out of the fingers, bearing grapes.

There are some 120 acres of grapes around the winery, 700 feet up above Keuka Lake, where he makes a dry and lovely Seyval Blanc, a full Baco Noir, a lighter Chelois and several others, including hybrid blends called Bully Hill Red and Bully Hill White. He refuses to call them hybrids, arguing that all grapes are crosses, preferring to call them direct producers because most of them go into the ground on their own roots. This is quibble, like his denunciation of standard practices, which become abhorrent when abused.

There is a process called ion exchange, for instance, which keeps tartrate crystals from forming on the cork or settling to the bottom of the bottle. They are harmless, actually a sign that the wine has developed properly, but wary consumers are suspicious. Walter Taylor thinks ion exchange is a terrible practice—it is unnatural handling of the wine—so he allows the crystals to form if they will. Sulphur is used everywhere in winemaking to keep unwanted bacteria from working on the wine, and Taylor uses it as he does other preservatives and manipulations, kept to a minimum, of course, but there is a feeling that his standards are arbitrary, if not cranky.

There is a steep road up to the old winery, which is a museum of tools and lore, the first wine museum in the country, expanded from a boyhood collection. And there is a good *Home Winemaker's Handbook* with drawings by Walter and text written with Richard Vine, a talented winemaker who started out at Great Western. And there is a railroad tank car up above the new winery, hauled there with great effort to flaunt the fact that the big wineries use vast quantities of out-of-state wines to improve their blends. The rebuke is gratuitous, even provoking, because state law permits the use of as much as a quarter of foreign wines, a practice common for blends in many regions and sensible when local wines lack basic qualities. Walter thinks it is wrong when you don't say so, and besides, the Finger Lakes wines are great and don't need such help. Good Bully Hill wines show he has right on his side, but do not necessarily prove all the others wrong. As always, taste tells. Bully Hill wines are not to be missed.

Gold Seal Vineyards. When your family has been involved with wines for a century, your great-grandfather being the first one to plant grapes in the Hudson Valley, you know exactly what to do when Repeal comes and you can begin making wines for everybody, not just church and pharmacy. You go to Champagne, where your three previous winemakers have come from, and ask one of the best to come and take over at Gold Seal. E. S. Underhill presented his problem to Charles Fournier, winemaker for the conservative Champagne house of Veuve Clicquot. Fournier wanted to experiment. He took the job, by so doing changing forever the making of wines in the East.

To illustrate just how much, consider the fact that his sparkling wine won the Gold Medal at the Sacramento State Fair in 1950. It was the first out-of-state wine ever to do so. This confounded the Californians so much that they limited their fairs to California wines. Twenty-five years later, feeling that their supremacy was firmly established, they opened the judging to outsiders. Charles Fournier Brut won the gold medal. Out-of-staters are no longer encouraged to enter.

When Fournier arrived in 1934, bringing along his own yeast culture from Veuve Clicquot, he tasted the wines and realized something had to be done in the vineyards. The grapes were too foxy. He sent to France for one of the Seibel whites and Ravat Blanc, amusing his complacent winegrowing neighbors, then found that Philip Wagner had a collection of hybrids in his Boordy Vineyard and began getting cuttings from him. His first Brut went to market in 1943, selling out at once, and the less hidebound of his neighbors began calling on Wagner to see what they could get. They even began taking looks at Fournier's new vineyards and asking questions.

As skilled a diplomat as he is a winemaker, Fournier calmly answered everything he was asked. In 1952 he heard about a field worker, just arrived at Geneva Station, who was going around muttering that hybrids were terrible and anybody who wasn't growing vinifera was an idiot, or even worse. The man was German, or maybe Russian, and claimed to know all about growing vinifera in cold climates, having done so in the Crimea. The Crimea runs along the western shore of the Black Sea, across from Romania. The Crimea is cold in winter. Fournier went to Geneva to see the man, name of Frank.

The Geneva staff thought Dr. Konstantin Frank was a nut, even a bit of a fraud, claiming to be a professor of both enology and viticulture, insisting vinifera was the only grape to grow, even though it had failed every time it had been tried for three hundred years. Fournier didn't think so. Frank explained how you could bury the vines against winter cold, how you left on an extra cane in case one would freeze and split. Fournier talked Underhill into trying an experimental plot.

Konstantin Frank came to Gold Seal in the spring of 1953. What was needed was root stock that stopped sending nutrients to the vine early in the fall so the bark would harden before the first freeze. The two of them, courtly Fournier and irascible Frank, went up to search the St. Lawrence valley. In the garden of a Québec convent they found some Pinot Noir that ripened enough every third year or so to provide a little wine. With the convent root stocks and California cuttings, 10 acres of Chardonnay and 10 of Riesling were planted each year.

By the early Sixties, Fournier was bottling Chardonnay, although most of it was used for his sparkling wines. Today there are some 100 acres, and Gold Seal markets ten thousand cases of Chardonnay and a thousand of Riesling to head its long list of blends. The company was taken over in 1959 by a group of investors and is now partly owned by Seagram, which markets the wines. Charles Fournier was named honorary president when he retired in 1967 but he continued to watch over the French winemakers he had installed and the vineyards he had planted, his knowledge of hybrids, vinifera and winemaking available to all.

* * *

Vinifera Wine Cellars. Konstantin Frank was born in the Crimea on Independence Day, the year before the century began. There may be something in the stars, for he celebrated the spirit of '76 every day of his life. His father was one of a group of Germans settled there by the last czar to establish vineyards, and Frank trained there, becoming a research professor in one of the institutes, then being made the director by German occupation forces. He got out after the war, put farms in production again for American occupying forces in Bavaria, and learned enough English to try his luck in America. He landed in New York in 1951 with his wife, three children and forty dollars, washed dishes until he had enough for train fare and turned up at Geneva Station one morning to get a job. Maybe it was his English, because he worked as a field hand until Charles Fournier brought him to Hammondsport in 1953.

He labored in the Gold Seal vineyards for ten years, with savings and help from friends like Fournier, slowly buying land and planting vines, licensing his own Vinifera Wine Cellars in 1965. Now there are close to 100 acres in Chardonnay and Riesling, Cabernet and Gamay, the first American plantings of Pinot Gris and many experimental vines, including Aligoté, a minor Burgundy grape that Frank believes in, the Russian Sereksia and others nobody ever heard of.

No hybrids.

His first wine was a sensation—a Riesling Trockenbeerenauslesen 1961 costing $45. Selected from dried grapes attacked by *edelfaule,* Dr. Frank liked to explain, the same noble rot of botrytis cinerea that the French called *pourriture noble,* and that was responsible for all the great Sauternes of Bordeaux. He had only a few bottles but its excellence—and price—made it the talk of the wine world. No modern American wine had ever cost so much or been so good.

Conviction triumphant, Dr. Konstantin Frank continued on his independent way, producing one fine wine after another—and keeping his prices up. Their novelty dimmed; other sensational wines came along; and Dr. Frank began having troubles with distributors who failed to do precisely what Dr. Frank wanted them to, which was to sell his wines at the top of the market. As the Seventies waned, wines were left too long in cask; bottles languished in the cellar. When his son was made head of the company in 1977, the struggle began to extend their availability. The wines are among the best ever made in America, but hard to find.

* * *

Widmer's Wine Cellars. The Swiss Alps are higher, but the Finger Lakes offered broader horizons, so John Jacob Widmer came to the chosen place, which was what the Indians called Lake Canandaigua. That was 1882 and Italians had preceded him, for he began setting out vineyards at the foot of the lake, in Naples. All three sons went into the business, but the legendary one was Will, who was sent to Geisenheim for training and came back to make wines from the native grapes. They were marvels unmatched and under his direction the vineyards expanded to 500 acres, with growers supplying grapes from more than 1,200 more.

The tradition continued when a group of Rochester businessmen bought the winery from his heirs and then sold it to the English firm that makes French's mustard. The new management expanded holdings, the first eastern winery to establish California vineyards, 500 acres in the Alexander Valley, now reduced to less than 200. The new wine is shipped east for aging, the Pinot Noir and Cabernet Sauvignon used in the firm's blends. Also marketed are wines with the grape names that are among the best buys to be had.

Wine lovers curious about native grapes can scarcely do better than try bottlings from Widmer, certainly Moore's Diamond and Delaware, Vergennes and Elvira—well-made white wines to serve with soft or slicing cheese or by themselves, good on a buffet or with seafood. Hybrids like Seibel Rosé or Cayuga White are exceptional; the most popular wine is a sweet white Lake Niagara. The firm produces more than a million cases a year.

Heron Hill Winery. On a wide bench above Keuka Lake, facing east and south near Bully Hill, are vineyards of Riesling and Chardonnay belonging to two growers who got tired of seeing their grapes going into big blends or being sold to home winemakers. Pushed into the rise overlooking them is the timber and stucco winery belonging to Peter Johnstone and John Ingle, built after a tasting of two of their Rieslings against five Auslesen from the Mosel of the 1975 vintage. Their first bottling of some five thousand gallons was in 1977 and included hybrids of Vignobles, Seyval Blanc and Aurora, some of which is made into blends. First bottlings sold out at the winery but a trickle reaches New York.

Glenora Wine Cellars. The largest of the Finger Lakes is Seneca, east of

Keuka, and growers there who watched the early plantings around them set out by Hammondsport wineries have begun to market their own wines from hybrids and vinifera. The first of these is Glenora Wine Cellars on the west side of the lake, where a quartet of businessmen including grower Edward Dalrymple made their first crush in 1977, amounting to some five thousand cases. First sales were made at the winery.

Wagner Winery. With sixty acres of hybrids and experimental plantings of vinifera above Seneca Lake to draw on, the farming family of Wagner built an octagon of a winery on the east side of the lake, starting with a first crush of some five thousand cases and more to come. Storage tanks holding fifty thousand gallons are clustered in the center of the lower deck, surrounded by the various offices, with pressing equipment above, sheltered by one of the gables. Built into a slope for natural insulation, the compact structure with its pleated roof works well because juice flows into the center of the building for fermenting and aging, then to the perimeter for bottling, with a minimum of handling. First sales at the winery will keep wines from city markets until the Eighties.

CHAUTAUQUA

Grapes grow all along the south shore of Lake Erie, mostly in Concords at the eastern end, but this is changing slowly. Leading the way is Johnson Vineyards Winery in Westfield. Frederick Johnson took his Cornell degree in tropical agriculture, pursuing that career in Hawaii and South America until 1960, when he came back to take over the family vineyard—more than 100 acres of Concords. He replanted them with hybrids, some native grapes, a few noble vines, and began offering Johnson Estate bottlings as far away as New York. They are among the most popular in the state.

Seneca Foods formed an alliance with Philip Wagner of Boordy Vineyards, planting hybrids in Chautauqua and in Washington State. Some pleasing wines were produced for a time, but the relationship was dissolved in 1977. Not in vain, though, because Wagner inspired other growers to try their hands. Any day now, Johnson may get some competition.

* * *

LONG ISLAND

A generation ago, Long Island's east end was farming and fishing, mostly potatoes and bluefish. First Nassau turned into bedroom towns; now Suffolk is faced with a choice: people or potatoes. Or vines.

Hargrave Vineyard. A China scholar really ought to marry a Chinese girl so as to get help with the language, but when you marry a Smith girl you really ought to switch to something else, like vineyards, so as to get help with the wines. And so you won't be a dull boy, you never work on Sundays, giving yourself time to write letters to the editor comparing smoking, mostly hot air, with drinking wines:

"Your choice is between the stale vapor of dried vegetable chaff with its tarry, creosoted precipitate and that of a myriad of esterified organic acids, languishing glycerols, buttery diacetyls and stringent tannins that tease the palate yet deny satiety—all unified in an unctuous solvent of ethanol which, as it slides down the glosso-epiglotic folds, awakens the senses, enlivens the past and civilizes the future."

The Hargraves had to wait five years for their own languishing glycerols, planting their first of forty-four acres in 1973. Acreage was equally divided between Louis Martini's superclone of Chardonnay and Davis stocks of Sauvignon Blanc, Pinot Noir and Cabernet. The first wines were released in the summer of '77.

They denied satiety to just about everybody, offering a couple of thousand cases of a rosé of Cabernet, a Sauvignon Blanc and a fast fermentation of Pinot Noir, feeling that light wines could best be made from the young vines. The wines had a depth of taste, though. People who chilled the rosés found them to be enclosed, only showing their charm when they were served a little cool, not much below room temperature, and when they had been allowed to breathe for an hour or so. Optimum production will be about 12,000 cases by the early Eighties.

Louisa Hargrave took chemistry courses for a couple of years, adding to what she had learned in an undergraduate course as part of her degree in education. Alexander Hargrave took charge of the planting, setting up the winery in a potato barn on the property and managing the farm, all three of which are full-time jobs. Alexander's brother, Charles, became interested and is now a partner in the corporation. The three do all the work, with extra help for pruning and during the vintage. Plus encouragement from everybody, including Vergil.

Alec Hargrave graduated from Princeton, took his master's at Harvard, then spent a winter recuperating from a back operation, giving Louisa and himself time to consider how to civilize the future. They thought of tending a vineyard and spent a summer touring the west, getting more and more discouraged. California was too hot; Oregon was too wet; and Washington was too cold. They decided to come home and plant a vineyard there. Alec had grown up in Rochester and knew the Finger Lakes region, but after searching, the two decided that they did not want to plant native grapes or focus on white wines, because they liked red ones best.

About to give up, they went for Thanksgiving to Louisa's parents in Huntington on Long Island, and on an off chance looked up an orchardist out on the North Fork who had been growing vinifera table grapes as part of an experimental program in conjunction with Cornell. John Wickham showed them his plantings in Cutchogue, took them around the area, pointed out that there were more than two hundred growing days compared to the one hundred sixty upstate, and showed them how the light, sandy soil encouraged vine growth. Alex remembered a line from the Georgics:

> If dirt is lacking, then your soil is loose,
> Most fit for fertile vines.

Just what Wickham said, corroborated by Vergil.

> But before we plough an unfamiliar patch
> It is well to be informed about the winds,
> About the variations in the sky,
> The native traits and habits of the place,
> What each locale permits, and what denies,
> One place is good for crops,
> One happier with grapes.

Soil without clods, plenty of light—it's the sunniest spot in the state—winters that rarely go much below freezing, a gentle slope to the south to catch morning light and dry the dew, extra space for experimental plots of

Merlot, Riesling and whatever else seems promising, Cutchogue is a perfect place for a vineyard.

* * *

There has been a curiosity about vines on Long Island since the first commercial plantings in the eighteenth century, but when these succumbed winemaking became an amateur endeavor until the Hargraves came along. Not far from Manhattan, at Lloyd Neck, an island off the North Shore, actress Diahn Williams and her husband, William McGrath, have a few vines in vinifera, with potential for and hopes to market several hundred cases from their Château Eastfair Vineyards by the Eighties.

All the other plantings are experimental. Near Hargrave, Michael Kaloski has an acre of vinifera and makes some Merlot and Chardonnay for himself, selling the rest of the fruit to home winemakers, as does an airline pilot with eight acres of vinifera, David Mudd. Potato and cauliflower farmers on the North Fork watch closely, aware that Long Island Sound tempers the weather, but that occasional hurricanes and cold spells may wipe out a commercial venture. On the South Fork, efforts have been made to stave off developers with a Suffolk County program through which the county buys development rights to the land. There are still miles of potato fields with vineyard possibilities. Artist John Little in East Hampton has had a small vineyard of native grapes for twenty-five years; a Southampton doctor, Sherburne Browne, has thirty varieties of hybrid and vinifera growing; and a local retailer, Ray Sanchez, is planting an acre of vinifera in East Hampton with the idea of selling cuttings to local potato farmers who want to take a flyer. Establishing a vineyard may cost $6,000 an acre, including land, so the success of Hargrave Vineyard may show the way to civilize the future.

"There's a mythic quality about growing wine," said Louisa Hargrave, in a *New Yorker* article written by Berton Roueché. "The vineyard is unique in agriculture . . . The grape is the only fruit of nature that has the power of transfiguration. It's as if wheat could turn itself into bread. Wine is mystery—ancient mystery. And I feel that Alec and I are part of it. We're attending a natural miracle—a miracle that goes back in time to the beginning."

* * *

New England: From New Hampshire to Sakonnet

Vineyards have gone into the long valleys and along the coastal moraine ever since pioneer days, but only in this decade have there been bottlings worth trying when you are passing through. Up in New Hampshire, a transplanted druggist from New York named John Canepa decided that if native vines flourished, then hybrids and vinifera could be made to do so. His White Mountain Vineyards, around Laconia now number more than one hundred acres, and there are more than forty plantings on the hardscrabble hills of Vermont and Maine, on river banks in Massachusetts, all growing grapes. Try Lakes Region White Dinner Wine or Canepa's estate bottlings when you come upon them.

The first vineyard was planted by Governor Winthrop on Governor's Island in Boston Harbor in 1632, which failed like all the rest, until 1971, when Chicama Vineyards was started on Martha's Vineyard. Vinifera grapes supply a few bottles for vacationers. There are home plots of vines, scarcely vineyards, all along the Connecticut shore, well back from the water, but the largest concentration is in Rhode Island, where locals of Portuguese and Italian ancestry make wines from backyard arbors of grapes of all sorts. How natural, then, for New England's finest winery to be set down among them, east of Newport, across Sakonnet Bay, nearly forty acres in a potato field in Little Compton. Optimum production is 15,000 cases.

211

Summer of '77 saw the marketing of America's Cup White from Sakonnet Vineyards, just in time for the races. A soft white of Seyval and Aurora with a little Ravat 51, it is not as dry as the Aurora, which is likened to a light Muscadet. It has about 15% Vidal and 10% Seyval, not as full and piquant as the Vidal, which has 15% Seyval and 10% Aurora. (Wine buffs may like to know such precise proportions, but Sakonnet labels identify the informing grape, which makes up 75% of the blend.) The labels show a cock crowing over a bunch of grapes, supposedly a Rhode Island Red. The wine so-called is 75% Chancellor, the other quarter made up of Maréchal Foch, Leon Millot, De Chaunac and Chelois; it is round but fruity. The wines retail for about $3, but the Chardonnays and Riesling, cost $1 more.

James Mitchell was a management consultant when he married Lolly McDonnell, who was an architectural publicist, and the two decided they wanted to combine some kind of farming with a small business they could run together. Considering his training, which included a chemistry degree, Mitchell made a feasibility study and somehow concluded that a New England vineyard was the answer. The potato field was the place, with a growing season like Bordeaux, only a couple of degrees hotter in summer and cooler in winter. It's a family winery, with friends helping out, and the family lives above it at one end of a long shingled barn built to house the equipment and store the wines.

Sakonnet is making the hybrid blends everyone thinks should be made, with no Labrusca. He has some Cayuga White to work with; he makes a rosé by blending reds and whites. The response will give a hint of what the Eighties will bring. Portions of his grapes come from New York State—when more than 25% of the blend is from out of the state, the wine is simply labeled American—and nobody keeps tabs on his wines more than New York growers. They would hate to have the best hybrid wines from their grapes come from Rhode Island. The Mitchells wouldn't mind at all.

Pennsylvania: From Erie Shores to the Delaware

Wineries cluster around Erie, the northwest corner of the state, tempered by the Great Lake. There are a few plots of wine grapes around Philadelphia; those in Bucks County to the north tempered by the Delaware and surrounding hills, those to the south by its bay, but most of the state's fifteen square miles of grapes are Concords grown for juice and jelly. William Penn had a vineyard a century before the Revolution; John Alexander came up with a grape named for him that spread west to the Mississippi; Rhinelanders and the early communes set out vines in valley after valley; but Concords were about all that survived Prohibition. Then in 1968, the state passed a model law permitting wineries to make as much as 100,000 gallons and sell them direct, through state stores and at the wineries. Sales don't go much beyond that, but more than a dozen wineries offer hybrid blends and vinifera bottlings, what would be called *vins de pays* in France, country wines to be drunk in the neighborhood.

Just about all the table wines of the East are country wines, and while a few New York companies like Taylor and Widmer's have regional distribution and the sweet kosher and cocktail wines go far and wide, only a few of the country wines get to Boston or New York, Washington or Chicago. In Philadelphia or Pittsburgh, though, you can taste Conestoga, Presque Isle, Pequea and Penn-Shore.

Melvin Gordon bought some hybrids from Phil Wagner and when the

213

new law passed he was able to offer a blend of Maréchal Foch and Rayon d'Or from his ten acres near Valley Forge. His Conestoga Vineyard wines are now in many of Pennsylvania's best restaurants.

So are those of Presque Isle Wine Cellars, founded by Douglas Moorhead, whose father grew Concords but tolerated replanting, and William Konnerth, a reporter in Erie. The group of growers supplies wines and a book on winemaking by Konnerth to homemakers. The group was instrumental in getting the new wine law passed. A new winery was built at North East to make Riesling, Chardonnay and hybrid blends.

Penn-Shore was started nearby by another group of growers, who make similar wines and one that sparkles. Near Lancaster, Pequea Valley Vineyards produces more hybrids. Others are coming along: Mazza Vineyards in North East has fewer today because the Mazzas sold most of them to buy their Spanish-style winery. They depend on other growers for most of their grapes and on the skills of Geisenheim graduate Helmut Kranich. His Labruscas, hybrids and some vinifera get no wood to keep them fresh and are made sweet because the belief is that the public likes them so.

New Jersey: Egg Harbor and Applejack

The Renault Winery at Egg ·Harbor has made wines for more than a century, weathering Prohibition by supplying wines for drug stores. There are 125 acres of vineyard, but much wine is bought and made into Renault sparkling wines, once a great favorite in Atlantic City. The company has recently been taken over by a local newspaper publisher, J. Milza.

Perhaps the largest New Jersey bottler is Tribuno Vermouth, made by Vermouth Industries of America and owned by Coca Cola.

There are a few family plots of grapes, but the main business is bottling California wines with labels of local distributors. Monte Carlo Wine Industries is said to use local grapes in their blends but there are few to be had. Gross's Highland Winery has something more than 50 acres; Tomasello Winery has a few less; John Shuster & Son buys grapes.

A grand old firm from Revolutionary days, Laird's, is still in business, mostly applejack and some cider. Laird's was the rage for generations; founded in 1780, it is about the last of the applejack makers. When apple wines became the fashion, Laird's began making some, but failed to find a market.

* * *

215

The South: Scuppernongs and Strange Fruit

The first wine marketed in this country was named after the first child born here, of English colonists, that is. Virginia Dare was made of Scuppernong in Virginia in 1835, startling all. The wines are startling today, strong and sweet, so popular that Scuppernong vineyards are being planted today throughout the south, reaching into Texas. The most celebrated planting is Mother Vineyard, owned by a firm of that name in Petersburg, Virginia. But most of the Scuppernong comes from Mac Sands, who started out as a bottler in Richmond after Repeal. One Scuppernong led to another, and finally to Canandaigua Wine Company, which is headquarters, but most of his wines come from southern branches of the family.

There is Richard's Wine Cellars of Virginia, Tenner Brothers in South Carolina peach country where Richard's Peach is made, Onslow Winery in North Carolina, Hammondsport Wine Company for sparkling wines. One of the wines is Wild Irish Rose—of Concord, Catawba, Delaware, Elvira and Niagara. Other wines are made from fruits.

Sands has gathered together most of the old wine names of southern wineries now defunct—he has most of the wineries still going—and for a taste of the Old South you might best try one of his.

Amateurs grow vines all along the Atlantic seaboard. Perhaps the most promising region is the Piedmont—foothills of the Blue Mountains that extend into Georgia. On the high slopes, the weather is cool enough for

217

vinifera and state agricultural bureaus are beginning to investigate. The same is happening on the western slopes and along the Alleghenies. Wines will come from them some day. Meanwhile, it's Richard's, Virginia Dare and Wild Irish Rose. Then there's Old Maude. And don't pass up Scuppernong. It's wild.

There is always rumor of a good new wine. A Baltimore visitor in the Fifties might have heard of a little vineyard out in Riderwood where a newspaper editor was making white wine from grapes he had developed. The most curious made efforts to get a bottle, usually driving out to see Philip Wagner at Boordy Vineyard, which seemed to be little more than a big backyard with vines and a converted garage that held a wine press, a couple of vats and a few casks. Wagner would tell you about the twigs he had got from France, each with the name of the man who had made the cross and its number—Baco Number One, Seibel 10,878, Seyve-Villard 5,276. Over a glass on the porch, Wagner would explain how the cross was made.

The cluster forms early in the spring, green pinheads along a stem. Before the bud flowers, the flower cap and stamen of one variety is removed and the pistil is dusted with pollen from another. All the other buds are removed, emasculated, says the hybridizer, and the cluster is bagged to prevent contamination. When the berries develop enough, seeds from them are planted. The resulting vine is the hybrid. Wagner had planted hundreds of these and the best wines from them seemed to be white. The wine was a little odd to one familiar with Chardonnay or Riesling, with some acidity, a little floweriness, a pleasant enough taste—but delicious compared to the rankness and feral quality of sweetish wines made from native grapes. Wagner had grown up drinking wines in Ann Arbor, where his father taught languages at the university, and he began making wines in the Thirties when he began working for the Baltimore *Sun*. When Repeal came he could no longer get Zinfandel from California, so he tried Delaware but disliked the taste. By the Forties, he had growing hybrids from Bordeaux and others he found in various nurseries and amateur plots. His wines pleased him; he began supplying Baltimore restaurants with them, wrote a book about winemaking and growing grapes; the newest version, *Grapes Into Wine*, published by Alfred A. Knopf in 1976, is the authoritative guide for amateurs. Amateurs everywhere and winemakers, like Charles Fournier at Gold Seal in the Finger Lakes region of New York, began planting his vines.

Neighbors like Charles Singleton and Hamilton Mowbray, professors at Johns Hopkins, began setting out vines, the first developing Caroli Vineyards, the second establishing Montbray Wine Cellars, which branched out into vinifera. Soon Wagner was supplying vines and advice to people across the country.

The vines and their wines improve with each decade, extending the range into every state. An amateur produces a few good bottles; local restaurants begin offering it; astonished drinkers decide to try their hand; more bottles appear. The state becomes interested, collecting the local lore, setting out experimental plots, passing around information and cuttings. Word spreads. Everywhere there are new wines to be tasted.

Down in Middleburg, Virginia, is a family winery called Meredyth Vineyards, now managed by Archie Smith, who holds a doctorate in philosophy from Oxford, taught there, and coached the drinking team while there. His wife, Suzelle, who has a baccalaureate in the same field, excelled in tastings against Cambridge, which may be useful when it comes to making Virginia vintages.

The Midwest

Vines followed the pioneers west, along the shores of the Great Lakes to Wisconsin, down the Ohio and Mississippi to Arkansas, up the Missouri to Nebraska. Prohibition did in most of them, but now there are new grapes bearing, scattered greenings in among the Concords and native grapes.

Ohio

Sparkling Catawba, made from thousands of acres planted around Cincinnati by Nicholas Longworth, established Ohio as the wine center of the New World just before the Civil War. The grape was a cross from a garden in Washington's Georgetown. There were said to be 10,000 acres along the banks of the Ohio and the river came to be called the Rhine of America. They languished, attacked by powdery mildew and black rot. By the time the war ended, the vineyards were gone. Some survived to the east, around Sandusky and on islands in Lake Erie, where vineyards have continued to supply Meier's Wine Cellars to this day. The firm, still producing Sparkling Catawba and other wines, is owned by Paramount Distillers of Cleveland. The wines are made by a graduate of the University of Chile, Galo Maclean, who studied at Montpellier, and are sparking

221

interest in the moribund wineries and vineyards that once flourished along the lake.

In Madison, a banker named William Worthy has 65 acres of hybrids and some vinifera in his Grands Vins Vineyard. He supplies all the grapes for the Cedar Hill Wine company, in the cellar of a fine small restaurant in Cleveland Heights, "Au Provence." The restaurant is owned by an ear surgeon named Thomas Wykoff, who became enthusiastic about French and Creole cooking while training in New Orleans. With chef Richard Taylor, the two opened the restaurant and Wykoff began making his Château Lagniappe wines to be served in it, several hundred cases each year. The restaurant is the only place where you can taste some of the best wines in Ohio.

Near the Pennsylvania border there are 10 acres of Chardonnay and Riesling in Markko Vineyards at Conneaut, owned by an admirer of Konstantin Frank. Arnulf Esterer and his family do most of the work themselves, producing not much more than a thousand cases a year and selling the wines for around $5 a bottle.

There are another 40 acres of vines near Madison— Labrusca, hybrids and some vinifera, which provide much of the grapes for the Chalet Debonné winery owned by the Debevc family. One of the most interesting wines is Ruby Debonné, made from Villard, and there are Debonné White and Red for the tasting, made of hybrid blends.

With the exception of Meier's Wine Cellars, Ohio bottlings are sold mostly in the state.

INDIANA

There are half a dozen wineries and perhaps 300 vineyard acres, mostly hybrids, thanks to an Indiana University law professor who drew up and pushed through a winery act in 1971, thereby ending prohibition among the Hoosiers. William Oliver has some 70 acres with more coming in on land across the Ohio River in Kentucky that had been strip-mined and left for worthless. His Oliver Wine Company offers ten wines.

Banholzer Wine Cellars, up near Chicago, has about the same acreage, including one of Cabernet, which sells for more than twenty dollars a bottle, and there are a thousand bottles each of Pinot Noir and Chardonnay, plus hybrids, lower in price. His Picnic White and Rosé sell for three dollars.

A retired navy flier has planted some 30 acres on his Possum Trot Farm in Brown County. Ben Sparks marketed his first hybrids in 1977. Not far away is another small plot of hybrids on the farm of Helen Hunt, a Latin teacher with a son-in-law in Connecticut, who flies out regularly to make the wines.

Most of the vineyards are along the Ohio, where the first plantings were made by Swiss settlers in the early 1800s. At Vevay, named after the Swiss wine town, they had a wine festival every year, even though there had been no vineyards for a century and a half. This lack was corrected when the Swiss Valley Vineyards of Alvin and Margaret Meyer were planted to 3 acres, tended by their eleven children and their offspring. Most of the grapes, though, come from Ohio growers, for the family lives in Cincinnati.

There are nearly 40 acres by the river that belong to Cape Sandy Vineyards, the wines made at the winery in Indianapolis, 160 miles away. There are nearly 100 acres on the Madison property of Cincinnati photographer Michael Mancuso, which is called Villa Medeo. Then there are a few acres of grapes, part of a large orchard near Evansville, where wines for the Golden Rain Tree Winery of Albert Weil are made by an Ohio State graduate in viticulture from India, Murli Dharmadhikari. More vines are sure to be planted, but it may be the end of the century before any wines get far beyond the state.

MICHIGAN

The vineyards lie behind the dunes of Lake Michigan's eastern shore, across from Chicago, more than 16,000 acres centered around Paw Paw. Most of them are Concords, but there is rebirth in an area that was an expansion of the Welch empire of the last century. The old plantings came in handy when a Detroit restaurateur got the idea of bottling a mixture of wines from Concords with sparkling Labrusca. He called it Cold Duck, a Rhineland drink made by taking leftover wines, Kalde Ende, and perking them up with sparkling wines. It was no time at all until the ends were corrupted to the German for duck; the translation was novel enough to appeal to casual drinkers. The fad lasted through the Seventies and scores of versions opened the market to all sorts of flavored drinks based on wines. New ones still appear, but Michigan growers have realized that their Concords were a wave of the past.

223

An amateur winemaker from Chicago began a search for vineyards and came to realize that the southwestern corner of Michigan, tempered by lakes, with a growing season of at least 180 days and sandy soil that drained quickly, might be just the place. By 1972, Leonard Olson was marketing wines in the Midwest from Philip Wagner's Maryland hybrids and vinifera from California and the Rhine. His Tabor Hill Vineyard encouraged others to follow his lead.

The largest Michigan winery is Warner, which started planting hybrids around Paw Paw and now has more than 300 acres, including vinifera, and buys more grapes from local growers to extend their lines. They make a full range from hybrids, including a rosé from DeChaunac and a sparkling wine that was named the "Agricultural Product of the Year" in 1973.

Almost as extensive is Bronte Winery and Vineyards in the Sister Lakes district south of Paw Paw, where there are some 200 acres in hybrids and some native grapes. They claim to have been the first to have bottled Cold Duck, in their Detroit winery, and they still make one of the best. About the same size and with a similar line is Fenn Valley Vineyard and Wine Cellar, over toward Lake Michigan, all 200 acres of their plantings being in hybrids and vinifera. South along the shore is Lakeside Vineyard, founded after Repeal by an Irishman named Ruttledge, whose Molly Pitcher wines based on Concords became famous. The company now makes a couple of dozen different wines from all types of grapes. The longest line of wines probably comes from Frontenac Vineyards, north of Paw Paw, and includes a dozen alcoholic fruit drinks called smashes, including one called Bahama Mama. Two small wineries with shorter lines, are Vendramino, north of town, and Boskydel, in a pine grove overlooking Lake Leelanau.

Another Paw Paw winery is St. Julian, started after the first world war in Windsor, Ontario, across from Detroit. The winery is named after the patron saint of the small town near Rome where Mariano Meconi came from. He kept the name when he moved across the river after Repeal and then on to Paw Paw. Still owned by the family, it has taken over the La Salle winery and vineyards, another winery that had moved over from Canada.

Most Michigan wines are sold in the state, but as those from hybrids and vinifera become known, the market is slowly expanding—and new wineries are being set up.

Wisconsin

Wisconsin's first successful winery was established at the time of the Civil War near Madison, not far from where Agoston Haraszthy had been frozen out of his first vineyard a decade earlier. A wily Rhinelander named Kehl planted native grapes that withstood the cold, built a handsome four-square house and winery out of dressed limestone blocks cut out of the hill and used the hole as a wine cellar, lining it with more stone. When Robert and Jo Ann Wollersheim bought it in 1972 the place needed a little work, the winery having been used for beer storage, a dance hall and piggery, the last most recently. The Wollersheims are still fixing things up, but have managed to plant more than a dozen acres of hybrids and produce upward of six thousand cases of wine aged in small oak, much of it from purchased grapes.

The Wollersheims started a supply business for home winemakers in 1966 and made a batch themselves, just to see. So delicious was the result that they determined to buy the old winery high in the back country. The trick was finding a market for their wines and they did so by installing their winemaker's shop, a gift shop, a cheese counter and delicatessen and a museum, with terraces for picnics to attract visitors from nearby Wisconsin Dells, one of the loveliest preserves in the states.

The area attracts balloonists, so they bottled The Great Balloon Race Red to celebrate the event. They contracted a local woodcarver to carve one barrel head per year, and this is bottled separately, with the carving on the label. They staged a vintage festival, so popular they had to raise wine prices so they wouldn't run out. The Wollersheims wanted to express the joy in wine, and have so delighted visitors that they scarcely have time to extend their vineyards. They sell T-shirts that say in German, "Life is too short to drink bad wine." Now if they can just find time to put out more good bottles . . .

The Ozarks and Elsewhere

St. Louis was a wine center a century ago, giving its name to a grape, the Missouri Riesling, which is now called Elvira. The biggest winery then was Bardenheier's and it is the biggest today. While hybrids and vinifera are being planted, they have mostly Catawba on their ranch down

225

near the Arkansas border. Their popular wines include Rosie O'Grady and Ozark Mountain.

Hermann, north of St. Louis, is reviving as a wine center, thanks to Stone Hill Wine Company. There is the St. James Winery in that town, along with Stolz Vineyards, venturing into hybrids, as has Peaceful Bend Vineyard, which began planting them in the Fifties. Mount Pleasant Vineyard has a little vinifera. The wines are drunk locally.

The major winery is in the Ozarks of Arkansas, Wiederkehr Wine Cellars, in the northwest corner of the state at Altus. The area was settled by Swiss and Germans, who established many wineries. The few left are growing, thanks to Alcuin Wiederkehr, who quit law school to study at Davis and then in Bordeaux, where he was joined by his brother Leo. The two of them returned to begin replanting the family's 400 acres of vineyard, starting with hybrids and ending with vinifera. The vast range of wines improves each year. Their hybrids are among the best available.

Not far away is Post Winery, founded the same year. Much of the 200 acres has been planted in hybrid. With their cousins, the Wiederkehrs, the Posts produce most of the state's wines. Another Post winery is Mount Bethel Cellar. Like others, it was established when dry Arkansas passed a law permitting sales of local wines in restaurants.

There are vineyards in every state, their wines to be tasted whenever you are in the neighborhood. Idahoans pay ten dollars a bottle for Sainte Chapelle Vineyards Riesling, produced in Emmet.

Ivancie Wines of Colorado was started by a Denver dentist who made wines from Napa grapes, then branched out with wines from Europe, Australia and New York, even Mexico. Vinifera was planted in 25 acres in Mesa County, watched over carefully by the experimental stations of Colorado State University, which has test plots that include hybrids. Colorado Chardonnay may be available in Denver in 1980, but vineyards on the western slope of the Rockies offer little competition to California producers and Ivancie has a tough time competing with out-of-state labels.

226

The Northwest: A New Region Heard From

The difference is light. The Northwest has long days—sixteen hours of daylight and more, an hour more than California—and mild weather at both ends of the growing season so that grapes can ripen well, perhaps even better than in Burgundy or Bordeaux, which are at the same latitude. The problem is water.

Clouds thrust up by the high Cascades drench valleys on the Pacific side, leaving those on the interior almost desert. Irrigation from the dammed waters of the Columbia River system corrected that. Harsh winters can kill the vines—but not if they go dormant early and form tough bark. They can be made to do this by cutting off the water in August. The Northwest can produce great wines.

The feeling was in the air. Richard Sommer took a course from Maynard Amerine while getting his agronomy degree at Davis and in 1961 bought a hillside in Oregon's Umpqua Valley near Roseburg. A decade later, the 20 acres of Hillcrest Vineyard were producing Riesling and other wines from noble grapes. Supply was augmented by neighboring growers and optimum production approached 10,000 cases.

Charles Coury quit his job as a wine salesman in the early Sixties, took a master's at Davis, spent a year in Alsatian vineyards and moved to a hill west of Portland in 1966. From nearly 40 acres of vineyard and some purchase of grapes, optimum production reached 20,000 cases in 1977.

227

Meanwhile, back down near Roseburg, Bjelland Vineyards was established in 1968, the 30 acres of vineyard producing something less than 4,000 cases a decade later.

Others were attracted to the cooler areas around Portland, Tualitin Vineyards becoming neighbors of Coury at Forest Grove, with plans for nearly 100 acres of vineyard; Oak Knoll to the east, with some vinifera, but several fruit wines; Ponzi Vineyards with some 10 acres of vines and plantings that include Pinot Blanc and Pinot Gris.

South of Portland in the Willamette Valley are the nearly 20 acres of The Eyrie Vineyards, already noted for their wines from various Pinot grapes; the small new Amity Vineyards with 12 acres and room for expansion; and the Knudsen-Erath Winery, which uses the 58 acres of grapes from Cal Knudsen's vineyard with the 22 from Richard Erath's, plus vinifera bought from neighbors and other Northwest growers to reach optimim production of perhaps 25,000 cases. Three other wineries in the state—Honeywood, Mt. Hood and Nehalem Bay—produce fruit wines.

Little production gets out of the state. The same is not true to the north, in Washington. Washington produces wines from noble grapes because a psychology professor at the University of Washington caught a cold in 1951. Looking for something to read, Dr. Lloyd Woodburne picked up Philip Wagner's book on making wines at home. It looked simple. He called a colleague, Angelo Pellegrini, and asked if that was so. "Easy as boiling an egg," said Pellegrini. The Woodburnes proceded to make some dreadful Zinfandel. A decade later, ten fellow amateurs got together and bought some land in the lower Yakima Valley and a decade after that, Associated Vintners' Gewürztraminer and Johannisberg Riesling was astonishing everybody, including Tschelistcheff, who encouraged them to plant more. Now there are 25 acres and Woodburne is devoting full time to the wine.

There are several new wineries in the southern part of the state: Bingen Wine Cellars with nearly 30 acres; Hinzerling Vineyards at Prosser, with nearly 20 acres, which has plans for as much as 20,000 cases, not including wines made for the new Salishan Vineyard near Bingen; and Preston Wine Cellars near Richland, which has nearly 50 acres and hope to reach some 50,000 cases during the Eighties. Manfred Vierthaler ran a successful German restaurant in Tacoma for years, but his interest in wines has led him to establish a winery near Sumner and make wines, mostly blends from Northwest and California grapes. Alhambra is an old wine company that in the past produced wines mostly from native and hybrid grapes, but on its some 130 acres vinifera has been planted and there is consideration of marketing some under the Old St. Charles Vineyard label. There were several wineries in the state before Repeal, the installations being taken over by existing wineries or new ventures. Most of the old ones specialized in Concord and various fruit wines, the newest of these being Puyallup Valley Winery, a corporation of fruit growers whose first success in 1976 was with a dry wine from rhubarb.

Ste. Michelle Vineyards. Washington's major winery was formed when two old ones were merged after Repeal into American Wine Growers by a group of Seattle businessmen. This was bought in 1974 by the United States Tobacco Company, which now owns more than 750 acres of vineyards, a handsome new winery, and the services of Andre Tschelistcheff, who has been their advisor since the beginning. Optimum production of 250,000 cases will be reached early in the Eighties, but wines already on the market indicate that bottlings will be among the best available.

The first wine to astonish California was a Johannisberg Riesling that ranked above fourteen California bottlings and four from Europe. Successive releases of Sémillon Blanc, Gewürztraminer, Chenin Blanc and Chardonnay confirmed the early tastings. The wines all have good acidity and balance, with good fruity qualities that are not overwhelming.

There is a lemony quality in the Sémillon, a crispness in the Gewürztraminer and a lightness in the Chardonnay that are almost a relief after the big fruit of California wines. Because the wines are influenced by California styles, the Chenin Blanc is lightly sweet to bring out fruitiness, and a Château Ste. Michelle is a rich Riesling reminiscent of some of the softer Rhine wines.

As if afraid to make fully dry wines, the first few vintages of Grenache Rosé and Cabernet Sauvignon were made with a little residual sugar to bring out fruitiness, the grapes left long on the vine to pick up plenty of sugar. These may find a market, so the chance for light and dry fresh reds and rosés may be lost.

What is found in the wines is good acidity in balance with the alcohol. The wines have a possibility for lightness probably not to be found in California, and then only if the new Monterey wineries feel that a market awaits such wines.

229

Canada—From Ontario to the Okanagan

Americans whose awareness is limited to cold fronts pushing down from Hudson Bay are surprised to learn that Canada produces wines at all, and they miss a shock unless they taste some of the native vintages before the end of the decade. Harsh and metallic blends, mostly from Concord and Labrusca, once made up most Canadian bottlings, but a brilliant winemaker named de Chaunac began changing all that in the Sixties, when he planted hybrids and vinifera. A century after the oldest existing winery was founded, issuing its first winery license in forty-four years, the glacial Ontario control board permitted the son of an Italian immigrant and a new Canadian from Austria to release Inniskillin bottlings in 1973.

Now there is Seyval Blanc and Gewürztraminer to be had when you can find it, several hybrids that are making big companies like Bright's, Jordan and Château Gai look to their blends, with Chardonnay, Riesling and Gamay Beaujolais coming along. Canadians can no longer take rueful pleasure watching friends from south of the border trying to be polite about Canadian wines.

Grapes come from the Niagara Peninsula, west of the falls and Buffalo, a strip of land twenty miles wide and thirty long between the tip of Lake Ontario above and the eastern end of Lake Erie below. Something more than 22,000 acres of grapes, mostly Concords, compete for space with orchards, industry and growing subdivisions. More grapes come from fur-

231

ther south around Windsor, at the western end of Lake Erie near Detroit. Like the vineyards along the south shore in New York, Pennsylvania and Ohio, they are tempered by the waters of the lake. Summer temperatures are not that much different from the Rhineland, but harsher winters, May and September frosts and dampness causing mildew, together inhibit growth of European grapes.

Donald Ziraldo of Inniskillin produces some 25,000 cases of wines, hoping to increase this five-fold during the Eighties. On some 100 acres of vineyard land he has plantings of 10 acres of Chardonnay, an expanding experimental vinifera plot of 20 acres and 30 acres of hybrids, but he also buys grapes from other growers. Bright's, the largest of the ten Niagara wineries, also buys grapes; of its 1,000 acres of vineyard, 700 are Labrusca, 250 are hybrids and only 50 are vinifera, all of which supply 20% of the production, which is 300,000 cases. They encourage the planting of hybrids by independent growers, as do Jordan and Château Gai, which are almost as large. Each of the big companies produces small bottlings of hybrids and even some viniferas, but most of the wines are Labrusca blends.

Karl Kaiser tasted one of them in 1968 while on vacation and instantly realized he had found a calling. In all his life in Austria never had he tasted such a miserable wine. He enrolled for chemistry courses in a local college and began making wines on the side, from whatever vinifera he could find. When Ziraldo tasted some he knew he had found a hand to help at Inniskillin. Kaiser became the winemaker. Torontonians discovered the wines.

Toronto had been settled by prohibitionistic Scots who considered drink and just about everything else immoral. Everything alcoholic is sold through provincial stores. Wines are bought by provincial employees, not necessarily considered the best of judges, and are offered to the public at twice their cost. Outside of Toronto, wines are not easy to come by, and even in Toronto choice is limited. This did not matter much until the Sixties, when the influx of new Canadians from Europe and elsewhere changed the city to one of the most cosmopolitan on the continent. The new Canadians turned their noses up at most of the Canadian wines until Inniskillin came along to give them hope. Imports keep rising, presenting the control board with a problem because it wants to keep a portion of the market for Canadian wines. Inniskillin is showing them how to do it.

Much wine is made from concentrates imported from Europe and California, to be reconstituted and blended with Canadian wines. None of them has developed a strong following. There is the chance for a new supply from the west.

Valleys of the Pacific Northwest are protected from harsh weather by the coastal ranges that catch the ocean rains and chilling winds—not so much as Rhineland vineyards on the same fiftieth parallel are tempered by warmer Atlantic currents—so that European grapes can grow in the Okanagan Valley of British Columbia. The valley is 120 miles from north to south with a deep lake along it that is one of the main feeds of the Columbia river system. When the owners of a hardware store and a grocery, both teetotalers, set up a winery in 1932 there were less than 300 acres of grapes in the Okanagan, all Labrusca, and now there are ten times as many, including hybrids and vinifera. Their Calona winery started out crushing the glut of apples, gradually switching to wines made from California grapes, then to grapes from their own vineyards, now more than 300 acres. The hardware man sold his interests when he entered politics, rising to premier of the province, when he was instrumental in passing laws that required all B.C. wines to be 80% from provincial grapes, and permitting wineries to offer tastings and sell wines to the public. The grocer sold his interest to Standard Brands, but his son, Tom Capozzi, stays on as board chairman.

The oldest British Columbia winery is Ste. Michelle of Victoria, founded in 1923 to make wines of a loganberry glut on Vancouver Island. It is no relation to the winery of the same name down in Washington, but is similar in that it has a new showplace winery, vineyards in the Okanagan, and a line of wines that includes a range of white wines from vinifera. It is owned by Jordan Valley Wines, which has a string of wineries across the country.

Another with a chain of wineries is Andres Wines, which was started in 1961 by a Hungarian brewmaster who sold his Ontario breweries to get into the wine business. Andres Peller hired Wallace Pohle to make the wines at the Port Moody installation and the two began encouraging Okanagan growers to plant vinifera and hybrids, launching the current trend. Two of their most popular wines are the red and white called Similkameen, named after the valley where the grapes grow.

One of the newest wineries in the Okanagan was started by a group of

Westbank businessmen, then sold to Uncle Ben's Industries. A long line of blends are made, including Hot Goose, Peacock, Red Red Robin and Fuddle Duck, variously flavored.

Fruit wines and ciders were the mainstay of most of the B.C. wineries and Casabello was no exception, offering its first varietals in 1976, from grapes grown in the Yakima Valley. The firm was started in the early Seventies by a hotel man, Evans Lougheed, who still heads the firm now owned by the brewers of Labatt beers. Among the forty-odd blends are Burgonay, Daddy Duck and Rosette.

There are a couple of dozen wineries across Canada, still busy with wines made from concentrate, many of them sweetened with fruit juice, but those from hybrids and vinifera grown on the Niagara Peninsula or in British Columbia will be readily available by the Eighties. Not that many will go south of the border. A new winery, the Podamer Champagne Company, started by a Hungarian winemaker, began releasing a few cases in 1976, made largely from Ontario grapes, but these scarcely get beyond Toronto. And the wines get better and better.

Fortified Wines

In the beginning, wine is simply the fermented juice of freshly squeezed grapes, quenching and good with food. They are light wines, for yeasts can only ferment a wine to about 14% alcohol, give or take a degree or two. Such wines for the table are without sweetness, dry, with flowery or fruity tastes. Some improve when aged in oak casks, a few improve still more in bottle, but most are best when drunk a few weeks or months after the fermentation has subsided. That is only the beginning.

Wines from warm climates vary widely because they are full of sugar and have little balancing fruit acid to hold them steady. Sometimes, no matter what is done to them, they never taste right. The Romans added honey and herbs and spices, the Greeks added pitch, to make them palatable. Over the centuries, what has been added has resulted in three classes of wines.

Add bubbles and you have sparkling wines.

Add herbs, like wormwood, and you have aromatic wines like vermouth. You can add quinine and sweetening to make other aperitifs, like Dubonnet or Byrrh. Neutral wines with no taste are used so the blender can make his own. Pop wines with fruit flavorings, usually with exotic names, fit here.

Add brandy and you have fortified wines, between 14% and 21% alcohol. If brandy is added after fermentation, you have Sherry, the best of which comes from Spain. Stop the fermentation by adding brandy and some of the natural sugar in the grape is preserved; the result is Port, the best of which comes from Portugal.

That is all the kinds of wine there are. Variations are endless, so confusing that defining the groups may be warranted. Drinks called wine are made from every kind of fruit—I have tasted a ferment of tomatoes—and they are called fruit wines. Consider them a separate group if you must. They have little to do with wine from grapes. You can make ferments from grains, as sake is made from rice, but these are usually called beers.

All these kinds are made everywhere, including California. The various aromatic wines from there are as good as any, being based on neutral wines, of which California has too much. Fortified wines call for good wines to begin with, and long aging. California borrowed the names and stuck them on millions of gallons of fortified wines, but these have nothing to do with what comes from Spain and Portugal. What has been passed off as Sherry and Port has been so dreadful that practically nobody drinks the real ones any more.

Sneaky Pete came to be the name for port, sherry and muscatel from California, the cheapest form of alcohol since Repeal. They were drinks for bums, sweet and strong, with nothing unpleasant in the tastes, but nothing pleasant, either. Except for the alcohol, of course, and the sweetness—substitutes for jelly and cookies, with a kick. A glass wouldn't hurt your grandmother; three glasses could send her spinning. Some people say Sneaky Pete was California's main production until the Sixties, when at last more table wines were sold than fortified wines.

The result of all this is not only that wine in general got a bad name, but that most Americans got the idea that wine was sweet. (This may account for the fashion for dry wine, as far as possible from Sneaky Pete, and a sign of Puritanism, rather than a national change in taste.) Surely, it must be good news to many that some of the best Sherries are dry and that some of the best Ports are sweet, for which we can be thankful. Most of us have never even tasted them.

In Spain, Sherry is fermented in small casks. The casks are then tasted and separated. Those that have a surface film of yeast called the flower, or *flor*, are made into Fino, which just means fine. Those with a nutty flavor are made into Amontillado, called that because they are like the wines of Montilla, a district near Cordoba, whose wines are never fortified and are marvelous with all sorts of seafood. (One of the grandest wines on earth, it is rarely imported.)

Still other barrels of Sherry have a wonderful, rich fragrance—the word is *oloroso* in Spanish—and the wines are so named. All three types are then aged for years, first in the cradle, or *criadera*, and then in the *solera*, or tiers of casks.

This may be more than you want to know about fortified wines, but great ones are so grand, imitations are so numerous and attitudes so negative that the curious may be encouraged to try them and Californians may be persuaded to make more good ones than they do.

There are several tiers of casks in a criadera, usually two or three, and the new wine goes into the youngest tier of its type. Wines from the oldest tier of the criadera are used to top off the solera; these are usually at least two years old. The solera, whose name means base or foundation, may have three tiers or more.

When wine is wanted for shipment it is drawn off from the oldest tier. Usually less than a third is drawn off each year. The oldest tier is replenished from the next oldest, and so on, so that a wine from the criadera may take nine years to flow through the solera. Then wines from different soleras are blended for shipment.

The wines are fortified before they go into the criaderas, which helps hold them to type; they become more typical—and darker and more intense—as the young Sherries take on the characteristics of the old wines in the soleras. Sherries start off with a special taste imparted by the chalky soil, a taste remarkably enhanced by the nurturing and blending skills of the winemaker.

Finos and Amontillados are not sweetened and are magnificently dry. The driest wine known is the Fino matured on the seacoast in a town called Sanlúcar de Barrameda, so unique that it is given a special name, Manzanilla. Most Olorosos for export are sweetened with wines made from raisinized grapes aged long in oak. It is called P. X., made from the Pedro Ximénez grape, and gives great character to the Olorosos, which are often called Cream Sherries because they are so rich. The Sherries themselves are made from the white Palomino grape, which grows in California and is often used for making fortified wines.

That is the only similarity between Sherry and the fortified wines so named in California.

Various techniques are used in California and elsewhere to speed the ancient process. Wines are successively heated and cooled, flor yeast is agitated in the wines, which are even aged in soleras. The wines bear only superficial resemblances to the Sherries of Spain, which are low in price and excellent buys because they are not fashionable.

Sherries taste best chilled.

Myron Nightingale made some good yeasty dry wines of the Fino type in the Sixties but they were used to give sweet blends some character; there is no doubt that classic dry styles could be made. Some firms even have solera systems, Sebastiani and Almadén, for example, and Widmer's in New York state. Although American styles bear little resemblance to classic ones, a market has been made for them and many find them acceptable.

Small batches of all the fortified wines can be made successfully—sun-baked Madeiras, the Sicilian Marsalas that were invented by an Englishman named Woodhouse as a substitute for Spanish Sherry—but markets are small and commercial quantities made in traditional ways would be costly to produce, so there is little incentive. Sweet, cheap versions of the Italian dessert wines called Moscato have been fortified to become American Muscatel, but have little distinction. A once-popular California fortified wine was Angelica, of dubious distinction, made of white grape juice and brandy, has occasionally been carefully made, but rarely in commercial quantites.

* * *

Port is a special wine. It was developed by the English and used to get the women away from the table after dinner so the men could talk. The table was cleared to the wood, a bowl of walnuts was set out, glasses were set around and the host picked up the decanter he had previously filled, poured some in his glass and passed the decanter to his left. Guests poured some in their turn, passing it to the left, and when each had served himself, the host raised his glass and said "To the king" (or "To the queen," if she was reigning), everybody sipped and silently considered the wine. The host mentioned something, perhaps the weather. Talk began.

There was an embargo on French wines in the middle of the seventeenth century so the British turned to Spain and Portugal. A couple of young men supervising shipments from Oporto tasted a red wine that was sweet because the fermentation had been stopped before all the sugar had been converted to alcohol. They named it after the port and shipped it to England where it created a sensation. Nobody knows quite how Port became relegated to its odd gastronomic role, but by the end of the eighteenth century, rules for drinking it were as rigid as they were artificial. Port was the fashion.

It is no longer. Its making has been perfected over three hundred years, a method as rigid as the drinking of it. Ten varieties of grapes and even more, all with high sugar content, are crushed and the fermentation is stopped by adding high-proof brandy so that the wine has something like 20% of alcohol. The wines are then sorted as to quality and put to age in long small casks called pipes. After two years in wood, good vintages are bottled and then cellared for decades, beginning to approach their peak after twenty years, often not drunk until they are half a century old. A style called late-bottled vintage Port is kept four years in wood and becomes drinkable quicker, perhaps after a dozen years. More popular are nonvintage Ruby Ports aged perhaps six years in pipes and ready to drink when bottled. Tawny Ports are aged in wood still longer, losing color and becoming softer; they are also ready to drink when bottled.

Winemakers willing to make the effort and starting with a good base wine from traditional varieties can make good fortified wines like Ruby and Tawny Port. A few are made in California.

There's the climate for it out in the hot Central Valley near Fresno near the town of Madera, where small Ficklin Vineyards have fifty acres of good Port grapes and painstakingly make fine wines from them. The plantings consist of Touriga, Sousao, Tinta Madeira and Tinta Cao, among others, and while the soil is not the crumbly rock called schist that contributes to the unique quality of the wine, great care is taken blending the wines and vintages. The Portuguese say the wine is bred to a style and there is no doubt that the manhandling is what sets Port apart. Ficklin ages the wines in small cooperage for four years, then bottles their Ruby and bins it for a year before releasing it to the market. Vintage Port is occasionally made, bottled after thirty months, sold after nine years of binning. Both sorts can be kept for twenty years and it is expected they will go on for another twenty. Nobody can be sure, for the first vintage was in 1948.

What Port drinking there is today is more relaxed. The wines are delicious with fruit, especially a pear or a peach. A grand dessert is melon with a couple of tablespoons of Port poured in the hollow; there are those that cut a plug out of a melon, spoon out the seeds, pour Port in the hole, replug and chill for a couple of hours. The same thing is done with Stilton, but without the chilling. In Oporto, bread is spread with cream cheese and a slather of guava jelly or paste—there are several kinds—and this is eaten until the Port is gone. Others prefer fruitcake or dry cookies.

Port shippers are not pleased by all the imitations, so to stand out from them, all wines shipped from Oporto are called Porto. Like the Spanish, who have seen their name bastardized, the Portuguese wryly accept the misappropriation of their name. Perhaps there is consolation that good though the imitations may be, they are not as good as the real thing. Few people are aware of this because hardly anyone drinks Port these days.

Some of the premium producers have made special bottlings of Port, notably Paul Masson and The Christian Brothers, and so have several smaller wineries. Look for bottlings from Llords & Elwood, Richard & Sons or J.W. Morris Port Works.

Sparkling Wines

Champagne is the most famous wine in all the world and the cheeriest, as exciting as fireworks or merry-go-rounds, as engaging as a new toy. No celebration is completely festive without the popping corks, the foaming in the glass, the fizz that tickles the nose, the bubbles bursting on the tongue. Champagne tastes best by itself, but it is good with all those things that white wines enhance. Some devotees claim it is best in the morning; others hold for afternoon; and many insist it is the wine for evening, to crown the day. No matter. Champagne brightens the moment, or makes it.

The wine was invented in the country of Champagne, sixty miles east of Paris, and the name has been borrowed for all sparkling wines—and usually been taken in vain. Sparkling wines made elsewhere rarely match real Champagne. The name is protected by international law to which the United States is not a party, so that our sparkling wines can put the name on the label when the state where the wines are made is identified; blends from various places can be called American Champagne. The same dubious legalism allows imitations like American Swiss cheese.

Champagne is made by fermenting the white juices of the Pinot Noir and Chardonnay, then blending the wines in vats. The resultant cuvée is then bottled with a little yeast and sugar in each, so that a second fermentation takes place in the bottle, forming bubbles of carbon dioxide and

241

some sediment. This is removed by jiggling the bottles upside down so that the sediment trails into the neck. The neck of the bottle is placed in brine to freeze the plug of sediment; the wire muzzle holding the cork is removed; the cork is pulled; the sediment pops out; and a sugar syrup of the same wine and some brandy is poured in, the bottle being quickly re-capped before the bubbles escape. The sugared brandy is called the dos-age, the amount governing the dryness of the wine.

Brut is driest of all, no more than 1½%. Extra Dry or Extra Sec may have up to 3%; Dry or Sec may have 4% or even more. Champagne Na-ture has no dosage at all, leading to confusion, because the phrase is also used for wines that have no sparkle. Brut is the most fashionable Cham-pagne. It is actually too dry for most tastes, particularly when served with food, and most people really prefer the taste of Extra Sec, even when they bow to fashion and drink Brut, which costs more.

Fermenting Champagne a second time in bottle, called *La Méthode Champenoise*, produces the best sparkling wines, distinguished by the fine string of bubbles seen rising in the glass. It is called the bead, and sparkling wines fermented in vats and bottled under pressure produce less distinctive, bigger beads. This Bulk Process, also called Charmat after its deviser, is much cheaper, much faster and much inferior. There are sever-al other ways to sparkle wines, including carbonating the wine like soda water, but all of them produce lesser wines.

Champagnes are usually bottled at four to six atmospheres of pressure, as are most sparkling wines, the broad term for the group being *vins mousseux*, or foaming wines. Good white mousseux from Burgundy and the Savoie are quite dry, at their best when made by the Champagne Method, which is always indicated on the bottle, often with the additional phrase, "Fermented in THIS bottle." Fine sweet sparkling wines are made in Vouvray and Saumur on the Loire, at St. Péray on the Rhône, and even in Bordeaux. The Italian term is *spumante*; the German term is *sekt*; and these can be found on American bottlings imitating the styles.

Wines bottled before the yeasts have fermented all the sugar of the grape will occasionally work to form carbon dioxide. Bubbles will form on the side of the glass when the wine is poured. Such wines are termed *pétillant*, or crackling, German versions are called *Perlwein*, Italians call them *frizzante*. The Swiss wine of Neuchâtel is made to have a little spar-kle, which is called the star. American law now permits wines to have as much as one atmosphere of carbon dioxide, so a lot of wines are now being made with this soda pop effervescence. Sparkling wines with more bubbles carry a high luxury tax that amounts to more than a dollar a bottle. People have been complaining for decades about the silly "tax on bubbles" to no avail. Wine people think taxing bubbles is like taxing the holes in cheese or the raisins in bread.

America's first famous wine was Sparkling Catawba from Nicholas Longworth's Cincinnati vineyards, hailed in Europe before and after the Civil War. Longworth used to complain when restaurants substituted real Champagne for it. Champagne was sweet then, varying wildly until Pasteur revealed the secrets of fermentation, and it was not until the Gay Nineties that Champagnes became dry. The English wanted a dry sparkle, satisfying their sweet thirsts with hocks, short for Hockheimer, from the Rhine. Dry Champagne dubbed English Cuvée became the rage of Paris. Sparkling Catawba disappeared from the international scene, but less syrupy blends can still be found from Meier's Wine Cellars in Ohio and Finger Lakes producers.

California began making sparkling wines long before the turn of the century, the first one to gain international renown being Paul Masson's, which won an award at the Paris Exposition of 1900. A San Francisco bottler had such success with his sparkling wines before World War Two that he established his Weibel Champagne Cellar at Warm Springs near Mission San Jose at the south end of San Francisco Bay. He replanted some abandoned vineyards in Chardonnay, which turned out to be the original ones planted by Leland Stanford. Weibel still produces sparkling wines there, but other wines come from the new cellars and vineyards in Mendocino.

Cook's Imperial Champagne Cellar in St. Louis was famous for its bottlings after the Civil War, languished, and became famous again after Repeal, when an Alsatian named Adolph Heck began making the wines, backed by capital from a Swiss investment firm. After the Second World War the secret Swiss investor turned out to be a former Sekt salesman named von Ribbentrop; the firm was seized. Heck made sparkling wines in Ohio for a few years, eventually becoming head of Italian Swiss Colony and finally setting up Korbel Winery with his sons on the Russian River. Cook's Imperial became a blend of California and Catawba made by the Guild Company in their Roma winery in Fresno.

Heck's sons began making some of California's best sparkling wines: Korbel Brut, Korbel Sec, Korbel Extra Dry, Korbel Rosé and Korbel

Rouge. They also worked out mechanical riddling racks that shake the bottles three times a day and tip them up so that the sediment goes to the neck. ʿɪne bottles quiver and clink awesomely and when the wine is clear, the bottles jiggle along a belt and through a freezing bath and to disgorging machines, then on to filling machines and labelling machines. It's all automatic. A few workers stand by to see that nothing goes wrong.

Much more traditional and among the best is one of the newest. John Davies, a management consultant, became enamored of wines, formed a group to buy Schramsberg—a vineyard, cellars and a gingerbread house on Mount Diamond that was made famous by Robert Louis Stevenson a century ago. Stevenson spent a honeymoon year in the Napa Valley in 1880 and wrote a book about it called *Silverado Squatters*. Davies kept the awkward name because of its history, digging the caves deeper into the slopes, replanting acres of vineyard in Chardonnay and Pinot Noir, then doubling it. He wanted to make wines in the classic style, buying the moribund establishment in 1965 and offering his first Brut in 1972.

There is a trend to lighter and lighter Champagnes, the lightest of all being made only from the Chardonnay grapes grown on the Côte de Blancs south of Epernay. Champagnes so made are called Blanc de Blancs, a name borrowed for blends of dry white table wines. Davies prefers an older style, where a predominance of wine in the cuvée comes from the white juice of the Pinot Noir. The wine so blended is full and fruity, a big wine that demands attention.

The French call such Champagnes *franc et loyal*, in the old tradition, and examples are Krug, Bollinger and Charles Heidsieck. Roederer Crystal and Lanson also have plenty of Pinot Noir in their cuvées, giving the wines body and balance. So does Schramsberg.

The Davies are the only free people in the valley when it comes to planning a dinner because they can serve the wines of others without offending anyone. They start with one of their sparkling wines and select the table wines of their neighbors. Dishes are usually seasonal and varied as much as possible, so there will not be two cheese dishes or two dishes with cream sauces. They select the main course first and the wines to go with it, the wines depending on the real interest of the guests. Sometimes people just want a simple wine that doesn't call for a lot of attention, and often enough a cheese course is eliminated. The dessert is fruit, as often as possible, with a sweet wine like a Barsac or Sauternes, and Port at the end. Champagne is rarely served all through the meal. Dinner is intended to be a pleasing sequence, not a display of wonders. Meals among winemakers tend to be simple, even modest.

Big wineries like to have sparkling wines as part of their lines, and firms like Almadén and Beaulieu Vineyards, Paul Masson and The Christian Brothers go to the trouble of making their own. Many other wineries provide the wines and have others perform the sparkling manipulations. This practice gave one of the best bottlers his start.

Hanns Kornell arrived in New York broke in 1939, after growing up in his grandfather's German vineyard, graduating from the wine school at Geisenheim and working in various European wineries. After stints making Kentucky's first sparkling wine and then Cook's Imperial, he rented a Sonoma winery and began making sparkling wines in his spare time while working as winemaker at Larkmead Vineyard.

The winery north of St. Helena in Napa had come to fame in the last century and had finally become a cooperative for local growers. After six years, Kornell had saved enough to buy the winery in 1958. He began at once sparkling wines for neighboring wineries and making his own. His wines were more in the European style than most of the others, perhaps less flowery and more fruity, and they became so admired that he made a sweet sparkling wine called Muscat Alexandria and an ultra dry one called Sehr Trocken.

The happy cheers that greeted the wines of Schramsberg, Kornell and Korbel and the growing market for those from older wineries encouraged the Moët-Hennesy-Dior complex of France to explore the future in the Napa Valley. The producers of Moët and Chandon, who also make Mercier and Ruinart Champagnes, had been successful in South America and a winery in North America could be even better. Taking a modest stance, they hired Americans to search out the ground, plan and build the winery, and run the company. Perhaps native winemakers would take offence at a French presence.

Napa was delighted. Winemakers had been arriving for generations, ever since Haraszthy, claiming that this was great wine country. Haraszthy's son had even trained at Moët, coming back to make an Eclipse Champagne, that was. Now the largest Champagne producer in the world was setting out to prove the point.

Moët began setting up Domain Chandon in 1973, throwing a party for

245

the valley when they opened the winery in 1977, serving Chandon Napa Valley Brut to all. The label said nothing about Champagne, but there was the familiar bottle wearing gold foil around its neck and the star of Moët as background on the label. Moët's most prestigious Champagne is Dom Perignon, named after the monk who was supposed to have invented it and who is quoted as saying when he took his first sip, "I am drinking stars."

The winery is on a broad sweep below the Mayacamas range, east of Yountville. Long stone walls extend along the ground and are cut into it, rows of barrel arches hovering over the winery and office quarters. Vineyards stretch away, there is a stream widening to a pond, shady oaks and madrones around terraces. Old vats and presses and equipment have been brought over for decoration, along with sets of the early Moët & Chandon posters. A restaurant is presided over by a French chef who's up at dawn to do the daily marketing. Moët's chief winemaker, Edmond Maudière, came over to make the first wines, including one made solely from Pinot Noir. Production is about a million bottles a year.

There are some 850 acres in prospect, about a third in bearing. There are three sections: more than 100 acres around the winery, twice as many up on Mt. Veeder, some 600 down in Carneros. The vineyards will be planted as the market grows. So far, everything is fine, even though the wines have to be priced above eight dollars a bottle. That is a little more than other sparkling wines, but Domain Chandon is not seeking to steal markets from others but to make one of their own. As Americans discover native sparkling wines they may be surprised to find that Chandon is one of them.

The same relaxed way is followed in the other major district producing sparkling wines, the Finger Lakes of New York. Great Western has been a favorite for generations, the portion of native grapes in the blend making the wine novel and distinctive. Widmer's has had marked success with their more flowery blend in recent years, but the prize goes to Charles Fournier of Gold Seal, who came from the Champagne country and who uses the Chardonnay to dominate his blends. His Gold Seal Fournier Blanc de Blancs is one of the most highly prized in the country.

Fournier likes to serve sparkling wine through a meal, particularly with poached fish, hot or cold, and with salty or smoked foods. When red meats are served, red wines usually accompany, Brut or Blanc de Blancs served before or after or with cheese. Sparkling wines can be delicious with fowl and veal dishes, but they are marvelous with cheese, particularly goat cheese.

Sparkling wines are accommodating, but there are certain niceties about service, some sensible. They should be served cold, not frigid, too much chilling blunting their tastes. Glasses should be those used for other wines or the narrow ones called flutes; shallow coupes dissipate the bubbles and slosh easily. Twiddlers and swizzle sticks are abominations; the bubbles took years to get into the wine and are part of the glory of the taste.

In Champagne, it is considered not proper to pop the cork, which is supposed to come out with a sigh, it is said. This is nonsense. The pop signals hilarity.

Opening a bottle is hard, and there's a trick. Remove the wire muzzle by twisting the little ring counterclockwise. Place one hand firmly over the cork, the other on the base of the bottle, and twist the bottle. Most people try to twist the cork, which is almost impossible. Twist the bottle not the cork and let it pop.

Sparkling wine is always poured twice, only about an inch in the glass the first time. This seems silly, but the small pour prevents the wine from foaming out of the glass. When the wine is poured a second time it will not foam, preserving the bubbles.

An open bottle stored in the refrigerator will retain its bubbles without recorking. It is always better, though, to finish the bottle.

Sparkling wine that has gone flat is marvelous for cooking, in a sauce, as a pan glaze, or whenever white wine is called for.

Pink sparkling wines are made by leaving the juice with the skins for a time, and these are often good. Sparkling red wines are made, but these are usually made of poor wines and have to be sweetened to be drunk; they are invariably second-rate.

Many cheap sparkling wines are made from common grapes, particularly Thompson Seedless, and these are generally insipid, oversweet and full of off-tastes. Even the cheapest carry the luxury tax and are poor bargains. A still table wine is always preferable to a cheap sparkling wine.

Some superior sparkling wines:

Brut	*Extra Dry*	*Bulk Process*
Gold Seal Blanc de Blancs	Korbel	Christian Brothers
Schramsberg	Kornell	Weibel
Korbel	Weibel	Almadén
Great Western	Mirassou	Italian Swiss Colony
Almadén Blanc de Blancs		
Domain Chandon		

Part IV:

Matters of Taste

Tasting Wines

Every bottle of wine is a mystery, most interesting when you know nothing about it and you let the wine in the glass speak for itself. A glance can tell you much.

The wine should be clear. If there is any cloudiness there is something wrong with the wine; you need not even taste it.

The smell tells you much more. If there is anything unpleasant in the smell—tasters call it the "nose"—there is something wrong with the wine. Any rank smell—of stale vegetables, of pigsty or chicken run, of a chemistry laboratory or a medicine chest, of burning tires or scorched toast or struck matches—is a sign that there was something wrong with the fermentation. A strong smell of wet wood or concrete, or a smell of cork, is a sign that the wine has been poorly kept.

A good wine smells good, with no sickly smell of flowers or rotting fruit. Any flowery or fruity smells should be pleasing and appetizing. Some wines seem to have no smell at all, or very little, which is a sign that there is not much to the wine or that the wine has not been opened long enough. Or maybe it's just too cold.

When you are tasting wines at home, most pleasure comes from choosing half a dozen bottles of a district or variety, preferably of the same year and not much more than a dollar apart in price. Tasting the wines alone can be deceiving.

251

With a buffet, a dozen people can spend a pleasant evening tasting six wines, and as many as twenty people could be accommodated. Six people at a dinner party would enjoy tasting four different wines.

Unfortunately, the host is most interested in wines and if he chooses them it is hard for him to taste blind. Retailers can help; they can select the wines, put each in brown bags, then the wines can be opened without taking the bottle from the bag. Some people think the effort isn't worth the trouble. For those who want to learn about wines, however, blind comparative tastings are the most revealing—of wines, and of the accuracy of your own tasting.

Sweet or Dry?

"I don't like sweet wines; they can't be dry enough for me," declares the one who's getting used to drinking white wine instead of highballs, pleased with his Chardonnay or Macon Blanc. Dry they are, but others trying them will say they're not dry enough, claiming to prefer Neuchâtel, which was supposed to be James Joyce's favorite wine, or Chablis, which is supposed to be the driest of the Burgundies, or maybe Pouilly-Fumé, which is supposed to be the driest of the Loires. Dry means not-so-dry to those who feel that all the above wines are fruity and claim to prefer Brut Champagne, the driest of sparkling wines—and also fruity. We need a standard.

To come to some agreement about what is truly dry, and what we can use as a guide in this book, you may want to taste some sugar water with your regular drinking companions. The aim is not to find out your threshold of awareness to sugar, which varies from time to time and from one person to another, but simply to agree on what can be considered dry, which in wine parlance is considered to be the absence of sweetness.

To get some idea of a sweetness range you might drink a few bottles of Champagne. Brut has up to 1½% sugar, and is much too dry for most foods, except perhaps for a sliver of ham, or oysters, or caviar or mild cheeses. Extra Dry Champagnes, often labeled Extra Sec, may have up to 3% sugar and taste good with many foods, while those called Dry or Sec may have 4% or more sugar and can taste good with chicken or fish—or even a not-too-sweet dessert.

Still more interesting comparisons can be made with Rhine wines: those labeled Kabinett will have little or no residual sugar and may taste

252

lightly flowery or fruity—and taste best by themselves or with bites of smoked or spicy foods. Those made from late-picked grapes are called Spätlesen and will be definitely flowery; those from grapes selected for extra sweetness are called Auslesen and will be definitely fruity. These last two may taste definitely sweet and are best by themselves, with fruit, or with dessert. The range is vast; there are even Rhine wines made from grapes that have dried on the vine, Trockenbeerenauslesen, and these are always sweet.

The trick is to agree about what constitutes sweetness and what does not. Eventually, you'll love the whole range. Take an ordinary highball glass; pour in a cup of water—eight ounces—and add half a teaspoonful of ordinary sugar, stirring until all the sugar is dissolved.* Taste it and you will just barely detect a very light sweetness, scarcely noticeable. Do this with soda water and the sweetness is less noticeable to some, even though some soda waters contain a little sugar. Add an ounce of vodka to the sugar water and the result may taste slightly sweeter; add a teaspoonful of lemon juice and the solution may taste sweeter still, for the lemon brings out the taste. You might try the same thing with a cup of hot tea and then a cup of tea that has cooled.

The sweetness you will notice is scarcely worth fussing about, even in the cooled tea with its tannic acid and with the citric acid from the lemon. The various fruit acids in a wine impart fruity tastes, while the various alcohols in a wine impart flowery tastes. Both are often called sweetness. Such wines are properly considered to be dry. They are so identified in this book.

There's still room for confusion. Tannin is the acid in wine that has a bitter taste, scarcely noticed when it is balanced by the other fruit acids. And there is glycerine in a wine as a by-product of fermentation and of aging, which is faintly sweet and slightly oily, a quality that is also described as sweetness. A quick sip can lead the unsuspecting to declare the complex taste of a wine with so much in it as sweetish. A wine is so complex we need further distinctions.

Wines of a dryness we have described may have a definitely flowery taste from the various alcohols therein. Rieslings and other white wines from the Rhineland and similar northern regions are often lightly flowery,

*This dilution is about 1 degree of sugar.

even though there is little grape sugar left in the wine. Other whites may taste fruity from the fruit acids, like Loire wines and those from such grapes as the Sauvignon Blanc. Descriptions mention such distinctions so that tastes won't be noted as sweetness.

All this spelled out is not confusing when you taste wines—only when you try to describe what you're tasting. "Maybe it's flower and maybe it's fruit and maybe it's glycerine, but it still tastes sweet to me," claims the one who doesn't want to focus on the taste, and there's no argument. Steaks are sweet to some, as are roast chicken done with herbs and fish with lemon. Those wines we call dry will taste fine with such dishes.

There are many wines in which all the grape sugar has been converted to alcohol, wines called bone dry. Winemakers say they are without residual sugar. In their tastes you may still note floweriness or fruitiness. Most people agree that a wine that tastes sharp with fruit acid is truly dry, like a Montrachet or a Chardonnay. Without the sharpness from the acid a wine is apt to taste bland and empty; some people think such bland wines are truly dry, really preferring them with meals. A good wine full of taste is simply too much for them to enjoy; they prefer the blandness.

Any wine with less than one percent residual sugar is considered dry—to expert wine tasters, but not to the trade. The wine world long ago discovered that people talk dry and drink sweet. Most blended wines—those with brand names or regional names—have some sugar left in the wine so your average drinker won't call it sour. (You may want to know that sour wine is wine that has gone bad, through the action of acetic acid, having turned to vinegar, *vin aigre* in French, sour wine.)

Wine always tastes drier when drunk with food. This fact fools people at tastings, where a flowery or fruity wine may seem to be sweet when tasted against a wine less pronounced. And both may taste dry when drunk at meals.

You begin to notice a definite sweetness in wines that contain more than one percent residual sugar—wines that may still be indentified as "dry" on the label. Most jug wines fall into this category, those called California Burgundy or California Chablis being blends that may have two or three degrees of sugar. Blends called California Chianti or Italianate names are blends that may contain more than three percent sugar and have come to be marketed as "mellow" wines. They can taste dry enough with a spaghetti sauce or something charred from the barbecue, the strong tastes of the food serving to mask the sweetness of the wine.

BODY

Everybody knows what is meant when a wine is said to have body—
until we try to put it into words. To come to some agreement we could
make a pot of tea.

Bring a quart of water to a rolling boil; rinse the teapot with a little of
it; then pour this off. Add three tea bags and pour the boiling water over
them. After three minutes, pour a cup, at four minutes pour another, and
pour a third cup when the tea has steeped for five minutes. The first cup
poured will taste watery, light in body; the second will taste strongly of
tea, full-bodied; the third will be too strong for most tastes. Tannic and
even bitter, the third cup will be more drinkable if you add half a teaspoonful of sugar, a teaspoonful of lemon juice and an ounce of vodka.

Wines pick up tannin from the stems, skins and pips of the grapes and
from the oak in which the wine is aged. A claret from Bordeaux—or a
California Cabernet—will taste strongly of tannin after three years in
wood and when it is first bottled it will not be pleasant to drink. After
three more years in bottle, some of the tannin will have dropped out of the
wine, precipitated as cream of tartar to form sediment in the bottom of the
of the bottle, and the wine will not taste so bitter. Some wines hold their
tannin so long that the wine may not be drinkable until ten years after the
vintage, even longer.

Most white wines spend little time in wood and are much lighter in
body. Not that they taste watery, because of the acids and alcohols they
contain, but few taste as full as red wines do. Some taste so light, like
those from Germany's Mosel, that they have been called glorious water.

Both reds and whites can be too light in body, like tea that has steeped
only two minutes. It's all a matter of balance.

Winemakers can control the amount of body a wine will contain, making light wines or full ones, depending on what they consider to be the
best wine to make from a particular harvest of grapes. Nobody wants a
watery wine, but if there is not much sugar in the grapes to be converted
to alcohol during fermentation, a winemaker may not have much choice.
If his grapes come in with a reading that shows 20 grams of sugar for 100
grams of juice (it's called 20° Balling on a hydrometer or 20° Brix on a
saccharometer; the scales are named after the men who devised them) you
can figure on a wine with 11% alcohol (you multiply by .55).

If the juice has a proper amount of fruit acids, the wine will be light in

255

body, with a fresh and lively taste, pleasantly tart. We call it the real acidity of a wine—the chemist will call it the pH—and it is a measure of intensity. A wine with a pH of 7 is neutral, while one of 8 or more will be alkaline and one of 5 or less will be acid. Stick a piece of litmus paper in a glass of wine and if it turns blue it's alkaline—and will taste empty and bland.

The winemaker talks of the fixed acidity of the wine, all the various fruit acids; tartaric, malic, lactic, citric and others. An acid he doesn't want is acetic acid, which results when air gets at a wine and allows a microorganism called an acetobacter to thrive; this converts the wine to vinegar. Less than one part in a thousand cannot be detected, but two parts can and such a wine is called sour, or spoiled. Some acetic acid is present in all wines and is called volatile acidity. When a winemaker talks about total acidity, he means the sum of all the acids, fixed and volatile. He keeps air away from his wines to keep the volatile acidity at a minimum.

Alcohol masks the acid taste, so the winemaker looks for grapes high in sugar—say 22°—so he can make a full-bodied wine of 12% and maybe leave a little sugar in the wine (by stopping fermentation) to mask tartness.

AN EXTENDED WINE LIST: WHITES, REDS, MID-VARIETALS

SAUVIGNON BLANC/FUMÉ BLANC

At their best after three years and before five, wines retailing for around four dollars are best buys. Those sold as Fumé Blanc are occasionally drier, perhaps with less fruit and flower, and are not necessarily preferable.

Wente Bros. California Sauvignon Blanc
Concannon Vineyard, Livermore Valley Sauvignon Blanc
The Christian Brothers Napa Fumé
The Christian Brothers, Napa Valley Sauvignon Blanc
Beringer Vineyards, Fumé Blanc
Beaulieu Vineyard, Beaulieu
Sterling Vineyards, Napa Valley Sauvignon Blanc
Robert Mondavi, Napa Valley Fumé Blanc
Inglenook Vineyards, Napa Valley Sauvignon Blanc

* * *

Limited distribution:
Spring Mountain Vineyards, Napa Valley Sauvignon Blanc
Joseph Phelps Vineyards, Napa Valley Fumé Blanc
Caymus Vineyards, Napa Valley Sauvignon Blanc
Dry Creek Vineyards, Sonoma County Fumé Blanc
Davis Bynum, Sonoma Fumé Blanc

NOTE: Try the new bottlings, coming into the market because of increasing popularity of the wine.

CHARDONNAY

$5 or under	*Above $6*
Louis Martini Winery	Heitz Wine Cellars
Beaulieu Vineyard Beaufort	Joseph Phelps Vineyard
Wente Bros.	Robert Mondavi Winery
Monterey Vineyard	Burgess Cellars
Pedroncelli Winery	Freemark Abbey
Parducci Wine Cellars	
Rutherford Hill	

$6 or under
Beringer Brothers
Mirassou Vineyards

RIESLING, alias JOHANNISBERG RIESLING or WHITE RIESLING

Under $4	
Ste. Michelle Washington State	
The Christian Brothers	*Around $4*
Paul Masson Vineyards	Weibel Champagne Vineyards
Wente Bros.	Simi Winery
Pedroncelli Winery	Beaulieu Vineyards Beauclair
Beringer Vineyards	Louis Martini Winery
Almadén Vineyards	Sebastiani Vineyards
	Sonoma Vineyards

257

$5 and up
Robert Mondavi Winery
Concannon Vineyard
Mirassou Vineyards
Chappellet Vineyards
Freemark Abbey

CHENIN BLANC

Dry	*Half-dry*
Dry Creek Vineyard	Charles Krug Winery
Chappellet Vineyards	The Christian Brothers
Sterling Vineyards	Wente Bros.
Rutherford Hill	Mirassou Vineyards
Stag's Leap Winery	Sebastiani Vineyards
Chalone Vineyard	

SEMILLON

Ste. Michelle, Washington	Concannon
Wente Bros.	Charles Krug
San Martin	

GEWÜRZTRAMINER

Wente Bros.	Louis M. Martini
Mirassou	Korbel
Monterey Vineyard	Pedroncelli
Sterling	Ste. Michelle, Washington

TRAMINER

Robert Mondavi	Charles Krug

CABERNET SAUVIGNON

Under $4
Paul Masson Vineyards
Widmer Vineyards
Sebastiani Vineyards

Around $4
BeautTour–Beaulieu Vineyards
Louis Martini Winery
The Christian Brothers
Korbel Winery
Cresta Blanca
Weibel Champagne Vineyards
Pedroncelli Winery
Sonoma Vineyards

Around $5
Beaulieu Vineyard
Simi Winery
Parducci Wine Cellars
Beringer Brothers
Mirassou Vineyards

Around $6
Robert Mondavi Winery
Freemark Abbey

MERLOT

.Sterling
Louis Martini

Stag's Leap Wine Cellars
Veedercrest

PINOT NOIR

Fruity style uniquely Californian:
Around $4
. The Christian Brothers
Wente Bros.
Louis Martini Winery

Beaulieu Vineyard Beau Velours
Sonoma Vineyards

Around $5
Geyser Peak Winery
Parducci Wine Cellars

Charles Krug Winery
Mirassou Vineyards

More like southern Burgundies in style:
Around $4
Widmer's Wine Cellars
Beringer Brothers
Pedroncelli Winery

Around $12
Hanzell Vineyards

Around $6
Robert Mondavi Winery
Caymus Vineyards
Freemark Abbey

ZINFANDEL

A wise buyer will get one case of Zinfandel a month for a year, starting with the cheapest, forget them for five years, then drink a bottle or so a month until they are gone. The wines will cost less than $400 and will last into the mid-Eighties, at which time he will wish that he had set aside more.

Sonoma
Pedroncelli Winery
Souverain
Sonoma Vineyards
Sebastiani Winery
Buena Vista Vineyard

Mendocino
Parducci Wine Cellars
Fetzer Vineyards
Cresta Blanca

Napa
Nichelini Vineyards
Clos du Val
Rutherford Hill
Sutter Home Winery
Louis Martini Winery
The Christian Brothers
Charles Krug Winery
Inglenook Vineyards

Santa Clara/Monterey
Mirassou Vineyards
Gemello Winery
Paul Masson Vineyards
Monterey Vineyards

Late Harvest
Trentadue Winery
Mayacamas Vineyards
Ridge Vineyards

Rosé
Pedroncelli Winery
Mayacamas Vineyards

Fermented for early drinking
Dry Creek Vineyards
Charles Krug Winery
Montevina
Grand Cru Vineyards

Low-Priced Zinfandel
Italian Swiss Colony
Gallo

* * *

PETITE SIRAH

$3.00–3.50
Souverain
Wente Bros.
Paul Masson Vineyards
Sonoma Vineyards
Mirassou Petite Rosé

Under $6
Burgess Cellars
Robert Mondavi Winery
Freemark Abbey

Around $4
Concannon Vineyard
Parducci Wine Cellars

GAMAY NOIR, NAPA GAMAY

The Christian Brothers
Robert Mondavi

Paul Masson

GAMAY BEAUJOLAIS

Louis M. Martini
Wente Bros.
Sonoma Vineyards
Sebastiani

Pedroncelli
Parducci
Monterey Vineyard
Mirassou

BARBERA

Louis M. Martini
Sebastiani
Paul Masson

Bear Mountain
Almadén

GRENACHE ROSE

Almadén
Paul Masson
San Martin

Sonoma Vineyards
Sebastiani
Ste. Michelle, Washington

GAMAY ROSE

Korbel

ZINFANDEL ROSE

Concannon

MID-VARIETALS

California makes an odd distinction between premium varietals—Pinot Noir and Chardonnay, Cabernet Sauvignon and Sauvignon Blanc, and Johannisberg or White Riesling—and all the others, which are lumped together as mid-varietals. This is a distinction for the trade, mid-varietals mostly costing $3 or less. A few, like some of the Sylvaners, can rise to $4; over that, wines are considered premium, regardless of variety. Here is a list of some of the best mid-varietals, those marked semi-dry being lightly sweet.

SYLVANER

The Christian Brothers Sylvaner Riesling
Louis Martini Mountain Riesling (Sylvaner)
Parducci Mendocino County Sylvaner Riesling
Paul Masson California Riesling
San Martin Vineyards Sylvaner Riesling
Mirassou Vineyards Monterey Riesling (Sylvaner)

GREY RIESLING

Sonoma Vineyards Sonoma County Grey Riesling
Wente Bros. California Grey Riesling
Beringer Vineyards Grey Riesling
Almadén California Mountain Grey Riesling
Cresta Blanca California Grey Riesling
Souverain Mendocino County Grey Riesling

EMERALD RIESLING

Paul Masson Emerald Dry (semi-dry)
San Martin Santa Clara Valley Emerald Riesling (semi-dry)

GREEN HUNGARIAN

Sebastiani North Coast Counties Green Hungarian
Weibel Green Hungarian
M. Lamont Green Hungarian
Buena Vista Green Hungarian

FRENCH COLOMBARD

Sonoma Vineyards Sonoma County French Colombard
Cresta Blanca California French Colombard
Almadén French Colombard
Inglenook French Colombard
M. Lamont French Colombard

RUBY CABERNET

Paul Masson Rubion
M. Lamont Ruby Cabernet
Sonoma Vineyards Ruby Cabernet
Paul Masson Ruby Cabernet
Inglenook Ruby Cabernet

CARIGNANE

Simi Parducci
Rapazzini

A Typical Wine Tasting

The best way to find out about wines is to try several at one time and find out which ones are best. This is easier than you might think. You taste them all blind, of course, so that you don't know beforehand what any of the wines are. That way you won't be influenced by names or prices, only by the taste of the wines.

Gallagher's, one of the New York steak houses, has begun to do this each year. Half a dozen writers on wine are asked to taste a collection of bottlings, choosing the five best, or those they like the best, to go on the wine list. A retailer familiar with California wines selected two dozen reds and the tasters made their choices. The wines were in brown paper bags, arranged in groups, and here are my notes on the wines, after the judges had made their choices. I started with L because there was a mob around the earlier letters and I tasted to find out which were the best wines:

Group I

A—Off nose, suffocating, green. /Very woody—not Limousin oak. Very light and acid.
B—Very little nose. /Good fruit, good balance, watery.

265

C—Off nose, full, familiar and off. /Off taste.

D—Very light, clean, some brackish. Good fruit. /Some odd, dead taste in middle.

Pick: D Best, but empty. D cleared up later.

Group II

E—Empty. /Watery.

F—Faint. /Watery.

G—Very light. /Something .

H—Vanilla. /Some fullness.

I—None. /Acid, clean.

J—Cooked. /Lots of wood. Clean enough.

K—Brackish. /Nice clean taste.

Pick: All thin, all way down. F best, if must choose.

Group III (I began tasting here, went through the next groups, then back to first two.)

L—Good nose, grape-y, light, round. /Very light, very dry, very thin.

M—Some nice fruit, but mostly flower: way down. /Good fruit. Light.

N—Good Burgundy nose. /Acid, not much character. Acid lingers, stays.

O—No nose. Some little flower. /Clean, light, dry. No character, short.

Pick: M stays in mouth, with some pucker. (This could be Pinot Noir because of smell of N. M is better wine.)

Group IV

P—Nice. /Even, dry taste. Acid lasts.

Q—Some nose, light fruit. /Very thin, acid.

R—Very light. /Wood, fuller but light. Good oak taste.

S—Some nose—flower. /Clean, long. Tannin too much.

Pick: S, but both R and S need time. Best group, all around. All with flower instead of bouquet, but nice.

Group V

T—Light nose. /Fat, but empty

U—Good fruit, developed. /Round, much tannin, clean. Falls out in middle.

266

V—Odd flavor, light, grassy. /Good balance, vinification off.
W—Very light flower. /Quite empty.
X—Fullest, brackish. /Good, long, watery. Empty in middle.
Pick: U, if choice is expected.

The first comment for each wine refers to what I got out of swirling the glass and then smelling the wine. The second comment is what the wine tasted like.

The groups were on separate tables. At each one, I poured a row of glasses, sniffed along the row, sniffed them all again, then tasted down the row, spitting out each mouthful of wine. This was all done quickly, with interruptions, but it was not too distracting. Easy enough, anyway, to smell the wines and taste them. After a couple of groups, I noticed I was tasting "light"; that is, all the wines tasted light to me. There was very little in the smells.

Either my smelling was off (not so because I was noticing slight differences) or the wines had been hustled to the restaurant and quickly opened; the wines should have come to the restaurant a couple of weeks earlier and been opened a couple of hours before the tasting. The wines had rested for a couple of days, I guessed, and had been opened an hour earlier for tasting by the judges.

Anyway, I concluded that the wines were light; there was very little smell to make it possible to identify which grapes the wines were made from. You could guess; I guessed that Group III was Petite Sirah because N had a definite smell, and if so, it was Parducci, which I like a lot. I also like Concannon, so Concannon might be M.

Talking with some of the judges, it became clear to me that they had assumed each group was a different grape, but the wines had so few varietal characteristics that they scarcely knew which was what, from the tastes. They could figure them out, by logic. The Burgundy smell, obvious in only one of the wines, must be Pinot Noir. The fruity smell of the next group must then be Petite Sirah, although maybe there was some Merlot in there, or Malbec. The last group was probably Cabernet, because they were driest, tasted most of wood. There was a progression, obviously, so the large Group II was certainly Zinfandel, and the first group certainly Gamay.

But taste didn't tell you that. The wines were generally light. They were flowery rather than fruity. There were some definite off-tastes, so the selection was a mixed bag. Looking over my notes, I selected a group of drinkable light wines: B and D, particularly with food, maybe hamburgers or pasta, or a platter of delicatessen. The wines would taste best chilled.

F, G and I were drinkable but very light. Maybe with sandwiches. Chill the wines. M and N, particularly M, with beef. The whole group good with stews, but very gentle wines. R is best balance; S has more to it, but needs time.

Of the last group, only U. Good with roasts.

The groups were haphazard; selections could have been better. Picking five of them all, I chose F, N, R, S, U.

There was some confusion among the judges, some of whom understood they should pick the preferred wine from each group. Others thought they should pick the best five wines from them all. After scoring, four wines were preferred by the judges: C, F, Q, U. In discussion, it became clear that the wines had been chosen because they were ready to drink, so that some fine bottlings had been kept out of the tastings. Obviously, many other good bottlings had simply not been available.

There were many wineries I would like to have seen represented. Among the larger ones, I would like to have tasted the wines of The Christian Brothers, Paul Masson and Almadén. From medium-sized wineries, I would like to have been able to judge Beaulieu Vineyards, Charles Krug Winery, Korbel, Concannon, Wente, Monterey. And there were a dozen small wineries: Heitz, Mayacamas, Chappellet, Freemark Abbey, Buena Vista, Pedroncelli, Hanzell, Bruce, Pedrizzetti, Weibel, Fetzer, ZD.

Still, the tasting was a good chance to judge a large group of wines. The two or three that tasted off to me may simply have been bad bottles; I wanted to taste them again, another time. Here is the list of wines:

A. Mirassou Vineyards, Gamay Beaujolais
B. Robert Mondavi Winery, Gamay
C. Sebastiani Vineyards, Gamay Beaujolais
D. Louis M. Martini Winery, Gamay Beaujolais

E. Sonoma Vineyards, Zinfandel
F. Ridge Vineyards, Lytton Springs, Zinfandel
G. Sutter Home Winery, Zinfandel
H. Chateau Montelena, Zinfandel

I.   Souverain of Alexander Valley, Zinfandel
J.   Callaway Vineyard & Winery, Zinfandel
K.   San Martin Vineyards Co., Zinfandel

L.   Sonoma Vineyards, Pinot Noir
M.   Sterling Vineyards, Pinot Noir
N.   Caymus Vineyards, Pinot Noir
O.   Inglenook Vineyards, Pinot Noir

P.   Burgess Cellars, Petite Sirah
Q.   Robert Mondavi Winery, Petite Sirah
R.   Parducci Wine Cellars, Petite Sirah
S.   Sonoma Vineyards, Petite Sirah

T.   Cuvaison, Inc. Lot #73-74, Cabernet Sauvignon
U.   Stag's Leap Wine Cellars, Cabernet Sauvignon
V.   Stonegate Winery, Cabernet Sauvignon
W.   Beringer Vineyards, Cabernet Sauvignon
X.   Simi Winery, Cabernet Sauvignon

Viewpoint: Afterthoughts On American Wine

"What do you really think of American wines?" asked my seatmate, as we jounced back to New York after judging the creations from some seventy wineries of the East and Midwest. They came from the Blue Ridge of Virginia and the White Mountains of New Hampshire, from the Ozarks and Ontario and hopeful plantings in between.

Trains seem to stir the spleen. I've never tasted a wine from native grapes, pure indigenous American grapes, I really liked, was my surly remark, including the Scuppernong. I detest Concord, Kosher wines are simple syrup to me, the sugarwater pinks should be outlawed.

Hybrids are another matter. The reds are just drinkable and may be more so in the Eighties, but will be best in blends. The whites are good now and are going to be wonderful—new wines for the Eighties from new places. And here in the east we are going to get wonders from the white viniferas, from Ontario vineyards like Inniskillin and Charal, from Michigan vineyards like Tabor Hill and Leelanau and Makana, from Markko and Cedar Hill in Ohio, Mazza in Pennsylvania or one of the dozen others, Montbray in Maryland, Meredyth in Virginia. Small vineyards are going in everywhere.

A new winery, Charal Vineyards of the Niagara Peninsula in Blenheim, Ontario, won the top award for a Chardonnay in the 1977 competition among eastern wines. While they only made a small batch, subsequent

271

competitions will have wines from some forty wineries that were licensed in 1977. These include ten in New York State: Cagnasso Winery, Clinton Vineyards, Demay Wine Cellars, El Paso Winery, Heron Hill Winery, Mack Fruit Farms, Northlake Vineyards and Windmill Farms. During the Eighties they may produce surprising bottles. And what about the six new ones in Ohio? There's Bushcreek, Colonial, Grand River, Heritage, Vinterra and Wyandotte. Or Pennsylvania's: Conestoga, Lafayette, Lapic, Lembo, Mazza and Wilmont. Minnesota has Lake Sylvia and Alexia Bailly; Missouri has Kruger's and Midi. New Mexico has La Vina. The South has several more: Berrywine, Byrd and Zim in Maryland; Truluck in South Carolina; The Winery Rushing in Mississippi. Enthusiasts are opening up a new world of wines, as they did a generation ago in California.

"What about California?"

New wineries are continuing to appear in California—Lower Lake Winery in Lake County; Keenan Winery in Napa; Channing Cellars, Château Vintners and Montclair Winery, across San Francisco Bay in Alameda County. Old ones like Villa Armando in Livermore are expanding operations; revitalized ones like Stony Ridge in Pleasanton are beginning to offer exceptional wines. A cluster of small wineries have been set up on the peninsula in the Santa Cruz range, including Sherill Cellars, Page Mill Winery, Ox Mountain; further south are Ahlgren Vineyard, Sunrise Winery, P and M Staiger, Frick, Parson's, Wines by Wheeler, Vines of Nepenthe and Santa Cruz Mountain Vineyard. There's Sycamore Creek to be heard from, Sommelier Winery, and one that claims to be the smallest in the state, Ronald Lamb. There will be a dozen new wineries from Monterey, many of them pursuing the perfect Pinot Noir, among them Turgeon & Lohr, Calera, Carmel Bay, Durney and Ventan. Down in Santa Barbara there is Sanford & Benedict, Santa Ynez, Santa Barbara Winery, Rancho Sisquoc, Zaca Mesa, Vega, Estrella River and Star Crest. As the names get more Californian, the wines become more and more typical of the places from which they come. By 2000, many will be famous.

Presently, California wines under two dollars are muck—what the English call plonk—nondescript blends from bulk production grapes, stretched wines from mediocre grapes, "mellow" wines bland with sugar to hide off-tastes. But there's a change coming—blends of wines with names of good grapes from bulk producers—wines that are left to be dry.

There's Barbera from Gallo, Colony Cabernet Sauvignon from Italian Swiss, the range from M. Lamont. Every big shipper in California is going to have a line of blends with grape names for two dollars and less. You just have to try them.

As for those called Burgundy, Chablis, and so forth—Californians insist on using the stolen names because they have been accepted on the low end of the market—the wines are usually mediocre, bland, sweetish—the lowest common denominator. Brand name wines or those called mountain wines are often better. As for pop wines—forget them.

"What about the ten-dollar bottles from the boutique wineries?"

Invariably good, invariably overpriced. Taking price alone, my interest can rise to 100% when the wine costs $5. Interest drops 20% for every dollar over that. There may be some fabulous ten-dollar bottles, but the expected delight occurs in maybe one bottle out of five. The proportion may rise in the Eighties, but the odds of getting a marvel today are long—about the same as those for buying estate-bottled Burgundies.

"So you think ten dollars is too much?"

Yes. But suppose you like the wines of Heitz or Chappellet, of Spring Mountain or Chalone? They are good buys if you like them, even at ten dollars.

"But they vary from year to year."

They do. And price reflects the valuation of the vintage. California claimed for years that every year was good. Actually, every year was mediocre, until they began finding isolated spots where the grape was pushed. They love their microclimates and they make a difference. The old regional classifications are too broad.

As to vintages, '68, '69 and '73 have been considered better than average. Cool weather in '74 and '75 produced fine wines, although fall rains in '75 meant that early grapes like Riesling and Chardonnay are best. Drought in '76 and '77 pushed the vines so good wines have been made.

Spring frosts made for light wines in those years unmentioned, around the decade's turn, but '70 reds that were left long on the vine can be fine. The fact of the matter is that the growing season is plenty long, that frosts limit quantity, that irrigation makes up for lack of rain and wet harvests are rare. Vintages are most useful to indicate the age of the wines.

"How old can the reds go?"

Wines mature faster than in Europe. The whites are ready when bottled. Few reds improve much after five years. Cabernets, Zinfandels and

273

Petite Sirahs can be vinified long and then put in small cooperage for two years or so, and these may take ten years to become ready to drink, but these wines are scarce and carefully identified on labels.

"So what are you finally saying?"

Be fearless about buying wines priced between two dollars and five dollars. Range wide. Try those from new wineries. When you find those you like, buy cases. And try them with meals. Don't have tastings.

"I like tastings."

Then have tastings. I am sometimes bored by tastings, after twenty-five years. They can take too long; the talk is not always scintillating. A professional wine buyer will be presented with a row of wines—maybe twenty—all from the same grape and the same vintage. In two minutes he can choose the three or four that interest him. He will buy them and enjoy them at leisure, with meals.

Most tastings present a hodgepodge—different grapes from different producers, from different years. Such a group is a sampling, not a tasting, good to go to if the wines or winemakers are unfamiliar. But such events are not meant for enjoyment of the wines. They are like guided tours, where you hit high spots. It's much more fun to settle down for a while, with a few bottles and a few friends at a meal.

"What about foods to go with the wine?"

Good cooks abound, city chefs are as pretentious as anywhere else, but the bounty of good vegetables and fish and seafood has tended to keep food simple. This is particularly true in the wine country, where foods too subtle or too full of taste might detract from the wine. That would never do. The great emphasis on salads has made a demand for simple wines. The growing number of subtle wines has further emphasized that good and simple cooking—when everything's perfect—is the best foil for wines. This is the hardest kind of cooking, of course. Bread, cheese and sausages make the perfect feast with wine, and this is served over and over again—maybe with something from the barbecue or the oven. But wine comes first. Masters of French, Italian and Oriental cuisines diligently adjust their dishes to the wines—most frequently in the direction of simplicity. It is not at all unusual to have a particularly noble wine served by itself, before a meal, so there will be no distraction. Some cheese may accompany it, but often not even that.

"How many wines are there to choose from, would you say?"

Under five dollars there must be a thousand to choose from, in the Napa

Valley alone. Add another thousand from the rest of California, at least another hundred from elsewhere. Of course, all of these aren't available. But there are at least a thousand different wines that are, through local stores, or in those of the major markets, or by mail from the vineyards.

Without any doubt at all, in the American market they are the best buys in the world of wines, matched only by odd bottlings occasionally available from the various European regions. American wines are simply not to be missed. A glorious renaissance of wonder has begun, and wines may lead the way to excellence in other realms of art. Certainly the brilliance of our wines should lead to a flowering in all kinds of creativity. The inspiration is there, in wine after wine.

There's a secret to buying wines, a simple one. Something makes you curious about a winemaker or shipper, so you buy a bottle and have it with dinner. If it's good, you try another. Those you like particularly well, you then buy by the case. You learn to trust your information, the hints you get from friend, merchant or label. Soon you get an instinct—a bird dog's sense—for when a wine you hear of or see on a shelf will be better than good.

This information does not often come from descriptions of past vintages, strangely enough. Those described in print are usually expensive. When they are not, the description is apt to be polite, or couched in vague language; this can only be negative. In California, especially, with winemakers moving from place to place, vineyards changing hands, techniques changing, vines coming to maturity, past wonders may not be repeated.

Wines are new every year. Explore them curiously. Don't depend on wine descriptions to lead you to the best vineyards on the shelves.

California hasn't found its soils yet. Rutherford dust may have something to do with the Napa Cabernets; limestone on Chalone's shelf certainly has something to do with their Chardonnays and Pinots, but elsewhere there is scarcely enough history to be sure the soil is important. Maybe the deep gravel along the Russian River benches has effect; maybe the rocky terrains high in the Mayacamas bring desired stress to the vines. But so far, most of it is winemaking with fully developed grapes that have held their acid. These are variables enough. More subtle marvels will be revealed in time.

A BRIEF BIBLIOGRAPHY

Buying the wines can be more revealing than the books about them, but there are those born to read first and savor after. A touring guide available free, which lists wineries that can be visited and their hours, is *California's Wine Wonderland,* to be had by requesting a copy from the Wine Institute, 165 Post Street, San Francisco, CA. 94108.

Here are available free winery newsletters:

THE WINES OF WARNER, Warner Vineyards, Paw Paw, MI 49079.
BOTTLES AND BINS, Charles Krug Winery, St. Helena, CA 94574.
SEBASTIANI VINEYARDS NEWSLETTER, Box AA, Sonoma, CA 95476.
VINEYARD VIGNETTES, Concannon Vineyard, Box 432, Livermore, CA 94550.
THE WOODINVILLE PRESS, Chateau Ste. Michelle, Box 1976, Woodinville, WA 98072.
NEWS FROM THE PEAK, Geyser Peak Winery, Box 25, Geyserville, CA 95441.
THE SIMI NEWSLETTER, Box 946, Healdsburg, CA 95448.
BERINGER'S VINEYARD REPORT, Box 111, St. Helena, CA 94574.
MONTEREY VINEYARDS, Box 780, Gonzales, CA 93926.

WINE AND THE PEOPLE, Berkeley Wine Company, 907 University Ave., Berkeley, CA 94710.

HANNS KORNELL CHAMPAGNE NEWSLETTER, Box 249, St. Helena, CA 94574.

ON TOP OF M. LAMONT, Bear Mountain Winery, Box 428, Di Giorgio, CA 93217.

PAPAGNI PRESS, Papagni Vineyard, 31754 Ave. 9, Madera, CA 93637.

MIRASSOU LATEST PRESS, 3000 Aborn Rd., San Jose, CA 95121.

NEWS FROM THE MONTEREY VINEYARD, Box 780, Gonzales, CA 93926.

California Wine Country is a quite extensive guide by a knowledgeable enthusiast, Bob Thompson, published by Lane Books, Menlo Park, California. With English expert, Hugh Johnson, he wrote *The California Wine Book,* published by William Morrow, New York.

For background there is *The Wines of America,* by Leon D. Adams, the first head of the Wine Institute, published in Boston by Houghton Mifflin.

A book of interviews with some of California's best is called *Great Winemakers of California,* by Robert Benson, published by Capra Press, Santa Barbara. Many of the questions are naive; some of the best winemakers are not included; but the book holds much interest for buffs.

Vintage Image, a publishing house in St. Helena, has been issuing a series of books on various California wine regions—a handsome pen drawing of each winery with a brief description on the facing page—that gives the feel of the wine country. Drawings are by Sebastian Titus, and text for each region is done by teams; the one for the *Napa Valley* was prepared by Michael Topolos, Betty Dopson and Jeffrey Caldeway, while the one for *Sonoma and Mendocino* is the work of Patricia Latimer and Deborah Kenly, aiding Topolos. There are maps, lists of restaurants and inns. The books can be used as travel guides.

There are many general books on wines, but perhaps the most useful, and the one with the best perspective on California wines is Frank Schoonmaker's *Encyclopedia of Wine,* published by Hastings House, New York. This, and the others mentioned, can lead you to many other books—and also to the wines.

278

Index

NOTES: *1. All wines referred to, unless otherwise indicated, are California wines.*

2. References to the wines of specific wineries are listed under the wines, not under the wineries.

Abby, 131
Acetic acid, 254, 256
Acidity of wine (pH of wine), 255–56
Adams, Leon, 107
Adriatica (Yugoslav wine), 31
Aestivalis (grapes), 190
After Hours (wine), Italian Swiss Colony, 96
Aging, 273–74
  of California wines, 67–68
    at Charles Krug, 130–31
    at David Bruce, 163
    at Dry Creek Vineyard, 98
    at Edmeades, 84
    at Fetzer, 82
    at Freemark Abbey, 131
    at Gemello, 164
    at Hanzell, 106–7
    at Mayacamas Vineyards, 137
    at Parducci, 78
    at Pedroncelli, 95

  of Petite Sirah, 52, 53
  at Robert Mondavi, 119
  at Sebastiani, 105–6
  at Stony Hill, 141
  at Trentadue, 94
  of Zinfandels, 50
  of fortified wines, 236
  of Spanish Sherry, 237
Ahlgren Vineyard, 272
Alameda region (Calif.), grapes planted in, 47
Albani White (Italian wine), 40
Alcoholic content, 235
  of Edmeades Dry Apple, 83
  of Felton White Riesling, 170
  of fortified wines, 235
  of Gallo wines, 184
  of Gemello Cabernets, 164
  of jug wines, 38, 39
  of Mayacamas Vineyards Late Harvest
    Zinfandel, 136

280

281

Mendocino Premium White as, 82
at Paul Masson, 168
with Petite Sirah wines, 51
at Simi, 92
at Sonoma Vineyards, 103
at Stag's Leap Wine Cellars, 143, 144
with Sylvaner wines, 53
Tokay as, 181
with Zinfandels, 49
See also Hybrid blends
Blooming Grove (winery), 198
Body, tasting for, 255–56
Bollinger (winery), 244
Bon Vin (marketing firm), 94
Bone dry wines, 254
Boone's Farm Apple Wine (wine), Gallo, 184
Boone's Farm Strawberry Hill (wine), Gallo, 54, 184
Boordy Vineyard, 194, 203, 206
Bo-Peeps, 77–78
Bordeaux Red, 41
Bordeaux region (France)
Classed Growths of, 137
grapes from, 24, 25, 31
See also specific grapes
regions of Napa Valley compared with, 70
Sonoma areas compared with, 89
Bordeaux Supérieur (French wine), 63
Bordeaux wines (French)
blends in, 36
bottles of, 18
Chappellet wines compared with, 153
fermentation of, 80
Gemello wines compared with, 164
as jug wines, 41
marketing of, 189-90
Mayacamas Vineyards Cabernet matched with, 137
1971 red, 69
as salad wines, 62
yearly production of, 68
See also specific Bordeaux wines
Boskydel (winery), 224
Bostwick, Reverend, 199
Botrytis, 49, 93, 204
Bottles & Bins (newsletter), 130
Boutique wineries, *see* Small wineries
Brandies, 45
of California Wine Association, 185

in making of fortified wines, 235–36
in making of Port, 238
sugared, in making of Champagne, 242
Bright's (winery), 231, 232
Bronco Wine Company, 182
Bronte Winery and Vineyards, 224
Brookside Vineyard Company, 176
Brotherhood Winery, 198
Brouilly (French wine), 29
Brounstein, Alfred, 141
Browne, Sherburne, 209
Bruce, David, 163
Brut sparkling wines
California
Korbel, 15, 101, 243, 248
Schramsberg, 15, 244
French, Champagne, 242, 252
New York State, Gold Seal, 202, 203
some superior, 248
Buena Vista Winery, 49, 72, 87–89, 110
established, 88
Green Hungarian grapes used at, 81
history and characteristics of products of, 107–8
Buffets, jug wines served at, 42
Bulk Process (Charmat process), 242
Bull, Ephraim, 192
Bully Hill Red (N.Y. wine), Bully Hill Vineyards, 201
Bully Hill Vineyards, 191, 201–2
Bully Hill White (N.Y. wine), Bully Hill Vineyards, 201
Burbank, Luther, 88
Burgella (Spanish wine), 41
Burger (wine), Gundlach-Bundschu, 110
Burgess Cellars, 68, 81, 160, 170
Burgonay (Canadian wine), Casabello, 234
Burgundy region (France)
California compared with, 21–22, 24
grapes of, 24, 26–28, 38, 176
See also specific grapes
Napa Valley compared with, 70
Sonoma region compared with, 87, 89
sparkling wines from, 242
Burgundy wines
California, 121, 254, 273
Gallo, 184
French
blends in, 36
bottles of, 18

283

Souverain, 14, 93
Stag's Leap, 143, 144, 145, 269
Stonegate, 269
Thomas Jordan, 94
Weibel, 259
Wente Bros., 172
Zepponi, 109
Indiana, Banholzer, 222
Israeli, Carmel, 193
New York State
Hargrave, 191, 207
Widmer, 15, 258
Washington, Ste. Michelle Vineyards, 229
Cabernet Sauvignon Special Reserve (wine), BV, 122, 123
Cadlolo winery, 182
Cagnasso Winery, 272
Cairanne (French wine), 30
Cakebread, John, 156
Cakebread Cellars, 156, 160
Calera (winery), 272
California
Burgundy region compared with, 21–24
premium growers and shippers from, 18–19
wines from
opinion on, 272–75
quality of French wines compared with, 68–69
yearly sales and production of, 67–68
See also specific California wines and wineries
California Growers Winery, 185
California Mountain label (Louis M. Martini Winery), 126
California Wine Association (CWA), 185–86
California Wine & Food Society, 130
Calistoga (grapes), 132
Calistoga Wineries, 155–60
Callaway, Ely, 177
Callaway Vineyards, 176–77
Calona (winery), 233
Calvet (firm), 133
Cambasio Sonoma County Cellars, 89, 110
Campari (Italian wine), 42
Canadian wineries, 231–34, 271
See also specific wineries
Canandaigua Wine Company, 217
Canepa, John, 211

Canepa (N.H. wine), White Mountain Vineyards, 211
Cantina Sociale de Soave Bianco di Verona, 41
Cape Sandy Vineyards, 223
Capozzi, Tom, 233
Cappello, Antonio (Tony Hat), 182
Carignane (grapes)
Mendocino Premium Red from, 82
plantings of
in San Joaquin Valley, 181
In Sonoma Vineyards, 87
total acreage, 47, 48
in Trentadue winery, 93
Carignane (wine)
Parducci, 14, 263
price of, 263
Rapazzini, 263
as salad wine, 59, 62
Carmel Bay (winery), 272
Carmel label (Israeli label), 193
Carnelian (grapes), 46
Carnenos Creek Winery, 156, 160
Carneros wineries (Calif.), 155–160
See also specific wineries
Caroli Vineyards, 219
Carpy, Charles, 131
Cartier Rouge (French wine), 41
Casabello (winery), 234
Cascade Mountain Vineyards, 199
Casey, William, 159
Cassis (French wine), 42
Castel 19637 (grapes), 197
Catawba (grapes), 191–92, 200, 217, 225
Catawba Red (N.Y. wine), Gold Seal, 15
Caymus Vineyards, 68, 146–47, 160
Cayuga White (grapes), 212
Cayuga White (N.Y. wine), 194, 195
Widmer, 15, 205
Caywood, Andrew J., 198
Cedar Hill (winery), 271
Cedar taste (redwood taste), 49, 71, 80-81, 115, 116, 128
Central coast of California, new wines from, 74–76
Centurion (grapes), 46
Certification program at Davis, 180
Chablis (wine)
California, 45, 254, 273
Gallo, 184
French, dryness of, 252

286

287

288

289

Lytton Springs Zinfandel (wine), Ridge, 50–51

McCrea, Eleanor, 140
McCrea, Fred, 114, 132, 140–41
McDonnell, Lolly, 212
McGrath, William, 209
Mack Fruit Farms (winery), 272
MacLean, Galo, 221
Macon Blanc (French wine), 252
Macon Rouge (French wine), 30, 62
McQueen, John, 176
McWilliams, Anne, 146
McWilliams, Jane, 146
Madeira (Spanish wine), 238
Madrone (winery), 89
Mahoney, Francis, 156
Main Riesling (grapes; Müller-Thuegan grapes), 52, 194
Makana (winery), 271
Malbec (grapes), 36
Malo-lactic fermentation, 91
Mancuso, Michael, 223
Mandia Champagne Cellars, 199
Manischewitz (company), 193, 200
Manzanilla Sherry (Spanish wine), 237
Maréchal Foch (grapes), 212
Margaux (French wine), 153
Marinade recipe, 174
Mark, 131
Mark West Vineyard, 110
Marketing problems, 189–90, 194–95
Markko Vineyards, 222, 271
Marlboro Industries, 199
Marsala (Sicilian wine), 238
Martha's Vineyard Cabernet (wine), Heitz, 124, 149–50
Martin Ray Vineyard, 163
Martini, Louis M., 125–26
Martini, Louis P., 70–72, 114, 115, 126, 154, 157
Martini and Prati (winery), 89
Maryland wineries, 218–19
   See also specific wineries
Massachusetts wineries, 211
Masson, Paul, 166
Maudière, Edmond, 246
Mayacamas Vineyards, 68, 69
   history and characteristics of products of, 136–37
   yearly production of, 160

Mayacamas wineries, 133–40
   See also specific wineries
Mazza Vineyards, 214, 271, 272
Meconi, Mario, 224
Médoc (French wine), 190
Meier's Wine Cellars, 221, 243
Mellow Red (wine)
   Rubino, 41
   Segesta 41
Mellow wines, 254
Mendocino Rain Wine (wine), Edmeades, 83
Mendocino region (Calif.), growers and shippers from, 18–19
Mendocino Riesling (wine), Parducci, 79
Mendocino wineries, 29, 47, 243
   selection from, 14
   touring, 77–85
   See also specific wineries
Mercier label (Moët and Chandon), 245
Mercurey (French wine), 30
Meredyth Vineyards, 219, 271
Merlot (grapes), 36
   plantings of
      in Diamond Creek Vineyards, 141
      in Hargrave Vineyards, 209
      in Napa Valley, 117
      in Ritchie Creek Vineyard, 140
      in Sonoma, 88
      in Stag's Leap Wine Cellars vineyards, 143
      in Sterling Vineyards, 131
      in Villa Mt. Eden vineyards, 146
   wines from
      Beringer blends, 128
      Freemark Abbey blends, 131
      qualities of, 31–32
      Simi blends, 92
Merlot (wine), 31
   Louis Martini, 127, 259
   Mill Creek, 94
   Stag's Leap Wine Cellars, 145, 259
   Sterling, 259
   Veedercrest, 259
Méthode Champenoise, La, 242
Meursault (French wine), 72
Meursault-Charmes (French wine), 69
Meyer, Alvin, 223
Meyer, Justin, 157
Meyer, Margaret, 223

300

301

302

at Concannon Vineyards, 174
in Napa Valley, 117
in 1970s, 181
in Sonoma, 88
in Stony Hill Vineyard, 141
Wente Bros. Sauvignon from, 87
Sémillon (wine)
Charles Krug, 258
Concannon, 173, 258
as salad wine, 61
San Martin, 258
Wente Bros., 121, 258
Sémillon Blanc (Washington wine), Ste.
Michelle Vineyards, 229, 258
Seneca Foods (firm), 206
Sereksia (grapes), 204
Seyval (grapes), 212
Seyval (N.Y. wine), 196
Seyval Blanc (wine)
Canada, Inniskillin, 231
New York
Benmarl, 199
Bully Hill Vineyards, 201
Heron Hill, 205
Seyve-Villard 5–276 (grapes), 196, 218
Seyve-Villard 19–307 (grapes), 196
Seyve-Villard 23–410 (grapes), 196
Sherill Cellars, 272
Sherry (wine)
California, 45, 236
Spanish, 235–37
Sherry Wines & Spirits (wine store), 105
Sichel, Franz, 167
Sichel (importer), 31, 133
Silver Oak Cellars, 157, 160
Silverado Cellars label (Château Mon-
telena), 155
Silverado Country Club, 142
Silverado Restaurant, 118
Silverado Squatters (Stevenson), 244
Silverado Trail wineries, 142-55
Simi (winery), 14, 68, 90–92, 95, 110
Similkameen (Canadian wine), 233
Simon, Norton, 39–40
Singleton, Charles, 219
Sirah (grapes; Duriff grapes), 33, 51, 152
See also Petite Sirah (grapes)
Sizes
of jugs, 38, 40
of wineries, prices and, 68
Skoda, Bernard, 157

Small wineries (boutique wineries)
from Carneros to Calistoga, 159–60
in Sonoma and Mendocino, 110
See also specific overall wineries
Smith, Archie, 219
Smith, Charles, 141
Smith, Stewart, 141
Smith, Suzelle, 219
Smith Vineyards, 141
Smothers, Richard, 164
Sneaky Pete (name for California Port,
Sherry and Muscatel), 236
Soave (Italian wine), 32
Folonari, 40
as salad wine, 62
Société des Vignerons, 198
Soils
California, 275
Central Valley, 239
in Monterey, 176
in Sonoma, 89
Long Island, 208
maturing of wine and types of, 71
Soleil Blanc (French label), 40
Sommelier Winery, 272
Sommer, Richard, 227
Sonoma County Cooperative, 110
Sonoma Red (wine), Pedroncelli, 41
Sonoma region
Gamay Beaujolais produced in, 29
grapes planted in, 30, 47
growers and shippers from, 18–19
Sonoma Vineyards, 90
architecture of, 152
distribution range of, 18
selection from, 14, 16
touring, 102–4
yearly production of, 68, 110
Sonoma White (wine), Pedroncelli, 40
Sonoma wineries, 87–110
of Alexander Valley, 90–98
along Russian River, 98–102
selection from, 14
in Valley of the Moons, 102–10
See also specific wineries
Sonoma Zinfandel (wine), Pedroncelli, 51
Sotoyome Winery, 110
Sousao (grapes), 239
South Carolina wineries, 217, 272
Southern wineries, 217–19, 272
See also specific wineries

305

310